Bude

rd

Launceston

Liskeard

hiel   Saltash

Looe

Polperro   Antony

25 miles

CORNWALL
THE TRAVELLERS' TALES

CORNWALL

THE
TRAVELLERS' TALES

Volume One

Edited by
Todd Gray

FOR BRIAN & ELIZABETH

First published in Great Britain by The Mint Press, 2000

© Todd Gray 2000

The right of Todd Gray to be identified as editor of this work
has been asserted by him in accordance with the Copyright,
Designs & Patents Act 1988.

ISBN 1-903356-05-9

British Library Cataloguing-in-Publication Data
A CIP record for this title is available from
the British Library

The Mint Press
18 The Mint
Exeter, Devon
England, EX4 3BL

www.themintpress.com

Designed and typeset in New Baskerville 10.5/12.6
by Mike Dobson, Quince Typesetting

Cover design by Delphine Jones

Main cover illustration, Penzance, *c*.1860 (MPr/P&D10279)
Title page, Wadebridge, *c*.1855 (LPr/P&D10409)
Both courtesy of Westcountry Studies Library.

Sciurus carolinensis circumforaneus by Tim Wormleighton

Printed and bound in Great Britain
by Short Run Press Ltd, Exeter.

CONTENTS

ACKNOWLEDGEMENTS

I would like to thank Tom Arkell, Dr Sadru Bhanji, David Reeve, Margery Rowe, Carole Vivian, Susan Conniff at the Devon & Exeter Institution and the staff of the Westcountry Studies Library, in particular Tony Rouse. I would also like to thank Major H. Porter, Sir John Quicke, the Berkshire Record Office, Bodleian Library, Devon Record Office, Dorset Archives Service, Isle of Wight Record Office and Worcester Record Office for their assistance with publishing archival material and the Westcountry Studies Library for permission to publish illustrations. Finally, I would like to thank Dr Mike Dobson, Delphine Jones and Hilary Tolley for their help in seeing this book through the production stages.

ILLUSTRATION SOURCES

Title page, Wadebridge, *c*.1855, Westcountry Studies Library, LPr/P&D10409; page 1, Lucy Toulmin Smith, *The Itineray of John Leland* (1907), frontispiece; page 33, detail from John Speed's map of Cornwall, 1610; page 40, Westcountry Studies Library, MPr/P&D10391; page 42, William Borlase, *The Natural History of Cornwall* (1758), 14; page 45, Westcountry Studies Library, SPr/P&D10068; page 49, William Borlase, *The Natural History of Cornwall* (1758), 22; page 52, William Gilpin, *Observations on the Western Parts of England, relative chiefly to Picturesque Beauty* (1808); page 65, Westcountry Studies Library, LPr/P&D10153; page 74, Westcountry Studies Library, SPr/P&D10347; page 78, Westcountry Studies Library, MPr/P&D10282; page 80, Westcountry Studies Library, SPr/P&D10413; page 87, Westcountry Studies Library, MPr/P&D10155; page 115, Westcountry Studies Library, MPr/P&D10278; page 121, Westcountry Studies Library, MPr/P&D10299; page 123, Westcountry Studies Library, LPr/P&D10409; page 128, Westcountry Studies Library, LPr/P&D40478; page 131, etching by William Bell Scott of Algernon Swinburne, 1860; page 134, Westcountry Studies Library, MPr/P&D10274; page 143, Westcountry Studies Library, MPr/P&D10253; page 167, Westcountry Studies Library, MPr/P&D10149; pages 179–191, private collection; page 192, S.P.B. Mais, *The Cornish Riviera* (1934), 3

'A RECIPE TO MAKE A TOUR'

Take of good humour as much as you have by you,
to this add a like quantity of a determination to
please and be pleased, throw in a few bank notes
by way of cement. Jolt these together in a coach &
my life don't they do wonders.

Sarah England, mid-nineteenth century
(Devon Record Office, 337b/4/3a)

INTRODUCTION

Cornwall has been popular as a holiday destination for several hundreds of years. Latterly it has been a place that tourists expressly journey to, not merely passing through en route to other places. But earlier generations, with their reliance on sea travel, found Cornwall convenient as the first, or last, contact with the United Kingdom and one of the visitors in this book, Louis Simond in 1809, was on such a journey. The vast majority of travellers in this collection made Cornwall their principal destination and they came not just in the summer months but at various times throughout the year. The subsequent accounts written by these tourists offer unique insights into the history of the county, providing details on the life of the Cornish people not found in other sources. Moreover, they are fascinating as outsiders' impressions of Cornwall because they reveal what was personally considered unfamiliar or distinctive. Finally, while it is interesting to note whether comments were complimentary, it is equally rewarding to try to understand why these attitudes were formed.

THE TRAVEL ACCOUNTS

In this volume there are two sets of travellers' tales. The main group comprises twenty-two accounts written by twenty-one travellers. Each offers unique information in that they are personal, snapshot views of Cornwall: for instance, one traveller recorded the search for a chicken egg thief by the Prideaux-Brune family at Place near Padstow. This vignette of Cornish life, incidental and unimportant in itself, is nevertheless a glimpse into the past at one place and point in time and is otherwise unrecorded. At least eight women, and possibly as many as nine, are amongst these writers. Several had family ties to Cornwall and at least three of them were Cornish born. The remaining travellers came from London, Dorset, Cheshire, Hampshire, the Isle of Wight, Worcestershire, France, the United States or from places unidentified. Two of the visitors were clerics. The majority of the travellers appear to have come from comfortable circumstances and several were accompanied by servants. The earliest traveller is John Leland who visited Cornwall twice in the early sixteenth century and the latest account is by Mrs Margaret Halsey, the wife of an American academic, who came in the late 1930s.

The second set comprises thirteen postcards sent by individuals, who were generally only identified by their first names, from 1902 to 1935. The postcards were sent to addresses throughout the country and the few sentences each wrote were generally favourable about Cornwall. They have been included to illustrate the variety of visitors and the formats in which travel accounts were written. In this book their use differs from what may be more usual where the images are important and the text of no consequence.

Only a few of the travellers are well known; many were merely quietly travelling the county and recording their impressions for their own private purposes. Their renown is partly dependent upon whether the accounts were published. At least seven of these visitors in the main collection wrote with the intention of reaching the reading public; this comprises John Taylor, William Gilpin, Louis Simond, H.G., Evelyn Burnaby, Margaret Halsey and an unidentified writer who published in 1855. Although their travelogues have long been out-of-print, they are nevertheless more easily available to the reader than the accounts of eleven of the remaining travellers which have never been published. Their impressions of Cornwall have remained personal and private: few individuals have hitherto read their views of the county and shared their experiences. The three remaining travellers include several of the best-known individuals in this collection although their accounts remained in manuscript until after their deaths. Two of them, Joseph Farington and Algernon Charles Swinburne, may have anticipated their writings being eventually published. The third writer, John Leland, probably had the greatest public impact but it is difficult to determine whether he imagined his work would reach beyond anything other than a very limited audience.

Nevertheless, each of these accounts, with only a few exceptions, was originally intended to be seen even if by only a single reader. Each writer's purpose must be considered. For instance, would the unidentified young woman, who described one Mrs Marsh as 'a very odd looking person decidedly primitive in appearance', have written quite so openly in 1836 had she thought they would be read by unknown strangers? Equally, would Mrs Florence Glynn have put on public record in 1884 her opinion of a woman she knew as 'rather fast'? Her letters were private and it is difficult to imagine that she considered anyone other than her husband would read them. Their content is personal and note such intimate details as her miscarriage at Padstow. The subject matter was so personal that she was unable to inform her husband of the event in anything but the briefest terms. In contrast, when in 1649 John Taylor wrote his *Wandering to See the Wonders of the West* he used the reader to get his message across: he intentionally flattered a number of Cornish men and women he met. In one instance Taylor identified a particular woman and then immediately described her as a 'virtuous and beautiful gentlewoman'. A gentleman was described as 'endowed with piety, humanity, affability and ability; he hath a heart charitable, a mind bountiful, and a hand liberal'. Irrespective of whether he believed this to be true, Taylor realised that many of their peers would read those passages. Travellers' comments should also be considered against the more restrained and guarded description given by Mrs Margaret Halsey of her hotelier in the 1930s:

> The owner of the hotel, a retired naval officer, has just been up to the room and built us a handsome fire. He is a strong-and-silenter. He builds fires and worms dogs and whittles out boats and evens off tennis courts, performing these and similar offices with an air of mani-fest enjoyment, and he never wastes a word – largely, I suppose, because he does not have to. His shrewd, weather-beaten face is a conversation in itself.

Although this was, presumably, largely a favourable assessment, it is telling that she felt unable to name him or even identify the location of this Cornish hotel: in her account the village is named as 'Purford'. It may have been that she, or her publishers, were concerned with issues of libel. Finally, the text on each of the postcards must be considered against the general assumption that once posted the cards passed through the hands of an unknown number of postal employees. Perhaps the comments made on Cornwall would have been very different had they not suspected that the postman might read their cards.

The travel accounts take the form of printed books, short articles, journals, diaries, letters and cards and have been selected from a wider body of material. It is hoped that a second volume will be published incorporating some of the unpublished remainder. The accounts in this volume provide a representative sample; there is a wide geographical and chronological range as well as a variety of travellers. This criterion was also used in the first two volumes in this series, on Exeter and East Devon, but the character of this collection is very different. In part it reflects the great differences in the nature of the Cornish topography. The traveller in East Devon inevitably commented on lace-making, the seaside resorts, the red soil and the great number of hills: the visitor laboriously climbed up one hill only to descend into another valley on the other side. But the traveller in Cornwall noticed other things. It may be that some travellers came with the expectation, or hope, of finding not only a distinctive landscape but a people different from those known at home. The traveller who wrote for the reading public or handed around travel journals to their friends, in the same manner in which photographs and the holiday video are shared today, may well have embellished the accounts to present Cornwall as every bit as strange and eccentric as it was generally presented and popularly perceived.

One of the first places that Joseph Farington saw on his visit to Cornwall in 1810 was the line of stones known as the hurlers. He explained that:

> The superstitious tradition respecting them is that they were men turned to stones as a punishment for having played at the game of hurling on a Sunday.

Farington also visited the Cheesewring and kept a watch for other possible relics of the Druids as well as for the curious and the uncommon. Comparisons between Cornwall and the rest of the country were made by nearly every traveller from John Taylor, who noted that one day he saw nothing 'strange to me' except choughs, to Mrs Halsey who commented that she enjoyed the 'rock-ribbed austerity' of Cornwall after the lushness of Devon.

One particular feature of this collection is the two sets of accounts describing large gentry house parties. These descriptions, for the middle of the eighteenth century and again in 1884, show the extravagance, food and entertainment enjoyed as ladies and gentlemen travelled to spend several days together. Among the activities were dances, sailing and hunting parties. There are strong similarities between the two sets of accounts even though they took place more than 120 years apart. All of the houses in which these parties took place still stand today.

THE LIFE OF A TRAVELLER IN CORNWALL

John Taylor's initial impression of Cornwall, when he arrived in 1649, was that it was the 'Cornucopia, the complete and replete horn of abundance for high churlish hills and affable, courteous people'. He wrote favourably about the people but occasionally he received a hostile welcome, notably at Blisland where the local inhabitants wrongly thought Taylor was there to serve legal papers and also at Mevagissey where he had considerable problems in finding lodgings. The people treated him as if he had been 'a strange beast or monster brought out of Africa'. Taylor wrote that he was threatened with eviction from an alehouse when he requested a room. More than a hundred years later a Hampshire gentleman wrote that he had 'heard that the inhabitants of Cornwall are not famed for their politeness towards strangers.' It is uncertain how widespread this perception was but this traveller's main concern, given that he was dressed in what he regarded as unusual clothes for Cornwall, was that the locals did not mistake him for being an escaped French prisoner-of-war.

Nearly all the travellers, those who visited for recreation as well as those on business, commented upon the food, their lodgings, the change in weather and the ease of transport. Perhaps the availability and quality of food was of the most immediate interest. In a short account by a male traveller, who had left Nanswhyden near Newquay with a large party for a trip to Bath in 1741, the jottings mostly refer to the quality of the roads and the food. At Launceston the group had wine, fruit tarts, cheese, bread and tea but he noted that later they were short one loaf of bread due to the actions of an unidentified canine traveller. A visitor to the Lizard in the late eighteenth century remarked upon the local method of making bread upon a covered hot plate. In 1809 one visitor commented that the French were better cooks. The traveller, not surprisingly perhaps a Frenchman, noted of his visit to Falmouth:

> We had three small dishes, dressed very inartificially (an English cook only boils and roasts), otherwise very good. The table linen and glass, and servants, remarkably neat, and in good order. At the dessert apples no bigger than walnuts, and without taste, which are said to be the best the country produces.

The following year Joseph Farington noted at Looe that:

> The fishermen & their families live upon fish, bread & potatoes, and never think of eating animal food, but on Sundays, & they are then the worse for it.

In 1866 one visitor was surprised to have ham and ducks' eggs for breakfast and in 1892 Evelyn Burnaby experienced his first Temperance house when he travelled to Cornwall. At his Liskeard hostelry he found no alcohol 'but the food was excellent and the beds clean.' Many of those who wrote postcards in the early twentieth century commented favourably upon the food but not Mrs Margaret Halsey in 1937. She had considerable difficulties in buying oranges in Cornwall and noted she was forced to in order 'to outflank the hotel carbohydrates'. Finally, two of the food items most popularly associated with Cornwall were mentioned by these travellers. In 1775 the Reverend William Gilpin experienced Cornish food at Cotehele similar to that enjoyed latterly by many thousands of visitors:

> Here we refreshed ourselves with tea, and larded our bread, after the fashion of the country, with *clouted* cream.

Finally, in 1929 a female visitor, only identified by the name 'May', wrote to a friend regarding her encounter with a pasty. She noted:

> I should think it was about a foot long. How I got through it I don't know but I did. I felt like bursting.

The quality of lodgings was also of great concern. It would be interesting to know the details of where John Leland stayed in the early sixteenth-century but presumably he lodged with members of the gentry for whom he had letters of introduction. John Taylor, in spite of his difficulties at Mevagissey in 1649, seems to have found some accommodation through contacts with the Cornish gentry although he did stay with a blacksmith and his wife in St Enoder amongst other places. In 1809 Louis Simond described his hotel at Falmouth. It was:

> a strange, old, low building, extremely neat inside, with a tempting larder full in view, displaying, on shelves of tiles, fish of all sorts, fat fowls, &c. Well-dressed servants, civil and attentive, wait our commands. We are put in possession of a sitting room and two bed-rooms.

The following year Joseph Farington wrote that his hotel in Truro was:

> an excellent house for a country town, with beds such as I do not recollect to have seen in any other Inn, and a chambermaid who attended to everything that could be required. This material point was very satisfactory, but there was too much noise & bustle in the house for me to approve it equally in other respects.

In 1866 'H.G.' stayed at the Queen's Hotel in Penzance which he thought was:

a first-rate house, situated in the centre of the Bay. Having secured a bedroom there, I was fortunate enough to induce a red-haired chamber-maid to bring me a cold bath, for I felt as dirty as a pig.

He later travelled on to the Isles of Scilly and stayed at:

the principal Inn at St Mary's (to call it an Hotel would be nonsense), and I accordingly intimated to him my wish to avail myself of his hospitality. He called a man to take my luggage, and accompanied by the lady and gentleman I have already mentioned, and who proved very agreeable people, we followed Mr Porter to the house, and of all the queer places I have put up at, this was certainly the queerest; a sort of village farmhouse with a long garden in front, and when you got inside it, exceedingly low and stuffy rooms, and reeking with the smell of tobacco and gin, for it is the head-quarters of the ship Captains who put into the Bay during contrary winds, or in stress of weather. The Captain's daughter, a very pleasant-spoken and good-looking woman (it would be absurd to call her young, though I don't believe she is more than thirty), showed me upstairs to a double-bedded room, and invited me to choose whichever of the two beds I preferred, but having a horror of sharing a room with anyone else (till I get a wife), I intimated that I should infinitely prefer even a closet to a fellow lodger, and she accordingly led the way to the pokiest little bed-room I ever occupied, and, after the grand room I had had at the "Clifton Down," it was anything but an agreeable contrast.

The following morning his concerns at Penzance, bathing and the female servants, again are mentioned in his journal. Even before he stepped ashore onto Cornish soil he had commented on the 'display of the ladies' legs'. At St Mary's he noted that:

Almost in despair of accomplishing my object, I had asked the chambermaid (or, to describe her more correctly, the serious-looking young woman, who was evidently either crossed in love, or the perpetrator of some horrible misdeed) to give me a bath in the morning, and she said she would; and soon after daylight I heard a sort of snorting outside my door, which I presently learnt was caused by her blowing into the interstices of an India-rubber contrivance which produces the identical thing, a circular flat-bottomed boat, that she handed into my room

with two kilderkin-looking receptacles of water, – and I
was soon enjoying the luxury of a thorough wetting.

Finally, in 1937 Mrs Halsey thought her Cornish accommodation
was far superior to the standard she had found in England. She wrote
that:

> The English hotels we have stayed in so far always seemed
> to me expressly planned to discourage people from
> remaining away from home overnight. The red plush.
> The black walnut. The framed engravings of lovers'
> quarrels. The Pampas grass. The fireplace blocked up
> with nasty little brutes of gas heaters. Whenever we
> checked out of a hotel this summer, it was with the moral
> certainty that the manager immediately retired to his
> office for a few minutes of private rejoicing. 'There,' he
> would say, looking out of the window after us, 'that'll teach
> 'em to go gadding about!'

Many of the travellers recorded the distances they travelled each
day and noted the merits of their modes of transport. For instance
in 1845, when the railway was just reaching the South West, Mrs
Jane Allen commented that she preferred travelling by train to the
carriage she used going to Cornwall. Several of those who travelled
by sea had difficult voyages: two unidentified visitors, who came to
Cornwall in 1793 and 1836, were relieved to reach land safely. Other
travellers wrote about the mere inconveniences of the Cornish lanes.
That same visitor of 1793 had an unpleasant experience at Polperro.
He wrote:

> I did at last however procure a little horse, or at least a
> part of one, for the poor creature looked so miserable &
> half starved, that I quite hurt to ride him. Its owner also
> I hired to show me the way to Plymouth, he was obliged
> to walk, indeed I walked a great part of the way myself
> for the hills were so high & so steep & the road so bad
> that it was impossible to ride.

Only a few years later Louis Simond remarked that Cornish roads
were narrow, crooked and dirty. He wrote that:

> The horses we get are by no means good, and draw us
> with difficulty at the rate of five miles an hour. We change
> carriages as well as horses at every post-house; they are
> on four wheels, light and easy, and large enough for three
> persons. The post-boy sits on a cross bar of wood between
> the front springs, or rather rests against it. This is safer,

and more convenient both for men and horses, but does not look well; and, as far as we have seen, English post-horses and postillions do not seem to deserve their reputation.

Many others also travelled by horse or carriage. The latter included the Hawkins family of Trewinnard near Hayle who, in the middle of the eighteenth century, travelled in their famous carriage formerly owned by the Spanish Ambassador, now on display at the Royal Cornwall Museum, to visit the St Aubyn family at Clowance between Camborne and Helston. Other travel accounts show the changes in transport to rail and then to the motor car, although Mrs Halsey's borrowed vehicle broke down in East Cornwall and she and her husband were forced to curtail their travels beyond the Rame Peninsula.

Finally, in 1884 language difficulties between a visitor and her French maid resulted in the confused girl trying to understand how she could travel by telephone.

Some travellers indicate prepared themselves before their tours by reading about Cornwall. For instance, the Reverend Gilpin read Clarendon's history of the Civil War and works by William Borlase. But many travellers were dependent on local knowledge from passing strangers and hired guides to bring them to places of interest; one such traveller was Joseph Farington who used a number of guides to bring him through Cornwall.

CORNWALL

Travellers continually commented upon the Cornish people and their ways. Farington recorded:

> Some peculiarities of the Cornish people I had before & did now notice. They speak in a singing tone; and, as *Yes sure* is always in the mouth of a Devonshire man, so when a Cornish Man, in this part of the country at least, answers in the negative he does it with this repetition *No, No Sir. No.*'

Another traveller was herself Cornish and noted a local saying. In the middle of the eighteenth century Mrs Hawkins of Trewinnard attended a dance and described it to a friend: she wrote that the partners were decided beforehand and 'twas all ordained, as we say in Cornwall, how it should be without either drawing or choosing'. Some forty years later another visitor, on a tour which included Polperro, was not impressed by the locals he met. He thought:

the inhabitants rude, stupid and uncivilized. I was shown a wretched looking house, which they called an inn, here I enquired if I could have a horse to carry me to Plymouth. Their dialect is uncouth and the answers I received were almost as unintelligible as they were dissatisfactory.

It is interesting to ponder how welcome any stranger was in Polperro during the French wars and the local attention to smuggling. In contrast, John Taylor found in 1649 the Cornishmen were strong and stout and the women handsome and beautiful. In 1809 a French visitor thought that the Cornish women, or at least those he saw in Falmouth, were:

highly dressed, or rather highly undressed, in extremely thin draperies, move about with an elastic gait on the light fantastic patten, making a universal clatter of iron on the pavement. Ruddy countenances and *embonpoint* [plumpness] are very general and striking.

There are many short descriptions of individuals such as Mrs Cortyon of Fowey ('at most fifty-five, she is well grown, has a good face, is very nimble, has good teeth'), of several female members of the Rashleigh family of Menabilly ('a particular woman, a great collector of curiosities for which she spares no cost or pains', 'tender spirits & a great dislike of Cards. She is in appearance vastly agreeable, received us with great politeness, is well made, I think pretty, & Miss Coryton says composed of sweetness, is very ingenious, makes flowers vastly well'), and a young female visitor to Penwith in 1836 was frank about the people she met including one Captain Marsh ('rather an odd-looking man, but very kind').

Perhaps one of the strangest descriptions is the tale retold by the Reverend Gilpin of James Tillie of Pentillie. In 1775 he wrote that Tillie was a 'celebrated atheist of the last age' and that:

He was a man of wit, and had by rote all the ribaldry and common-place jests against religion and scripture; which are well suited to display pertness and folly, and to unsettle a giddy mind, but are offensive to men of sense, whatever their opinions may be, and are neither intended nor adapted to investigate truth. The brilliancy of Mr Tilly's wit, however, carried him a degree farther than we often meet with in the annals of profaneness. In general the witty atheist is satisfied with entertaining his *contemporaries*; but Mr Tilly wished to have his sprightliness known to *posterity*. With this view, in ridicule of the resurrection, he obliged his executors to place his dead body, in his usual garb, and in his elbow-chair, upon the top of a hill, and to arrange, on a table before him, bottles, glasses, pipes and tobacco. In this situation he ordered himself to be immured in a tower of such dimensions, as he prescribed; where he proposed, he said, patiently to wait the event. All this was done, and the tower, still inclosing its tenant, remains as a monument of his impiety and profaneness. The country people shudder as they go near it.

The story was later repeated by C.S. Gilbert in his *Historical Survey of Cornwall* but Gilpin may have heard the tale while travelling through Cornwall.

Perhaps Joseph Farington is the most consistent observer of individuals. He has been criticised for being a gossip but his diary is nevertheless full of human interest. At Polperro he met 'a woman of very respectable appearance' who was the mother of Robert Jeffries, the sailor famously abandoned on a desolate Caribbean island.[1] Farington provides a long passage on the unfortunate seaman. He also described Mr Job of Polperro ('very respectable and wealthy') of whom his guide later reported had 'larger property and greater influence than any other inhabitant of *Polperrow*, is a native of Penzance & came from thence without a shilling. He said Mr Job is King of the place, and held in much respect for his good qualities.' His most heart-rending description is of a fisherman employed to row him along the coast. The seaman had:

been blind 34 years, caused by his having struck one of his eyes with a needle whilst mending a sail. He said he did not suffer much pain. "It was like the touch of a fly upon his eye," but he lost the sight of it, and in two years the sight of the other eye. Yet, in this apparently helpless state, this industrious man continued his occupations, went out to fish and placed his nets with more judgment than most of those who were so employed; could mend sails and in short seemed scarcely to want eyesight. He brought up a large family of children, five of whom he told me he never saw; and never had assistance or applied for relief. This he modestly expressed, but with seeming satisfaction. I met him walking alone in the town, and

---

[1] For more on Jeffries see James Derriman, *Marooned: the story of a Cornish seaman* (Emsworth, 1991).

when he was recommended to me I objected to him on account of his unfitness; but I was assured I could not employ a better man, & so it proved.

Cornish houses were also commented upon. In 1793 one visitor described Falmouth ('the houses are tolerably good'), Helston and Manaccan ('the houses in it, or rather huts, are very wretched and bad ... we went into one of the cottages and found it equally miserable with its inhabitants'), Mevagissey ('of all the places I ever was in this is the most wretched and disagreeable. In the whole town there seemed to be scarcely a habitation fit for a human being to dwell in') and Polperro ('the houses are in general mean, dirty and disagreeable'). There are scores of other descriptions including of Falmouth in 1809 ('the houses, in a confused heap, crowd on the water; the tide washes their foundation; a black wall, built of rough stones, that stand on end, to facilitate the draining of the water, and steps, overgrown with sea-weeds, to ascend to the doors ... I have been introduced to several respectable citizens of Falmouth; they all live in very small, old habitations, of which the apartments resemble the cabins of vessels. A new house is a phenomenon'), of 'Purford' in the 1930s ('green hills rise baldly up at the back of it. These, combined with the stretched-out pieces of water, make the houses, which in other English villages seem to be rubbing up against each other like puppies in a basket, seem in Purford to be huddling together for the definite purpose of protection') and of dozens of individual houses.

Visitors felt that certain things symbolised Cornwall for them such as the choughs seen by John Taylor. But perhaps it has been St Michael's Mount that most represented Cornwall. As early as 1649 it was described as 'this so much talked of famous mount' and nearly all travelled to the far west to see it. In 1836 one visitor provided an unusual vignette:

> Must not forget to mention the romantic appearance of the Water Carriers with their red pitchers on their heads and some were very pretty girls, also the girls before we left bringing their clothes out to whiten had a pleasing effect as they were scattered about among the rocks, but oh, the smell of the rabbits that really was a sad nuisance.

The landscape occupied the attention of every traveller. Leland's commentary of the early sixteenth century is concerned solely with the degree of productivity[2] and never with issues of beauty: even when he used the word 'pretty' he intended the now obsolete definition of 'considerable'. This view of the landscape is in stark contrast with the Reverend Gilpin who was only interested in the picturesque qualities of the countryside. He was pleased with the Tamar valley and, strangely, compared the river with the Mississippi. Gilpin must be the only writer to have mused on alligators and the Tamar. He was however disappointed with Cornwall and its 'deserts of dreariness'. He only visited the eastern part of the county and recorded:

> From Launceston we travelled as far into Cornwall as Bodmin, through a coarse naked country, and in all respects as uninteresting as can well be conceived. Of wood, in every shape, it was utterly destitute. Having heard that the country beyond Bodmin was exactly like what we had already passed, we resolved to travel no farther in Cornwall; and instead of visiting the Land's end, as we had intended, we took the road to Liskeard.

Gilpin had no interest in mining, being as he explained, only interested in what was on the surface, and was, in many ways, a disappointing observer of Cornwall. His description is interesting to compare with that of the Reverend John Swete, Devon's leading proponent of the Picturesque, who visited the Tamar valley some seventeen years later.[3] Swete was more complimentary although they were both writing about the same aspect of the landscape. Interestingly, Swete visited the county not long after Gilpin's tour but before Swete himself had developed an awareness of the Picturesque. His travel account of that tour was concerned with more traditional subjects other than to what degree the countryside was beautiful, sublime, gothic, romantic or picturesque.[4]

Gilpin's disinterest in Cornwall is in great contrast with the opinion of the Reverend Thomas Rackett who in 1794 felt that the further west he travelled, the more interesting Cornwall became. Had Gilpin continued beyond Bodmin he may have noticed a division in the

---

[2.] For Leland, see John Chandler, 'John Leland in the West Country', 34–49, in Mark Brayshay (ed.), *Topographical Writers in South-Western England* (Exeter, 1996).

[3.] Todd Gray (ed.), *Travels in Georgian Devon: The Illustrated Travel Journals of the Reverend Swete, 1789–1800* (Tiverton, 1997), I, 127–45.

[4.] Rosemary Leach, 'A Tour in Cornwall in 1780', *Journal of the Royal Institution of Cornwall* (1971, part 3).

county's landscape. In 1866 one traveller, who was travelling eastward on the railway, thought there were two halves of Cornwall and that the west was:

> rather wild looking and spotted with Mine shafts, and the latter more like Devonshire, with splendid apple orchards, the fruit still on the trees, well cultivated fields, and abundance of foliage.

In the depths of winter in 1810 another visitor noticed how green the county was and remarked upon the trees being covered with moss. The milder temperatures of Cornwall elicited some comments as did the strength of the winds. Many of the travellers visited Land's End and, like John Taylor in 1649, were attracted to the notion of being in the most westerly part of the country. Taylor was even driven to cut his name, four inches deep, in the earth: he wrote 'I am sure no man can go thither and set his name or foot half a foot before me'. Another visitor, in 1836, enthused that:

> to attempt description perfectly useless. Three of us stood on the last stone, some few hundred feet over the Sea, the green coral rocks the most splendid colours I have ever seen, yet one in particular appeared quite transparent, saw for the first time the celebrated Cornish Chough, the roar of the sea from the Land's End awful, and the shriek of the cormorants, the plaintive cry of the other sea fowl under the spot melancholy and romantic. I remained there some time, there you forget the world and feel indeed alone.

Cornish towns also received considerable comment: Fowey in the early sixteenth century was 'a market town walled defensibly to the sea coast, and hath gates also. The houses of the town be well builded of stone, and ill-inhabited', in 1764 'the finest harbour I ever saw' and in 1794 'one of the most beautiful situations that can be imagined, it being surrounded with high hills covered with wood, down to the rocks which rise out of the sea'. Tintagel also received some attention possibly because of the Victorian interest in King Arthur. But some of the greatest praise was for Mount Edgcumbe. As the most famous garden in Cornwall, or even Devon, the well-heeled visitor expected to be allowed into the grounds and see the extensive grounds and experience the views which remain unparalled in the South West.[5]

Two other features of Cornwall were also in the expectations of the visitor. Mining was of considerable interest. Many visitors descended into at least one mine to see for themselves how the tin or copper was extracted and took home a sample rock. Fishing was the other great interest even if in 1793 one visitor found the smell of pilchards in Mevagissey overpowering.

Many thousands of travel accounts for Cornwall continue to be written; despite electronic communication lessening the volume of traditional hand-written letters, travel accounts carry on, for now at least, to be written on postcards. Also, some visitors continue to keep their own personal journals. For example, Keith Gabler, an American University student who was on a visit to Polperro in the summer of 2000, wrote in his travel journal:

> In 2000 most of the houses have been made up to look a bit nicer for the tourists. It seems as if Disney Land bought the place, renamed it Pirate Land and invented some traditional Cornish merchandise that is available in one of the many gift shops. Polperro once again showed just how awful life has been for a great number of people who have lived on this planet. The next two stops [Cote-hele and Saltram] for the day were quite the opposite. We got to see rich people's homes.[6]

This personal view will some day be of interest to historians. Hopefully it, along with at least some of the others now being written, will be archived and examined by future generations in order to help understand the nature of Cornwall at the start of the twenty-first century just as this collection of accounts assist us appreciate the complexities of Cornwall history over the last five centuries.

[5.] Douglas Ellory Pett, *The Parks and Gardens of Cornwall* (Penzance, 1998), 229–31; Helen McCabe, *Houses and Gardens of Cornwall* (Padstow, 1988), 27–31; Todd Gray, *The Garden History of Devon* (Exeter, 1995), 156–60.
[6.] Communication with Dr Joe Steiff, Columbia College, Chicago.

NOTES ON EDITING

Punctuation and spelling has largely been modernised and American English retained. Words in foreign languages appear in italics, except Cornish, as normally do unusual spellings of place names with the modern spelling generally given afterwards, in the first instance, in square brackets. A place of residence, where known, has been given for each traveller. The date given which follows the traveller's name indicates the year in which travel was undertaken. There are further travel accounts on Cornwall and these will hopefully be edited as an additional volume.

JOHN LELAND
of
ST MICHAEL LE QUERNE,
LONDON, *c.*1536, 1542

Engraving of John Leland from bust formerly in All Soul's College, Oxford

Bodleian Library, MS.Gen.Top.e8–15. There are a number
of imperfect manuscript copies of Leland's itinerary. The
earliest edition is by Thomas Hearne, *The Itinerary of John
Leland the Antiquary* (Oxford, 1710–1712) in nine volumes
with Cornwall in volume two, 108–116, and volume three,
11–42. However, the following extract is derived from that
edited by Lucy Toulmin-Smith, *The Itinerary of John Leland
In or About the Years 1535–43* (1907), 173–212 and 315–
26. The latter pages, noted as an appendix, comprises
Leland's later amended version of his Cornish account.
The Cornish section was included by Richard Pearse
Chope in his *Early Tours in Devon and Cornwall* (Devon &
Cornwall Record Society, 1918, reprinted Newton Abbot,

1967), 8–53 and there are considerable differences in both the wording and arrangement of text between the Toulmin-Smith and Pearse Chope editions. Also see John Chandler, *John Leland's Itinerary: Travels in Tudor England* (Stroud, 1993) who has modernised Leland's language. For example, his version of Leland's description of St Ives is 'The majority of houses on this peninsula are badly afflicted and smothered by sand which is thrown up during high winds and storms; it has been a problem for more than twenty years' whereas Toulim-Smith edited it as 'Most part of the houses in the peninsula be sore oppressed or overcovered with sands that the stormy winds and rages casteth up there; this calamity hath continued there little above 20 years.'

John Leland is now principally remembered for his travels but he was also an accomplished writer, and greatly concerned with identifying, locating and collecting, if not rescuing, ancient manuscripts and books. His *Itinerary*, with the lengthy detail on religious houses, would have been of interest to a wide audience during the English Reformation. Leland undertook the tours over the course of some eight years and visited Cornwall twice. The first visit was sometime before 1536 and the second in 1542. He was in his thirties when in Cornwall, suffered mental illness only a few years later and died in 1552. Some of Leland's terminology differs from modern use, such as the words 'pretty' by which he meant considerable, 'quick' which meant lively, and 'mean' by which he meant inferior or insignificant.

*c.*1536

...From *Depeford* to *Lanstoun* is a 12 miles by hilly and much moorish ground barren of wood. Or ever I came to *Lanstown* by a mile I passed over a bridge of stone having 3 arches, and a small, called New Bridge, through the which the river of Tamar runneth, that almost from the head of it to the mouth divideth *Devonshir* and *Cornewaule*. This New Bridge was of the making of the abbots of *Tavestok* [Tavistock] and maintained by them; for *Tavestoke* Abbey had fair possessions thereabout. The river of Tamar riseth a 3 miles by north east from *Hertelande* [Hartland], and thence cometh to *Tamertun* [Tamerton] a village on the east ripe in Devonshire; and there is a bridge over

Tamar of stone; and from this bridge to *Padestow* [Padstow] 20 miles.

Yalme [Yeolm] bridge of stone 2 miles lower; New Bridge 2 miles lower; *Polstun* bridge 2 miles lower; *Greistoun* [Greystone] bridge a 2 miles or more lower; *Tavestoke* about a 4 miles from *Greston* bridge, and *Grestown* bridge being about a 3 miles from *Launston* is the way from *Launston* to *Tavestok*; *Hawte* bridge; another bridge called New Bridge; *Caulstok* [Calstock] bridge next the sea begun by Sir Perse Eggecumbe. *Lideford* [Lydford] bridge is not on Tamar.

After that I had entered a little into the suburb of *Launstown* [Launceston], I passed over a brook called *Aterey*, that runneth in the bottom of the steep hill that *Launstown* standeth on. This water, as I there learned, riseth a 10 miles of by west north west towards *Bodmyne* [Bodmin], and passing by *Launstoun* goeth in Tamar by east, as I did gather, a little above *Pulstun* bridge. After that I had passed over *Aterey* I went up by the hill through the long suburb until I came to the town wall and gate, and so passed through the town, conscending the hill until I came to the very top of it, where the market place and the parish church of St Stephane, lately re-edified, be. The large and ancient castle of *Launstun* standeth on the knap of the hill by south a little from the parish church. Much of the castle yet standeth and the moles that the keep standeths on is large and of a terrible height, and the arx of it, having 3 several wards, is the strongest, but not the biggest, that ever I saw in any ancient work in England. There is a little purl of water that serveth the high part of *Lanstoun*.

The priory of *Launstoun* standeth in the west south west part of the suburb of the town under the root of the hill by a fair wood side and through this wood runneth a purl of water coming out of an hill thereby and it serveth all the offices of the place. In the church I marked 2 notable tombs, one of Prior Horton and another of Prior Stephane. One also told me that one Mabilia, a countess, was buried there in the chapter house. One William Warwist, Bishop of *Excestre*, erected this priory, and was after buried at *Plymtown* [Plympton] Priory that he also erected. Warwist, for erection of *Launston* Priory, suppressed a collegiate church of St Stephan, having prebendaries, and gave the best part of the lands of it to *Launstown* Priory, and took the residue himself. There yet standeth a church of St Stephan about half a mile from *Launstoun* on a hill where the collegiate church was. Gawen Carow hath the custody of the priory. There is a chapel by west north west a little without *Launstowne* dedicated to St Catarine, it is now profaned.

From *Launston* to *Botreaux* Castle, vulgo *Boscastel* [Boscastle], first a 2 miles by enclosed ground having some wood and good corn.

Thence an 8 miles by moorish and hilly ground and great scarcity of wood, insomuch that all the country thereabout burneth furse and heath. And thence a 2 miles to *Boscastel* by enclosed ground meetly fruitful of corn but exceeding barren of wood, to the which the bleak northern sea is not there of nature favorable. The town of *Boscastlle* lyeth upon the brow of a rocky hill by south east, and so goeth down by length to the north toward the sea, but not even full hard to it. It is a very filthy town and ill kept. There is a church in it, as I remember, of St Simpherian. The Lord Botreaux was lord of this town, a man of an old Cornish lineage, and had a manor place, a thing, as far as I could hear, of small reputation, as it is now, far unworthy the name of a castle. The people there call it the court.

There cometh down a little brook from south east out of the hills thereby, and so running by the west side of the town goeth into Severn sea betwixt 2 hills, and there maketh a poor havenet, but of no certain safeguard. One of the Hungrefordes married with one of the heirs general of *Botreaux*, and so *Boscastel* came to Hungreford. Then came *Boscastlle* by an heir general of the Hungrefordes onto the Lord Hastinges. Hastinges Earl of *Huntendune* and the late Lord Hungreford had a lordship of the Botreaux in partition, called Parke, and there is a manor place or castlet; it is 6 miles from *Botreaux* by south. There is no very notable town or building from *Botreaux* by east north east along upon the shore upper on Severn to *Hertland* point but *Strettoun* [Stratton], and that is 12 miles from *Botreaux*, and there is a pretty market; it standeth about a mile from the sea.

There is a place near to *Stretton* called *Ebbingford*, but now commonly Efford, where John Arundale of *Trerise* was born, and hath a fair manor place; in the which Sir John Chaumon now dwelleth, that married the mother yet living of John Arundale of *Trerise* [Trerice]. Old Treviliane, a man of pretty land but coming of a younger brother of the chief house of that name, dwelleth toward *Stretton* at a place called [blank]. *Hertland* point is a ten miles upper on Severn from *Strettoun*.

From *Botreaux* to *Tredewy* [Trethevy] village on the shore is about a mile, and there cometh down a brook rising in the great rocky hills thereby. From *Tredewi* to *Bossinny* [Bossiney] on the shore is about a mile. This *Bossenny* hath been a big thing for a fisher town, and hath great privileges granted onto it. A man may see there the ruins of a great number of houses. Here also cometh down a brook, and this brook and *Tredewy* water resort to the sea at one mouth betwixt 2 hills, whereof that that is on the east side lyeth out like an arm, or cape, and maketh the fashion of an havenet, or pier, whither shiplettes sometime resort for succour. A friar of late days took upon him to make an haven at this place, but he little prevailed therein. There lie 2 black rocks as islets at the west north west point or side of this creek, the one, saving a gut of water, joining to the other. And in these breed gulls be all likelihood.

From *Bossinny* to Tintagel Castle on the shore is a mile. This castle hath been a marvelous strong and notable fortress, and almost *situ loci inexpugnabile*, especially for the dungeon that is on a great and high terrible crag environed with the sea, but having a drawbridge from the residue of the castle onto it. There is yet a chapel standing within this dungeon of St Ulette alias Uliane. Sheep now feed within the dungeon. The residue of the buildings of the castle be sore weather beaten and in ruin, but it hath been a large thing. The castle standeth in the parish of *Trevenny*, and the parish church thereof is of St Symphorian, there called Simiferian.

Passing a mile from the church of St Symphorian by hilly and heathy ground I came over a brook that ran from south east north to Severn sea, and about half a mile beyond the mouth of this brook lay a great black rock like an islet in the sea not far from the shore. *Porthissek* [Port Isaac], a pretty fisher village, lyeth about a 3 miles from the mouth of the aforesaid brook lower by west on Severn Shore. There resorteth a brook to *Porthissek*; and there is a pier and some succour for fisher boats. *Porthguin* [Port Quin], a fisher village, lyeth a 2 miles lower on the shore, and there is the issue of a brook and a pier. And a 3 miles lower is the mouth of *Padestow* haven.

From *Dindagelle* [Tintagel] to *St Esse* [Teath or Issey] village is a 4 miles, [and there is] meetly good ground about *St Esse's* self. From *St Esse* to *Trelille* [Trelill] village is 2 miles, and from *Trelille* [I went] to [blank] where master Carniovies, *alias* Carnsey, hath a pretty house, fair ground, and pretty wood about it. Thence 3 miles by good corn ground, but no wood, to Wadebridge.

Where as now Wadebridge is there was a ferry a 80 years since, and men sometime passing over by horse stood often in great jeopardy. Then one Lovebone, vicar of Wadebridge, moved with pity began the bridge, and with great pain and study, good people putting their help thereto, finished it with 17 fair and great uniform arches of stone. One told me that the foundation of certain of the arches was first set on so quick sandy ground that Lovebone almost despaired to perform the bridge until such time as he laid packs of wool for foundation.

The river of *Alawne* [Allen] runneth through Wadebridge, evidently seen at lower. The first memorable bridge on *Alane* is called *Helham*

[Helland] bridge ... miles lower than *Camilforde* [Camelford], but *Alane* is almost a mile from *Camilford* town. *Dunmere* bridge of 3 arches a 2 miles lower. Here doth *Alaune* river run within a mile of *Bodmyn*. Wadebridge a 3 miles lower by land and 4 by water. This is the lowest bridge on *Alane*. There cometh a brook from St *Esse* 5 miles from Wadebridge, and a little above Wadebridge goeth into *Alane* by the east side of the haven. This brook riseth a 2 miles above St *Esse* by east north east. There cometh a brook from Mr Carnsey's house and goeth into *Alane* by the east side of the haven a 3 miles lower than Wadebridge, and here is a creek at the mouth of this brook that ebbeth and floweth up into the land.

In the way passing from *Dunmere* [Dinham] bridge toward *Bodmyn* there runneth a pretty brooket through a bridge of one stone arch, a very little way beyond *Dunmer* bridge; and a little lower goeth into *Alane* beneath *Dunmer* bridge by the west ripe of *Alane*. This little brook serveth the mills and runneth by the east end of the town of *Bodmyn*. There cometh a brook into *Alaune* about a 2 miles beneath *Dunmere* bridge on the west ripe. This brook riseth by south east and at St *Laurence* [Lawrence], scant a mile out of *Bodmyn*, I passed over a bridge on this water in the way to Michael.

From Wade Bridge to *Padestow*, a good quick fisher town but uncleanly kept, is a 4 Miles. This town is ancient, bearing the name of Lodenek in Cornish, and in English, after the true and old writings, Adelstow – *Latine Athelstian locus*; and the town there taketh King Adelstane for the chief giver of privileges onto it. The parish church of *Padestow* is of St [blank]. There use many Britons with small ships to resort to *Padestow* with commodities of their country and to buy fish. The town of *Padestow* is full of Irish men. *Padestow* is set on the west side of the haven. *Padestow* town is a [blank] miles from the very haven mouth. From the mouth of *Padestow* have to St *Carantokes* [Crantock] a [blank] miles.

From Wadebridge to *Dunmere* is a 3 miles, and thence a mile to *Bodymn*. *Bodmyn* hath a market on every Saturday like a fair for the confluence of people. The show and the principal of the town of *Bodmyn* is from west to east along in one street. There is a chapel of St [blank] at the west end of the town. The parish church standeth at the east end of the town, and is a fair large thing; there is a chantry chapel at the east end of it.

The late priory of black canons stood at the east end of the parish churchyard of *Bodmyne*. St Petrocus was patron of this, and sometime dwelled there. There hath been monks, then nuns, then secular priests, then monks again, and last canons regular in St Petroke's church in *Bodmine*. William Warlewist, bishop of *Excestre*, erected the last foundation of this priory, and had to himself part of the ancient lands of *Bodmyn* monastery. I saw no tombs in the priory very notable but Thomas Viviane, late prior there and suffragane by the title of the bishopric of Megarense. The shrine and tomb of St Petrok yet standeth in the east part of the church. There was a good place of gray friars in the south side of *Bodmyn* town. One John of London, a merchant, was the beginner of this house, [and] Edmund, Earl of *Cornwaul*, augmented it. There lay buried in the Gray Friars Sir Hugh and Sir Thomas Peverelle, knights, and benefactors to the house. There is another chapel in *Bodmyn* beside that in the west end of the town, and an almshouse, but not endowed with lands. The town of *Bodmyn* taketh King Edelstane for the chief erector and giver of privileges onto it. From *Bodmyn* to St *Columbes* [St Columb] 8 miles.

From *Bodmyn* to St *Laurence*, where a poor hospital or lazar house is, about a mile. One of the Peverelles gave a little annuity unto this house. Here I passed over a stone bridge, and under it runneth a pretty brook that cometh out of the hills from south east and got into *Alane* a 2 miles above *Padestow* by the west ripe, and by the means of the sea and creek it ebbeth and floweth up into the creek of this river. From St *Laurence* I passed by moorish ground all barren of wood, a 6 miles, leaving about this 6 miles end St *Columbes* about a 2 miles off on the right hand. And there about I left *Castle Endinas* [Castle-an-Dinas] on the same hand, a good mile of. But I saw no building on it, but an hill bearing that name. Thence to *Michal* [Mitchell], a little thoroughfare a 2 or 3 miles by moorish ground all barren of wood. Thence a 5 miles to a little village and parish church called *Aleine* [Allen]. And hereabout very good corn. And so a mile to *Guarnek* [Gwarnack], Master Arundel's house.

This Arundale giveth no part of the arms of great Arundales of *Lanhiran* [Lanherne] by St *Columbes*. But he told me that he thought that he came of the Arundales in base Normandy that were lords of Culy Castle, that now is descended to one Monsieur de la Fontaine, a Frenchman, by heir general. This Arundale is called Arundale of *Trerise* by a difference from Arundale of *Lanheron*. *Trerise* is a lordship of his a 3 or 4 miles from *Alein* Church. Arundale of *Trerise* had to his first wife one of the 2 daughters and heir of Boville alias a Beville, and Granville had the other, and they had betwixt them little lack of 400 marks of lands by the year in partition. The house that John Arundale of *Trerise* dwelleth in was Boville's; and this Boville gave the ox in gules in his arms. There is yet one of the name of the Beviles, a man of a £50 land purchased by the grandfather of [blank]

Bevile now living. This Beville had [blank] brother of John Arundale of *Trerise*. Humfrey Arundale a man of mean lands brother to old Arundale of *Lanheron*. Humfrey Arundale a man of mean lands nephew to Arundale. Sir John Arundale a son and heir to Arundale of Lanheron. Sir Thomas Arundale brother to Sir John. [blank] Arundal brother to Sir John and Thomas hath land of his fathers [blank]. Arundale of [blank] in Falmouth haven came out of the house of *Lanheron* [blank] Cirihais where Trevagnion now dwelleth was once the Arundalles.

Arms in Castle Cairdin

Sir William Godolchan and Strowde's daughter his wife of *Perham* [Parnham] in Dorsetshire. Sir William Godolchan and Margaret Glynne his first wife. Margaret was one of the 3 heirs of Glyn of *Morevale* by low water towards St Germans. Vivian of *Trelawaren* had another. Richard Kendale of Worngy had the 3rd. Vivian's grandfather was a man of mean land.

William Godolchan the son and Blanch Langdon his wife. Langdon dwelleth at Kenerel by St *Germanes*. St Albine his stock came out of *Britaine*. There is another house of the St Albines in Somersetshire. Graineville. Milatun dwelleth at Pergroinswik.

All in Devonshire: Fortescue of *Phile* [Filleigh], Fortescue of Preston, Fortescue of *Sprillestun*, Fortescue of *Wymestun*, Robert Fortescue of Wood

Fulford a Knight at Fulford in Devonshire.

Campernulphus *alias* Chambernoun *Dns olim de Trewardreth et fundator prioratus monachorum, qui post domini erant ejusdem monaster. manerii.* Campernulphus *nunc Dns de Modbyri in com.* Devoniæ. He was lord of *Bere*, toward *Excestre*.

Men of fair lands: Carrow of Mohuns *Oterey*, Carrow of *Hacham* [Haccombe] by Torbay, Carrow of Antony in *Cornewaulle* by *Aisch*.

Vivian.

all 3 in Menek. Reskimer

Erisi at Erisi in Menek.

Cowlin at Treueglis.

Cavel married Sir William Godolcan sister.

Petite was a man of very fair lands in *Cornewaulle*: and among other things he was lord of the Isle of Pryven that now descendeth to Kiligrew.

Bewpray: *id east de Bello prato*.

Archedeacon.

Tresinny at *Penrine*, a man of 40 mark lands, most part of it lyeth about *Padestow*.

Ex vita Sanctae Breacae.

Barricus socius Patritii, ut legitur in vita St Wymeri.

St Breaca nata in partibus Lagoniae & Ultoniae.

Campus Breacae in Hibernia, in quo Brigida oratorium construxit, et postea Monasterium in quo fuit et St Breaca.

Breaca venit in Cornubiam comitata multis Sanctis, inter quos fuerunt Sinninus Abbas, qui Romae come Patritio fuit, Maruanus Monachus, Germmocus rex Elwen, Crewenna, Helena.

Tecla appulit sub Revyer come suis, quorum partem occidit Tewder.

Breaca venit ad Pencair.

Breaca venit ad Trenewith.

Breaca aedificavit eccl. in Trenewith et Talmeneth, ut legitur in vita St Elwini.

Leyland.

Pencair an hill in Pembro parish, *vulgo* St [Banka].

Revier [Rivier] *Castlelum Theodori in orientali parte ostii Hayle fluvii nunc, ut quidam putant, absorptum à sabulo.* It was on the North Sea. Trenewith a little from the parish church of *Pembro* [Penbro], where the parish church [Breage] was or ever it was set at *Pembro*. Talmeneth a mansion place in *Pembro*. *Cairdine* [Kerthen] an old mansion of the Cowlines, where now William Godalcan dwelleth. Carne Godalcan on the top of an hill, where is a ditch, and there was a pile and principal habitation of the Godolcans. The ditch yet appeareth, and many stones of late time hath been fetched thence; it is a 3 miles from St Michael's Mount by east north east. Cair Kenin, *alias Gonyn et Conin*, stood in the hill of Pencair. There yet appeareth 2 ditches. Some say that Conan had a son called Tristrame.

St Germocus [Germoe] a church 3 miles from St Michael's Mount by east south east, and a mile from the sea. His tomb is yet seen there. St Germok there buried. St Germoke's chair in the churchyard. St Germoke's well a little without the churchyard. Garsike, *alias Pengarsike* [Pengersick] near the shore a 3 miles by east from St Michael's Mount. One Henry Force was lord of it. One of the Worthe's wives gave this land with a daughter of hers to one of the Milatuns of *Devonshir*.

[Milatum] hath Milatun in Devonshire; [Milatun] hath part of Mewis land [in Devonshire] by one of the heirs general of Mewis of … Mewes.] Urth, a daughter and heire of the Godalcans, married to Henry Force. Young Milatun hath Sir … Godalcan's daughter to his wife.

Marksin [Marazion] a great long town burned 3 *aut* 4 *anno* Henr. 8. *à Gallis*. The parish church of *Markine* a mile off. A pier by the

Mount. *Markine* and the Mount be both in St *Hilaries* parish. *Comes Moritoniæ et Cornubiæ* made a cell of monks in St Michael Mount. This cell was once given to a college in Cambridge. Since given to Syon. A fair spring in the Mount. *Ludewin, alias Ludevaulles* [Ludgvan], where, as some suppose, was a castle a mile by west from *Marksin,* it belonged to the Lord Brooke.

Pensandes [Penzance] 2 miles of by west; there is a little pier. *Newlin* [Newlyn] a mile lower on the shore; there is a pier. *Newlin* is an hamlet to Mousehole. Mousehole a mile lower. There is a pier. Mousehole in Cornish *port enis, portus insulæ.* A bay from *Newlin* to Mousehole called *Guaverslak.* A little beyond Mousehole an islet and a chapel of St *Clementes* in it. There hath been much land building, and wood devoured of the sea betwixt [*Pen*]*sandes* and Mousehole. There was found of late years since spear heads, axes for war, and swords of copper wrapped in linen scant perished, near the Mount in St *Hilaries* parish in tin works. There is an old legend of St Michael that speaketh of a townlet in this part now defaced and lying under the water. King Ethelstan founder of St *Burien's* College and giver of the privileges and sanctuary to it. St Buriana an holy woman of *Irelond* sometime dwelled in this place, and there made an oratory. King Ethelstane going hence, as it is said, onto *Sylley* [Scilly] and returning made *ex voto* a college where the oratory was.

Tredine Castle ruins at the south west point of Penwith. *Manifesta adhuc exstant vestigia.* I heard say that one Myendu was lord of it. Myendu, black mouth or chimney.

Revier [Rivier] Castle almost at the east part of the mouth of Hayle river on the North Sea, now, as some think, drowned with sand. This was Theodore's Castle. Combe Castle, *ubi tamen loci vestigia*: and Pencombe a little foreland about a mile upper then Kenor on Severn. Basset hath a right goodly lordship called *Treheddy* [Tehidy] by this combe. There cometh a good brook down by Combe. Cayl Castle a mile by east from river in St *Filakes* [Phillack] parish. Nikenor a 2 miles from *Ryvier,* sometime a great town, now gone. 2 parish churches is yet seen a good deal several on from the other, sometime in the town, but it is now commonly taken to be in St *Guivian's* [Gwithian] parish, and there cometh a brooket to the sea. *Carnbray* [Carn Brea] on an hill a castlet or pile of Bassets a mile to west of *Revier* town. There was sometime a park now defaced.

Scylley

There be counted a 140 islettes of *Scylley* that bear grass exceeding good pasture for cattle. St Mary Isle is a 5 miles or more in compass, in it is a poor town and a meetly strong pile: but the roofs of the buildings in it be sore defaced and worn. The ground of this isle beareth exceeding good corn; insomuch that if a man do but cast corn where hogs have rotted it will come up.

Iniscaw [Tresco] belonged to *Tavestoke*, and there was a poor cell of monks of *Tavestoke*. Some call this *Trescaw* it is the biggest of the islettes, in compass a 6 miles or more. St Martines Isle. St Agnes Isle is so called of a chapel therein. The isle of St Agnes was desolated by this chance *in recenti hominum memoria*. The whole number almost of 5 households that were in this isle came to a mariage or a feast into St Mary Isle, and going homeward were all drowned. Ratte Island. Saint Lides Isle, where in times past at her sepulchre was great superstition. There appear tokens in divers of the islettes of habitations now clean down. Gulls and puffins be taken in divers of these islettes. And plenty of conies be in divers of these islettes. Divers of these islettes beareth wild garlic. Few men be glad to inhabit these islettes, for all the plenty, for robbers by the sea that take their cattle of force. These robbers be Frenchmen and Spaniards.

One Davers a gentleman of *Wilshir*, whose chief house is at Daundesey: and Whitington, a gentleman of *Glocestreshire*, be owners of *Scylley*; but they have scant 40 marks by year of rents and commodities of it. *Scylley* is a kenning, that is to say about an 20 miles from the very westest point of *Cornewaulle*. Petites principal house was at *Ardeueranian* in *Gaulmouth* Haven by the peninsula called *Ardeuerameur*. Petites lands be now descended to Arundale of *Trerise*, Granville knight, and Killigrew. Thomas Levelis about St *Burianes*. Kiwartun at *Newlin* by Mousehole. John Godolcan at Mousehole. Cauelle in St *Cua* [Kew] parish at Trearach. Carnsew at *Bokelley* [Bokelly] in St *Cua* parish. Nicolle in St *Tedy* parish by Bokelly. Trecarelle at *Trecarelle* [Trecarell] by *Launston*. From Mr Godalcan to Pembro where the parish church is to Mr Godalcan. The personage impropriate to Heyles in *Glocestreshir*. The South sea is about a mile from *Pembro*. From Mr Godalcan to *Lanante* [Lelant] a 4 miles.

No greater tin works in all *Cornwal* then be on Sir William Godalcan's ground. *Heyle* haven choken with sand of tin works. *Heile* River cometh of 4 principal heads or brooks. One riseth by south, and other by south west, another by south east, the 4 by north east. Passage at ebb over a great strand: and then over *Heyle* River. Mr Mohun hath a fair lordship by St *Erthe*'s [Erth] called...

Trewinard, a gentleman, dwelling at *Trewinard* [Trewinnard] in St Erth parish. St Erth a good mile above *Lanant*. St Erth bridge a good mile from *Lannante* of 3 arches a little beneath the parish that standeth on the east side of the haven. This bridge was made a 200 years since and hath a 3 arches, afore there was a ferry. There came to this place once, the haven being unbarred and since choked with tin works, good tall ships.

There was a castle called Carnhangibes, as appeareth, or manor place now clean down, not far from the bridge. Dinham, as some say, was lord of this place, and to the court thereof belonging many knights and gentlemen's services. The town of *Lannant* is pretty, the church thereof is of St Unine.

St *Iës* [Ives] a 2 miles or more from *Lannant*. The place that the chief of the town hath and partly doth stand in is a very peninsula, and is extended into the sea of Severn as a cape. This peninsula to compass it by the rote lacketh little of a mile. Most part of the houses in the peninsula be sore oppressed or overcovered with sands that the stormy winds and rages casteth up there. This calamity hath continued there little above 20 years. The best part of the town now standeth in the south part of the peninsula up toward another hill for defence from the sands. There is a block house and a fair pier in the east side of the peninsula, but the pier is sore choked with sand.

The parish church is of Iä, a noble man's daughter of Ireland and disciple of St Barricus. Iä and Elwine with many other came into *Cornewaul* and landed at *Pendinas*. This *Pendinas* is the peninsula and stony rock where now the town of *Iës* standeth. One Dinan a great lord in *Cornewaul* made a church at *Pendinas* at the request of Iä, as it is written in St Iës legend. There is now at the very point of *Pendinas* a chapel of St Nicolas, and a pharos for light for ships sailing by night in those quarters.

The town of St *Iës* is served with fresh water of brookets that rise in the hills thereby. The late Lord Brooke was lord of St *Iës*, now Blunt Lord Monjoy and young Poulet. St *Piranes* [Perrans] in the sands is an 18 miles from St *Iës* upward on Severne. And St *Carantokes* is a 2 miles above that on the shore. Else little or no notable thing on the shore for so far.

The shore from St *Iës* is sore plagued to St *Carantokes* [Crantock] with sands. There dwelleth a gentleman of 50 marks land by year called *Glynne* [Glynn] in St *Iës*. From Mr Godalcan's to *Trewedenek* [Trewennack] about a 4 miles, where Thomas Godalcan [younger] son to Sir William buildeth a pretty house, and hath made an exceeding fair block house and mill in the rocky valley thereby. All the brooks that cometh from the hills thereabout gather toward this bottom and go into *Lo* [Loe] pool a 2 miles lower. *Lo* pool is a 2 miles in length, and betwixt it and the main sea is but a bar of sand. And once in 3 or 4 years what by the weight of the fresh water and rage of the sea it breaketh out, and then the fresh and salt water meeting maketh a wonderful noise. But soon after the mouth is barred again with sand. At other times the superfluity of the water of *Lo* pool draineth out through the sandy bar into the sea. If this bar might be always kept open it would be a goodly haven up to *Hailestoun*. The common fish of this pool is trout and eel.

Hailstoun, alias Hellas [Helston] standeth on an hill, a good market town having a mayor and privileges, and coinage twice a year for tin blocks. There hath been a castle. One parish church at the north west end of the town. An hospital of St John yet standing at the west south west end of the town, of the foundation of one Kylligrin.The fresh water that goeth to *Lo* pool cometh down on the west side of the town, but not even hard by it.

Wike [Gweek] mill water cometh within about half a mile by the east side of *Hailstoun*. From *Hailstown* to Mogun bridge about a 2 miles *dim*. Thorough this bridge runneth at ebb a little brook that riseth a … miles upper by west. It ebbeth and floweth about a mile above this bridge. I saw on the left hand a little beside this bridge the principal arm of *Hailford* Haven called *Wike*, the which floweth about a 3 miles upland by north to *Wike* Mill, and this arm is beaten with 2 little fresh brooks bearing the name of *Wyke*.

A flight shot beyond this bridge I came to a causey of stone, in the middle whereof was a bridge having but one arch. It floweth above this bridge: and at the ebb there resorteth a brook through this bridge that cometh down from south west. A little beneath these bridges both these brooks in one ran into *Wik* water. These bridges be a 4 miles or more from the mouth of *Heilford* haven.

About a 2 miles beneath this confluence runneth up on the east side of the haven a creek of salt water called *Poulpere* (*Poul Wheverel* [Polwheveral] about half a mile lower, having a brook resorting to it) and hemmeth in a piece of Mr Reskymer's park at *Merdon* [Merthen], so that with this creek and the main sea water of the haven upon a 3 parts the park is strengthened.

There is on the same side half a mile lower another creek called Cheilow *alias* Calm..ansak. [Calamansack] There be 4 creeks on the south side of the haven thus named: (each of these creeks hath a brooket resorting to them). Pen *Kestel* [Kestle] the first from the mouth, 4 miles beneath the bridges, whither ships do resort, and here is a *trajectus* from the one side of the haven to the other. This is a mile from the haven mouth, and here the ships commonly do lie. Caullons half a mile upward. Then *Mogun* [Mawgan] a 2 miles higher, where the bridge is with the broken stone. St *Mogun's* church up upon *Mogun* creek. *Gaire* [Gear], where the bridge is with the causey and one arch: so that this breaketh as a creek out of *Mogun*. St *Mawnoun* [Mawnan] church at the very point of the haven on the side toward *Falmuth* [Falmouth] a sea mark.

Gelling [Gyllyng] creek again St *Mawnoun's* on the other side, hard without the haven mouth. *Gilling* Creek breaketh at the head into 2 creeks. The patronage of St *Antonies* belonged to *Trewardreth*. [St] *Antonie's* church or chapel beside at … sand. [St] *Antonies* standeth in the point of the land of *Gilling* Creek, and the mouth of *Hailford* Haven. St *Keverin's* [Keverne] 2 miles from *Gilling* Creek and not a mile from the sea. St *Keverin's* belonged to *Bewle* [Beaulieu] Abbey in *Hampshir* a sanctuary privileged at St *Kevern's*. St *Piranes* [Piran/ Perran], *alias Keuerine*, where the sanctuary was … mile from St *Antonies*: and not a mile from the main sea.

Mr Reskimer hath a manor called by his own name a mile from *Moredon*. There hath been a fair house, but it fell to ruin in time of mind. Mr Reskimer beareth in his [coat of] arms a wolf. One of the Reskimers gave land to St *Keverines*, for sustentation of certain poor folks. From Gaire Bridge to *Tremain* [Tremayne], where Mr Reskimeur now dwelleth a good mile. This little house belonged to Tremain, and in time of mind came by heir general to one Tretherde. This Trederth hath beside lands and a pretty manor place at … John Riskimer's mother was Tretherth's daughter. There is in *Devonshir* one of the Tremains *a man of fair lands*.

From *Tremayn* over *Heilford* Haven to *Morden* where Mr Reskimer hath a ruinous manor place and a fair park well-wooded, whereof 3 parts is with the principal stream of the haven, and a creek called pool Penreth, hemmed in. *Morden* in *Constentine* [Constantine] parish. Then I rode half a mile and more of, from *Morden* over the fresh water that riseth no far distance off in the hills and goeth straight into *Poulpenrith*[Polpenwith] Creek. About half a mile farther I rode over an arm of the brook that cometh down to *Poulwitheral* [Polwheveral] Creek, and sone after I rode over the greater arm of the same brook, the salt arm lying in the bottom hard under it.

Then I rode a 4 miles by moory and rocky ground. And then within the space of half a mile I came to St *Budocus* [Budock] church. This Budocus was an Irish man and came into *Cornewall* and there dwelled. A little from the church there entered betwixt 2 hills on the shore a short creek like an havenet, but it was barred. And a quarter of a mile farther I came to *Arwennak* [Arwennack] Mr Keligrewis place, standing on the brim or shore within *Falemuth* Haven. This place hath been of continuance the ancient house of the Killigrewes. There was another house of the Keligrewis descending out of this: and it was in the town of *Penrine* [Penryn]. Now both these houses be joined in one.

The very point of the haven mouth being a hill wheron the king hath builded a castle is called *Pendinant* [Pendennis] and belongeth to Mr Keligrewe. It is a mile in compass by the compass and is almost environed with the sea, and where it is not the ground is so low, and the cut to be made so little that it were insulated. There lyeth a little cape or foreland with the haven a mile *dim.* almost again Mr Kiligrewis house called Penfusis.

Betwixt this cape and Mr Keligrew's house one great arm of the haven runneth up to *Penrine* town. *Penrine* 3 good miles from the very entry of *Falemuth* Haven and 2 miles from Penfusis. From St *Mawnon* to *Pendinas* by water a 4 miles. The king hath set his castle on *Pendinas* at one of the points of *Falemuth* Haven. *Pendinas* almost an isle. *Levine Prisklo, alias Levine Pole* [Swan Pool], betwixt St *Budocus* and *Pendinas*; it were a good haven but for the bar of sand.

The first creek or arm that casteth out on the north west side of *Falemuth* goeth up *Perin*, and at the end it breaketh into 2 arms the less to the college of *Glasenith, unus viridis nidus*, or Wag Mier at *Perin*, the other to St Gluvias the parish church of *Penrine* thereby. Out of each side of *Penrine* Creek breaketh out an arm or ever it come to Penr[yn.] Stakes and foundation of stone set in the creek at *Penrine* afore the town a little lower then where it breaketh into arms. A gap in the middle of the stakes and a chain. Good wood about the south and west side of Penryn.

One Water Good Bishop of *Excestre* made in a moor called *Glesnith* [Glasney] in the bottom of a park of his at *Penrine* a collegiate church with a provost, 12 prebendaries, and other ministers. This college is strongly walled and encastleated, having 3 strong towers and guns at the butt of the creek.

Betwixt the point of land of *Trefuses* [Trefusis] and the point of *Restronget* Wood is *Milor* [Mylor] [Creek,] and there is St *Milor's* church, and beyond the church is a good road for ships. *Milor* Creek goeth up a mile. Good wood in *Restronget* [Restronguet]. The next creek beyond the point in Stronget Wood is called *Restronget* and going 2 miles into the land and breaketh into 2 arms, and St. Pe... church standeth in the land betwixt; and on the arm is a stone called [Carr] Bridge in the way thence to *Truru*.

Betwixt *Restrongith* Creek [and the] Creek of *Truru* be two creeks that are called *Feoke* [Feock], and there is St Scaf... called St Cay.

Trure creek is next, and goeth up a 2 miles creeking up from the principal stream. This creek breaketh within half a mile of *Truru* and casteth in a creek westward by Newham wood. This creek of *Truru* afore the very town is devided into 2 parts, and each of them hath a brook coming down, and a bridge, and the town of *Truru* betwixt them both. The White Friars House was on the west arm in Kenwyn street. *Kenwen* Street is severed from *Truru* with this arm: and *Clementes* Streat by east is separate on the east side from *Truru* with the other arm. One parish church in Truro self. *Kenwen* and *Clementes* Streetes hath several churches, and bear the name of the saints of the parish churches. Coinage of tin at Midsummer and Michaelmas at *Truru*. *Truru* is a borough town and privileged.

There is a castle a quarter of a mile by west out of *Truru* belonging to the Earl of *Cornwale* now clean down. The site thereof is now used for a shooting and playing place. Out of the body of Truro Creek on the east side breaketh a creek eastward a mile from *Truru*: and goeth up a mile *dim.* to *Tresilian* [Tresillian] bridge of stone. There is a parish of St *Michell*.

At the entry and mouth of this creek is a road for ships called *Maples* [Malpas] Road, here fought a late 18 sail of merchant Spaniards, and 4 ships of war of *Depe*. The Spaniards chased hither the Frenchmen. A mile and half above the mouth of *Truru* Creek called *Lan Moran* [Lamorran] Creek of the church of St Moran. This creek goeth into the land a quarter of a mile from the main stream of the haven.

The main stream goeth up 2 miles about *Moran* Creek, ebbing and flowing, and a quarter of a mile above is the town of Tregony, *vulgo* Tregny; here is a bridge of stone *aliquot arcuum* upon *Fala* [Fal] River. *Fala* River riseth a mile or more of Rochehill, and goeth by *Granpond* borough where is a bridge of stone over it. *Graunpond* a 4 miles from Rac... and 2 little miles from Tregony. Mr Tregyon hath a manor place richly begun and amply but not ended called *Wuluedon*, *alias Goldoun* [Golden]. *Fala* River betwixt *Graunpond* and Tregony.

From Tregony to pass down by the body of the haven of *Falamuth* to the mouth of *Lanyhorne* [Lanihorne] creek or pill on the south east side of the haven is a 2 miles. This creek goeth up half a mile from the principal stream of the haven. At the head of this creek standeth the castle of *Lanyhorne* sometime a castle of a 7 towers, now decaying for lack of coverture. It belonged as principal house to the archdeacons. This lands descended by heirs general to the best Corbetes of *Shorpshir*, and to Vaulx of Northamptonshir. Vaulx part since bought by Tregyon of *Cornewaul*.

From *Lanyhorne* Pill is a place or point of land of 40 acres or thereabout as a peninsula, and is called *Ardeueraueur*, and is a mile from *Lanyhorn* Creek; and the water or creek that cometh or runneth into the south south east part is but a little thing, as of an half mile up into the land. The creek that hemmeth this peninsula in on the west south west side is the greater. The main land betwixt Crameur Creek and this...

From the mouth of the west creek of this peninsula to St *Juste* creek a 4 miles or more. In this creek is St *Justes* [Just-in-Roseland], parish church to St *Mawns*. From St *Juste* Pill or Creek to St Manditus creek is a mile *dim*. The point of the land betwixt St Just Creek and St *Maws* is of some called Pendinas. On this point standeth as in the entry of St *Maws* Creek, where is a castle or fortress late begun by the king. This creek of St *Maws* goeth up a 2 miles by east north east into the land, and so far it ebbeth and floweth, and there is a mill driven with a fresh brook that resorteth to the creek.

Scant a quarter of a mile from the castle on the same side upper into the land is a pretty village or fisher town with a pier called St *Maws*, and there is a chapel of him and his chair of stone a little without, and his well. They call this saint there St Mandite, he was a bishop in Britain and painted as a school-master. Half a mile from the head of this downward to the haven is a creek in manner of a pool with a round mark made in the chart on the which is a mill grinding with the tide.

A mile beneath that on the south side entereth a creek half a mile, and this is barred only by a small sand bank from the main sea a mile beneath this and almost again St *Maw*, a creek or pool going up a little in... , at the butt of this is a mill and a cell of St Antonie belonging to Plympton Priory: and here of late days lay 2 canons of *Plymptown* Priory.

All the creeks of *Fala* well wooded. From St *Antonies* point at the main sea to *Penare* [Nare] Point a 3 miles *dim*. Gref Islet lyeth scant half a mile east of *Penare* wherein breedeth gulls and other sea fouls. This Gref lyeth north from the Forne, a point or foreland in Britain, between the which is the entry of the sleeve of the ocean. And betwixt Forne and Grefe is a 5 kennings, and here is *breviss. trajectus* by estimation from *Cornewaulle* into *Britaine* continents.

About a mile by west of *Penare* is a force near the shore in the parish of St *Geron's* [Gerrans]. It is single diked, and within a butt shot of the north side of the same appeareth an hole of a vault broken up by a plough in tilling. This vault had an issue from the castle to the sea. A mile *dim*. from this force is another in the side of an hill.

And a little by north of the castle a 4 or 5 burrows or cast hills.

...are a quarter ... from the lordship of ...thy, sometime the Archdeacons now Corbettes and Tregions.

Dudeman [Dodman] Foreland or Point is about a 5 miles from Grefe. No wood on the very cost from St *Antonies* Point to *Dudeman*. Inward in the land some wood... This chapel land or point is in the park of *Bodrugam* [Bodrugan]. And in this park was the house of Sir Henry Bodrugam, a man of ancient stock attainted for taking part with King Richard the 3 again Henry the 7 and after flying into Ireland Sir Richard Eggecomb, father to Sir Pers Eggecombe, had *Bodrigan* and other parcels of Bodrigan's lands. And Trevagon had part of Bodrigan's lands, as *Restonget* and Newham, both in *Falamuth* Haven. From Chapel Land to *Pentowen* [Pentewan] a sandy bay, whither to fisher boats repair for a succour, a 2 miles. Here issueth out a pretty river that cometh from St *Austelles* about a 2 miles *dim*. off. And there is a bridge of stone of the name of the town.

This river runneth under the west side of the hill that the poor town of St *Austelles* standeth on. At St *Austelles* is nothing notable but the parish church. From *Pentowen* to the *Blake Head* about a mile. There is a fair quarry of white free stone on the shore rocks betwixt *Pentowen* and *Blak-Hed*, where of some be used in the inward parts of St *Mawre* fortress. The residue of moor stone and slate. And *Pendinas* Castle is all of moor stone except the filling. And in the cliffs between the *Blak-Hed* and *Tywartraith* [Tywardreath] Bay is a certain cave, wherein appeareth things like images gilted. And also in the same cliffs be veins of metals, as copper and other.

There is a mile from the entry of *Tywartraith* Bay up in the land, at the butt end of it a parish church of St *Blasé* [Blazey] and there is a new bridge of stone of the saint's name over a brook that there cometh into the bay. *Tywardreth*, a pretty town but no market, lyeth a quarter of a mile from the east side of the bay. There is a parish church, and there was a priory of black monks, cell sometime to a house in Normandy.

Some say Campernulphus was founder of this Priory. Some say that Cardinham was founder. Arundale of *Lanhern* was of late taken for founder. I saw a tomb in the west part of the church of the Priory with this inscription.

Haec east Tumba Roberti *filii* Wilihelmi.

This Robert Fitz Williams was a man of fair lands *tempore Edwardi 3 reg. Ang.*

From Tywardreth Town to *Fawey* Town a 2 miles. The point of land on the east side of *Tywardraith* Bay is called Penarth-Point. From Penarth to the haven mouth of *Fawey* is about a 2 miles. There is at the west point of the haven of *Fawey* mouth a block house devised by Thomas Treury and made partly by his cost, partly by the town of *Fawey*.

A little higher on this point of the hill is a chapel of St Catarine. And hard under the root of this hill a little within the haven mouth is a little bay or creek bearing the name of *Catarine*. About a quarter of a mile upper on this the west side of *Fawey* Haven is a square tower of stone for defence of the haven made about King Edward the 4 time, and little above this tower on the same side is *Fawey* town lying along the shore and builded on the side of a great slatey rocked hill.

In the middle of the town upon the shore self is a house builded quadrantly in the haven which shadoweth the ships in the haven above it from 3 parts of the haven mouth and defendeth them from storms. The name of the town of *Fawey* is in Cornish Couwhath. It is set on the north side of the haven, and is set hanging on a main rocky hill, and is in length about a quarter of a mile.

The town belonged to one Caridinham, a man of great fame; and he gave it to *Tywartraith* Priory, of the which some say that Cardinham was founder, some say Campernulph of *Bere*. But at this gift *Fawey* was but a small fisher town. The parish church of *Fawey* is of St Fimbarrus, and was impropriate to the priory of *Tywartraith*. The glory of *Fawey* rose by the wars in King Edward the first and the third and Henry the 5 day, partly by feats of war, partly by piracy, and so waxing rich fell all to marchandise: so that the town was haunted with ships of divers nations, and their ships went to all nations.

The ships of *Fawey* sailing by *Rhie* and *Winchelsey* about Edward the 3 time would vale no bonet being required, whereupon *Rhy* and *Winchelsey* men and they fought, where *Fawey* men had victory, and thereupon bear their arms mixed with the arms of *Rhy* and *Winchelsey*: and then rose the name of the gallants of *Fawey*.

The Frenchmen divers times assailed this town, and last most notably about Henry 6 time: when the wife of Thomas Treury the 2 with her men repelled the French out of her house in her husband's absence. Whereupon Thomas Treury builded a right fair and strong embattled tower in his house: and embattling all the walls of the house in a manner made it a castle: and unto this day it is the glory of the town building in *Faweye*.

In Edward the 4 day 2 strong towers made a little beneath the town, one on each side of the haven, and a chain to be drawn over. When war in Edward the 4 days ceased between the French men and

English, the men of *Fawey*, used to pray, kept their ships and assailed the Frenchmen in the sea against King Edward's commandment; whereupon the captains of the ships of *Fawey* were taken and sent to London, and *Dertemouth* [Dartmouth] men commanded to fetch their ships away; at which time *Dertmouth* men took them in *Fawy*, and took away, as it is said, the great chain that was made to be drawn over the haven from tower to tower. Thomas Treury now living and the town made a blockhouse on St Catarine's Hill bottom.

From Fowey town end by north in the haven is Chagha Mille Pill a little upward on the same side. A good mile above Chagha Mille Pill is on this west side *Bodmyn* Pill having for wares then to be carried to *Bodmyn*. A quarter of mile from *Bodmyn* Creek mouth up into the haven on the same side is *Gullant* [Golant] a fisher townlet. From *Gullant* to *Lantian* [Lantyan] Pill or Creek about half a mile: it goeth up but a little into the land. Barret a man of mean lands dwelleth betwixt *Gulland* and *Lantient* Pill. *Lantiant* lordship belonged to the Earl of *Saresbyri*.

From *Lantiant* Pill to Bloughan Pill or Creek near a mile, it creeketh up but a little. Carteis a gentleman almost of an 100 mark land dwelleth betwixt Blowghan and *Penknek* [Penknight] by Lostwithiel. From Bloughan to Lostwithiel scant a mile on the principal stream of *Fawey* River. It hath ebbed and flown above Lostwithiel, but now it floweth not full to the town. In Lostwithiel is the Shire Hall of *Cornewaul*. Thereby is also the Coinage Hall for tin. The town is privileged for a borough: and there is weekly a market on Thursday. *Richardus Rex Ro. comes Cornubiæ* privileged this town.

The parish is of St Barpholome. There cometh a brooket from west through the side of Lostwithiel; and goeth east into *Fawey* River dividing *Penkhek* from Lostwithiel. *Penknek* is in *Lanleversey* [Lanlivery] parish. The park of Restormel is hard by the north side of the town of Lostwithiel. Tin works in this park. Good wood in this park. There is a castle on an hill in this park where sometimes the Earls of *Cornewal* lay. The base court is sore defaced. The fair large dungeon yet standeth. A chapel cast out of it, a newer work then it, and now unroofed. A chapel of the Trinity in the park not far from the castle. The castle of Cardinham a 4 miles or more by north from Lostwithiel.

To this castle belongeth many knights services: Arundale of *Lanhern*, the Lord Souch, Compton and … parteth Cairdinhams lands. The river of *Fawey* riseth in *Fawey* Moor about a 2 miles from *Camilford* by south in a very wagmore [quagmire] in the side of an hill. Thence to Draynesbridge of flat moor stones. Thence to Clobhā Bridge drowned with sand 2 miles and more. Thence to Lergen

Bridge of 2 or 3 arches a mile lower. Thence to Newbridge of stone arched a 2 miles. Thence to Resprin bridge of stone arched, *alias* Laprin, about 2 miles. A little above Lostwithiel Bridge of stone the river of *Fawey* breaketh into 2 arms. Whereof at this day the less goeth to the stone bridge, the bigger to a wood bridge even again and but a little way of from the stone bridge, and after a pretty way lower the arms come again to one bottom.

The great part of *Fawey* Water is by policy turned from the stone bridge for choking of it and for to put the sand off from the bottom of the town. The stone bridge in time of memory living was of arches very deep to the sight, the sand is now come to within a 4 or 5 foot of the very head of them. The sand that cometh from tin works is a great cause of this: and in time to come shall be a sore decay to the whole haven of *Fawey*. Barges yet come with merchandise within half a mile of Lostwithiel.

From Lostwithiel down along *Fawey* River to St *Winnous* [Winnow] an abbot church a good mile. By the which church of old time inhabited a gentleman John de St Winnoco. After the Lords Hastinges were owners of it: and then sold to William Loures great grandfather now living. This Lower hath to wife one of the 2 daughters of Thomas Treury. By this church is a wharf to make ships on. Much good wood at St *Ginokes* and on the other side of the haven again it. From St *Guinows* church to the point of St *Winows* Wood half a mile. Here goeth in a salt creek half a mile on the east side of the haven, and at the head of it is a bridge called *Lerine* [Lerryn] Bridge, and the creek beareth also the name of *Lerine*. At the north side of this *Lerine* Creek almost at the head is Trenthey, Laurence Courtineis house. It belonged once to Stonnard, since to Cayle: and now last to the Courteneis of the house of *Devonshir* descending.

From *Lerine* Creek to St Carac Pill or creek [Penpoll] about half a mile lower on the said east side of the haven, it goeth a mile *dim.* up into the land. In middle of this creek on the north side was a little cell of Saint Cyret and Julette belonging to *Montegue* Priory. From the mouth of St Carak Pill to *Poul-Morlande* Pill about a mile, it goeth scant a quarter of a mile up into the land; and at the head goeth into 2 arms. From the mouth of *Poulmorland* [Polruan] to *Bodenek* [Bodinnick] village half a mile, where the passage is to *Fawey*, and from...

Mr Mohun hath a manor place called the *Haul* [Hall] on an hill above this village. From *Bodenek* to Pelene Point a quarter of a mile, and here entereth a pill or creek [Pont] half a mile up into the land. At the head of this pill is a chapel of St Wilow, and by it is a place called *Lamelin* [Lamellyon] in late belonging to Lamelin, now to Trelauny by heir general. Trelauny's house is at *Meneheneth* [Menheniot] by *Liscard*. On the south side of this creek is the parish church called *Lanteglise juxta Fawey* [Lanteglos] being the parish church of *Bodenek* and *Poulruan*.

From the mouth of this creek to *Poulruan*, a good fisher town, a quarter of a mile. Here by on the hill is a chapel of St Salvator. And at this *Poulruan* town is a tower of force marching again the tower on *Fawey* side. There was once, as it is said, a chain to go over the haven from tower to tower. The haven mouth of *Fawey* is a 2 bow shots off. The very point of land at the east side of the mouth of this haven is called *Pontus* [Pont] Cross, *vulgo* Paunch Cross.

From Lostwithiel to *Castledour* [Castle Dore] now clean down 3 good miles by plentiful ground of corn and grass. *Castledour* belonged to the Earl of *Saresbyri*. A mile off is broken cross thus inscribed: Conomor *et filius come Domina* Clusilla. From *Pontus* Cross to *Poulpirrhe* [Polperro] about a 6 miles, where is a little fisher town and a pier, with a very little creek and a brook. There is a creeket betwixt *Poulpirrhe* and *Low* [Looe] From *Poulpirrhe* to *Low* creek dry at half ebb a 2 miles. On each side of the entry of this creek is a town, the one called *Estlow*, the other *Westlow*. *Estlow* is a pretty market town. There is a great bridge of a 12 arches over *Low* Creek to go from the one town of *Low* to the other. Good wood about *Low* Creek. There is a manor place called *Trelaun* [Trelawne] about this *Low* Creek, sometime Bonvilles, now the Marquise of *Dorsetes*. Salmon taken in this creek.

Kendale and Code, gentlemen, dwell in *Morel* [Morval] parish on the east side of this creek. From *Low* creek to *Seton* [Seaton] Bridge of stone of a 2 arches and *Setown* River a 3 miles. From *Seton* to *Ramehed* about a 9 miles. From *Fawey* over the haven to *Bodenek* a fisher town, whereby Mr Mohun hath a manor place. Thence a 5 miles by very pleasant enclosed ground pretty wooded plentiful of corn and grass. Then a 3 miles by moory and heathy ground. Then 2 miles by hilly and woody ground to *Liscard* [Liskeard]. About half a mile or I came to *Liskard* I passed in a wood by a chapel of our Lady called our Lady in the Park, where was wont to be great pilgrimage. This chapel of ease belongeth to *Liskard*, and so doth 2 or 3 more.

Liskard standeth on rocky hills, and is the best market town at this day in *Cornwaul* saving *Bodmyn*. In this town the market is kept on Monday. The parish church is of St *Martine*, stondeth on an hill, and is a fair large thing. The personage is impropriate to... There was a castle on an hill in the town side by north from St Martin. It is now all in ruin. Fragments and pieces of walls yet stand. The site of it is magnificent and looketh over all the town. This castle was the Earls of Cornwall; is is now used sometime for a pound for cattle. The town acknowlegeth freedom and privileges by the gift of Richard King of Romans and Earl of *Cornewaul*. There is a goodly conduit in the middle of the town very plentiful of water to serve the town.

From *Liskard* to *Fawey* 10 [miles]. From *Liskard* to *Launstown* 12 miles. From *Liskard* to Lostwithiel 10. From *Liskard* to *Bodmyn* 10. From *Liskard* to *Low* market 7. From *Liskard* to St *Germaines* a 6 miles. From *Liskard* to *Plymmouth* a 12 miles. Coming out of *Liskarde* about half a mile I left *Cortyder* [Cartuther], a goodly lordship, and an old manor place on the right hand; it is a hundereth pound by the year. This is now fallen onto heir general in partition. Cotyder and the lordship of Tregelly now called *Minheneth* lordship belonged, as Mr Trelawny told me, to one Heling or Eling, an oder came after ...e therof na... *Cotyder* ... had male... *Cotyder* now Beket hath *Cotyder* self. Corington and another of them had ... From *Liskard* to *Minheneth* 2 miles, where is a fair large old church. The personage of it is impropriate to ... The manor of *Minheneth* was sometime called Tregelly, whereof the name and some ruins yet remain. Trelawney now living is the 4 of that name that hath be Lord of *Minheneth*. There was one Sir John Trelawney an ancient gentleman father of the first Trelawney of *Minheneth*. But be likelihood he had an elder son, for Trelawney now living hath none of the lands: but is is descended to heirs generals. From *Mynhenet* to the ruins of Bodulcan's place a 2 miles.

Half a mile of a great brook after the course of a 4 miles resorting to *Liner* [Lynher] and St *Germane's* Creek a this side St *Germane's*. Another brooket a quarter of a mile beyond that resorteth to the other. Thence to *Natter* [Notter] bridge of 2 or 3 arches 4 miles, it standeth on the *Liner* River. This river, as far as I could learn, riseth by north east up towards the quarters of *Launstoun*. The soil betwixt *Minheneth* and *Natter* Bridge very good, and enclosed, and meetly well wooded. From *Natter* Bridge to St *Germane's* about a 2 mile. The town of St *Germane's* is on the hither side of *Liner* as I came to this bridge. St *Germane's* is but a poor fisher town. The glory of it stood by the priory. St *Germane's* standeth about a 3 miles in *Liner* creek from the main strand of Tamar Haven. From *Liner* Bridge to *Asche* about a 4 miles by much like ground.

Asche [Saltash] is a pretty quick market town and is set from the top of a rocky hill as by west to the root of the same and very shore of Tamar Haven by east. The townsmen use both merchandise and fisher. There is a chapel of ease in *Asche*. The parish church is called St Stephan's, about half a mile off by south, the personage whereof is impropriate to *Windesore* College.

By St Stephanes and in St Stephanes parish is the great and ancient castle of *Tremertown* [Trematon] upon a rocky hill: whereof great pieces yet stand and especially the dungeon. The ruins now serve for a prison. Great liberties belong to this castle. The Valetortes, men of great possession, were owners, and, as far as I can gather, builders of this castle, and owners and lords of the town of *Aische*. Morwel the Abbot of *Tavestok* House about a mile from *Morleham* [Morwellham]. Tamar a little from *Morwelle*. From *Tavestok* to *Greston* [Greystone] Bridge a 6 miles: and then 3 miles to *Launston*. Tamar 2 miles and more from *Tavestock*. *Calstok* [Calstock] Bridge or New Bridge two miles from *Milbrok* [Millbrook] the first creek. St John the next. *Liner* [Lynher] the 3. The 4 a little above *Asche*. The 5 without fail is the main stream of Tamar.

From Reddon the land lying south west on St Nicholas Isle to Cair Grene where Tamar turneth west a 6 miles, Tamar going a mile west for the most part after goeth north. These creeks I noted on the west side of the Tamar: first I marked in sight about *Aschetown* a 2 miles or more the principal arm of Tamar Haven going up into the land about a 10 miles from that place to *Caulstoke* Bridge, whither to it almost ebbeth and floweth. And ships come up within a mile of this bridge to a place called *Morleham*. And this place is but 3 miles from *Tavestoke*. *Tavestoke* is counted to be but 10 miles from *Asche* to go the next way. Betwixt the 2 miles from *Asch* to the main arm of Tamar in sight I marked descending in the haven 3 creeks breaking out into the land, whereof the first lyeth by north west creeking up into the land. The second lyeth west north west. The 3 plain west and this creeked in to the land scant half a mile. Scant a mile lower lyeth *Liner* Creek going up onto *St Germane's*.

The town of *Asch* standeth between these 2 creeks. Then breaketh a little creek out called St John's or Antony. And at the mouth about St Nicholas breaketh in a creek going up to *Milbrok* 2 miles up in land from the main haven. This *Milburne* is a rich fisher town. *Penle* aforeland lyeth 3 miles lower from this creek into the land. And the promontory of *Ramehed* a mile lower…

1542

The Middle Part of *Cornewale*.

By the river of Tamar from the head north north east issuing out toward the south, the country being hilly, is fertile of corne and grass with some tin works wrought by violence of water. *Hengiston* [Hingston] being a high hill, and near Tamar, in the east part, barren of his self, yet is fertile by yielding of tin both be water and dry works. The middle of *Cornewale* to the east part high mountains, rochel ground, very barren with some tin works in them. *Cornewal* thorough out from the east part to the west, nearer to the north part then to the south, is high mountains barren ground. Fruitful from *Launston* to *Bodman*, in a dry summer good for pasturage for cattle with some tins work.

Look for Dosmery Poole, otherwise called Dounëuet, almost by St Annes Hill. From *Bodman* to *Redruthe*, village nearer to the north sea then to the south be high mountains barren also, yielding bare pasture and tin. From Redruth to Carne Gotholghan the country is hilly, very barren of grass and plenteful of tin. From *Lanant* to *St Juste alias Justinian*, being the very west point of all *Cornewayle*, the north part is mountains and barren grown, but plentiful of tin. The very west point as it is called now in Cornish is Penwolase, *id est, infimum caput*.

The North Part of *Cornewale*.

From Stratton, not very far from the head of Tamar, to Padstow the country by the north sea is rather hilly then mountainous, and is very fertile of grass and corn. And the cliffs of the said north sea between the places aforesaid hath good fine blue slates, apt for house covering, and also hath divers veins of lead and other metals not yet known.

Also about Camelford are certain old mines, wrought in times past, but of what metal it is now unknown. Within a mile above that poor village south runneth the river that goeth into the Severn sea at *Paddistow*; and it is the greatest river on the north side of *Cornewale*, and is called in the common speech there Dunmere, and in the Kings grant of privilege to the canons of *Bodmynne*, and the burgesses of the same town, *Alan*, it may fortune for *Aluane*. Some histories called Cablan. By this river Arture fought his last field, in token whereof the people find there in ploughing bones and harness.

Within 4 miles of the said *Camylford* upon the north cliff is Tintagel, the which castle had by likelihood 3 wards, whereof 2 be worn away with gulfing in on the sea, in so much that it hath made there almost an isle, and no way is to enter into it now but by long elm trees laid for a bridge. So that now without the isle runneth all only a gatehouse, a wall, and a false bray digged and walled. In the isle remain old walls, and in the east part of the same, the ground being lower, remainth a wall embattled, and men alive saw there in a postern door of iron. There is in the isle a pretty chapel with a tomb on the left side. There is also in the isle a well, and nigh by the same is a place hewn out of the stoney ground to the length and breadth of a man. Also there remaineth in the isle a ground quadrant walled as it were a garden plot. And by this wall appear the ruins of a vault. The ground of this isle now nourisheth sheep and conies.

Paddistow [Padstow], a haven town of one parish of fishermen, where ships come not in but at the flowing water. In the east part of *Paddestow* haven be 2. ...kketes that ...yth sea... The east ... is called ...tyre, and so is the land that lyeth against it. The ground by the sea coast from *Paddestow* to Saint Anne's hill, whereon (*i.e.*, *super montem Annæ*) is no manor of building, the ground somewhat hilly, is fruitful of corn and grass, but with little tin.

Upon an 8 miles from *Paddestou* is a little house of canons secular called *Crantoke*. From Saint Anne's hill to *Lanant* a village the country by the north sea is somewhat hilly, sandy, and barren, and in sundry places of the same well replenished with tin.

By *Conarton* cometh a river called *Dour Conor*, and goeth to the sea not far from *Lanant* river mouth. In the mouth of the river that cometh by *Lanant* is the rocket *Godryve* wherein breedeth seafowl. From *Lanant* by the north sea to St Just, *alias* Justinian, where is no thing but a parish church of divers sparkled houses at the west point of the shore called ... The ground is but barren, but it hath in divers places good tin works. By all the north sea in *Cornewale* be sundry creek, whereas small fishers boats be drawn up to dry land, and in fair weather the inhabitants fish with the same.

At *Paddestow* haven, *Lanant*, and St *Yes*, the balingers and ships are saved and kept from all weathers with quays or piers. Dosmery pool standing in the east part of the same somewhat toward the south is of length by estimation 2 arrow shots, and of breadth one, standing on a hill, in the east part of the which pool is a vale of 14 or 15 fathom deep by estimation; and out of this pool issueth a river, the which running by the space of a mile and a *dim*. is of 3 fathom deep, and is called Depe Hatche. Look where he issueth into the sea.

Also in the said hilly ground and moorish be red deer, the which when they be chased take the said pool for soil. There be of the Isles of *Scylley* 147 that bear grass (beside blind rockettes) and they be by estimation a 30 miles from the west part of *Cornewale*. In the biggest isle (called St Nicholas Isle) of the *Scylleys* is a little pile or fortress, and a parish church that a monk of *Tavestoke* in peace doth serve as a member to *Tavestoke* abbey. There be in that parish about a 60 households. There is one isle of the *Scylleys* called Rat Isle, in the which be so many rats that if horse, or any other living best be brought thither they devour him. There is another called Bovy Isle. There is another called *Inisschawe*, that is to say, the Isle of Elder, because it beareth stinking elders. There be wild boars or swine.

From St Just to *Newlin* eastward the ground is somewhat hilly and fertile of grass, with tin works both wet and dry, without haven or creek, saving in diver places there remain capstans like engines as ships doth way their anchors by, wherewith they draw their boats up to dry land, and fish but in fair weather. Also in the south-west point betwixt St Just and Newlyn is a point or a promontory almost environed with the sea wherein is nothing but as it where a hill enclustered with rocks as it had been in times past a castle, and for the declaration thereof there remain yet toward the land 2 wards clean fallen down; but the stone of them remain there very fair and well quadrated. The ruin of the fortlet in the point is at this day a hold irrecoverable for the fox.

There lyeth betwixt the south-west and Newlyn a mile or more of of the sea St *Buryens* [Buryan] a sanctuary, whereby, as near to the church, be not above 8 dwelling houses. There belongeth to St *Buryens* a dean and a few prebendaries that almost be never there. And St *Buryens* is a 4 miles from the very south-west point.

Newlin is a poor fisher town, and hath all only a quay for ships and boats with a little succour of land water. Within a arrow shot of the said quay or pier let directly a little low island with a chapel in it. And this little islet beareth grass.

Mowsehole is a pretty fisher town in the west part of *Montesbay* lying hard by the shore, and hath no safeguard for ships but a forced pier. Also in the bay be east the same town is a good road for ships called *Guaves* Lake.

Pensants about a mile from *Mowsehoole* standing fast in the shore of *Montbay*, is the westest market town of all *Cornwayle*, and no succour for boats or ships but a forced pier or quay. There is but a chapel in the said town as is in Newlyn. For their parish churches be more then a mile off.

Marhasdeythyou, alias forum Jovis, is a fisher town with a market, and standeth fast upon the shore of the bay directly against the foot of St Michael's Mount northward. Be the west end of the town is a lake, or a *rivulus* the head whereof riseth within a mile of *Lanant* northward from *Marhesdeythyou.*

In *Marhasdeythyow* is but a poor chapel in the midst of the poor town, and little chapel in the sand near by the town toward the Mount. Betwixt the head of this *rivulus* and the nearest part of the river of *Heyle,* that cometh in to the sea at *Lanant,* is not a mile. And the ground of breadth between the full sea mark at *forum Jovis* and the full sea mark of *Lanant* river is not 2 miles.

The compass of the root of the Mount of St Michael is not *dim.* mile about. The south south-east part of the Mount is pasturable and breedeth conies. The residue high and rocky. In the north north-east part of the Mount is pasturable and breedeth conies. The residue high and rocky. In the north north-east is a garden with certain houses with shops for fishermen. To the north north-west is a pier for boats and ships. The way to the church entereth at the north side from half ebb to half flood to the foot of the Mount, and so ascendeth by steps and grasses westward, and thence returneth eastward to the utter ward of the church. Within the said ward is a court strongly walled, wherein on the south side is the chapel of St Michael, and in the east side a chapel of our Lady. The captain and priest's lodgings be in the south side and the west of St Mich. chapel. The Mount is enclosed with the sea from *dim.* flood to *dim.* ebb, other wise men may come to the Mount afoot.

In the bay betwixt the Mount and *Pensants* be found near the low water mark roots of trees in divers places, as a token of the ground wasted. There be found from the inward part of the ...ivers ...re stones ...wes and ...ois 5 miles ... the sea. The compass of the bay is from *Lyzart* point to Newlyn about a 20 miles.

Within 3 miles of *Lyzart* point is a little isle within the bay, called *Inispriuen,* and containeth 2 acres of ground wherein be birds and conies. The ground from *Neulin* to *Loo* pool by the south sea is not very fertile, but hath good tinwork. From the point of *Lyzart* to *Hayleford* Haven the ground is fertile of corn and grass by the south sea.

Also within 3 miles of the south sea betwene *Haylford* and the east side of *Montesbay* is a wild moor called *Gunhilly, i.e.,* hilly heath, where is brood of cattle. Also in the west side of the point of *Hayleford* Haven, and within the land of *Meneke,* or Menegland, is a parish church of St *Keueryn,* otherwise Piranus, and there is a sanctuary with 10 or 12 dwelling houses, and thereby was a cell of monks, but now gone home to their head house. The ruins of the monastery yet remaineth.

Within 2 miles of the head of the full sea mark of *Heyle* river is *Heylston* a market town, within the which there is a court for the coinage of tin kept twice in the year. In the town is both a chapel and a parish, and yet appeareth in the town *vestigia castleli* in the west part; and a river running under the same *vestigia* of the castle issueth toward the south see, stopped there with south east winds casting up sands maketh a pool called *Loo*, of an arrow shot in breadth, and a 2 mile in compass in the summer. In the winter, by the reason of floods flowing to *Heylston* town, whereby the mills near *Heylston* being stopped men be constrained to cut the sandy bank betwixt the mouth of the pool and the sea, whereby the water may have issue, and the mills grind; by the which gut so opened the sea floweth and ebbeth in to the pool, whereby sea fish entering with a south east wind is closed in the pool, the gut being again choked and filled with sand, and so after taken with trouts and eels drawn in the same pool.

The country from Newlyn to *Heylston* is meetly fertile of grass and corn, and plentious of tin by the south sea. From the mouth of *Heylford* to *Falemuth* be water is 4 miles. *Falemuth* is a having very notable and famous, and in a manor the most principal of all *Britayne*. For the channel of the entry hath be space of 2 miles into the land 14 fathom of deeps, which commonly is called *Caryk* Road because it is a sure harbour for the greatest ships that travel by the ocean. At the entry of the haven lyeth a blind rock covered at full sea, nearer the west side of the haven then the east, called Caregroyne, *i.e., insula vel rupes potius vitulorum marinorum, alias Seeles.* Seals when they cast their calves they come to land, and lay their *foetum* in a dry bank, the which they may come to, and there they suffer their *foetum* to tarry a while or the bring him to the sea.

In the east side of the said haven entereth a creek flowing by the space of 2 miles into land, and is fed at the head with fresh water. Upon the south side of this creek is a cell belonging to the house of Plympton called St Antony's, having but 2 canons. On the very north shore of the said creek toward the haven's mouth is a poor fisher village called St *Mausa* [Mawes] alias La Vousa, and nigh to this village toward the same haven is a fortlet lately builded by the country for the defense of the haven.

In the west side of the haven is a creek that floweth up from the haven's mouth into the land above 3 miles, at the very head of the which standeth a pretty town called *Peryn*, of merchandise, and victual market. Within the town is a college well walled and diked defensibly called St Thomas, where be secular canons and a provost. Also in the town is a chapel, and a quarter of a mile out of the town is the parish church. Also 8 miles and more above the said haven's mouth is a market town east north east called *Trureu*, wherein is a mayor, and also coinage for tin, with a parish church and a black friars. Also on the south east side at the head of the old full sea mark of *Falemuth* is a market town 12 miles and more up into land called *Tregoney*, wherein is an old castle and a parish church of St James standing in a more by the castle: also a ch... standing in the midst of the town, and at the east end of the town a parish church.

St *Austol's*, a poor village with a parish church, is 62 miles east from *Tregoney*. *Trewardreth* Bay hath at the head on the east side a poor village, with a parish church, and a priory in the same town of Cluny monks. From *Falemuth* to *Trewardreth* by the south sea the ground is meetly fertile of corn and grass, and no tin works from *Falemuth* to *Dudman* foreland.

In the mid way between *Falemuth* and *Dudman* is an islet or rock bearing grass called Grefe, a 2 acres about, but standing in the midst torring up right. There breedeth in the isle sea fowl. From *Dudman* Foreland to *Trewardreth* the country somewhat barren of grass and corn, and replenished with tin works, with veins in the sea cliffs of copper. Pasture, corn and wood, meetly plenty.

From *Trewardreth* to Fowey town is 2 miles. Between these towns by the south sea there is plenty of corn and grass, but no tin works. The town of Fowey is a market town walled defensably to the sea coast, and hath gates also. In the town is but one church, but the houses of the town be well builded of stone, and ill inhabited. Also at the entry of the haven on the west side is a block house and a chapel of St Catarine be the same. Also there is on the same side a tower with ordinance for defence of the haven. On the west side a 2 miles up in the haven is a fisher town called *Gullant*.

At the head of the full sea mark of this haven, and a quarter of a mile more is the town of *Lost Whythyel* having a market, and is the shire town of *Cornewal*. For there the shire is kept by the sherrif once in the month. Also at this town is coinage of tin twice a year. And by the shire hall appear ruins of ancient buildings, a house of the Duke of *Cornwal*. It is evidently known that it hath flowed to *Lost Whythiel*; but the spewing of the sands of the tin works hath stopped it now. The little round castle of Restormel standeth in the king's park nigh to *Loswithiel*. At the east side of the haven's mouth of Fowey standeth a tower for the defense thereof, and a chapel of St Savyor a little above the same. Nigh by the said tower standeth a fisher village called *Porthruan*.

A mile beyond *Polruen* on the east side of the same haven standeth a poor fisher village called *Bodennek*. There is the passage or *trajectus* to Fowey. 2 miles above *Bodennek* into the land northward is a creek upon the north side, wherein is a cell of 2 black monks of *Montegu*, and is dedicated to St Sirice and Julit. By east the haven of Fowey upon a 4 miles is a small creek called *Poul Pier*, and a simple and poor village upon the east side of the same of fishermen, and the boats their fishing be saved by a pier or quay.

In the east side also of this *Poul Pyrre* 2 miles off is another creek called *Loow*, being but a tide creek. For at low water beneath the bridge a man may both wade and ride over in the summer. There is on either side of this small creek a small fisher village hard on the sea shore, the one called east and the other West *Loowe*, east *Loowe* being a market town, and in either of them a chapel. Also in the said creeks mouth near somewhat to the south west is a low isle called St Nicholas Isle, not a quarter of a mile from the main shore, and containeth a 6 or 8 acres in compass, and feedeth sheep and conies, nourishing also brood of sea birds.

There is a bridge somewhat above these 2 villages of 10 or 12 stone arches, over the which men pass when the sea is in. From Fowey Haven to *Lowe* creek the ground nigh the sea side is very fertile of corn and grass, and no tin works. From *Loowe* Creek to Tamar is a 12 miles toward the town of *Plymmuth*. In the west side of Tamar within 3 miles of the haven mouth of Tamar is a simple fisher town called *Mylbrooke*. Also upon another creek west of the said river and nearer up is a town called St *Germayns*, wherein is now a priory of black canons, and a parish church in the body of the same. Beside the high altar of the same priory on the right hand is a tomb in the wall with an image of a bishop, and over the tomb a 11 bishops painted with their names and verses as token of so many bishops buried there, or that there had been so many Bishops of Cornwall that had their seat there. And at this day the Bishop of *Exceter* hath a place called *Cudden Beke* joining hard upon the southest side of the same town.

North east of St *Germaynes* 6 miles upon the river of Tamar is a market town called *Asshe* [Saltash]. And near to the same westward within 2 miles is a round castle of the kings called *Tremeton*, as a man should say the second fortress on Tamar. At the town of *Asshe* is a passage or ferry of a quarter of a mile over. Also 2 miles from *Asshe* northward into the land is a small village called *Caregrin*. East of this is *Bere* park and house in Devonshire, divided from *Caregrin* [Cargreen] *tantum Tamara*. From *Low* to Tamar by the south sea the ground is fertile of corn and grass, but without tin works.

[?Cornw]ail is now ...d by ... hundreths that is to say on the south ...e from the east part west ward the hundreds of east, and west, Powder and *Kyrer*. On the north westward Stratton, *Lesnewith*, *Tryg*, Pyder and Penwith.

Launston, otherwise called *Lostephan*, in old time called Duneuet, standeth 2 miles beyond *Powlston* Bridge on Tamar westward. The said town Duneuet, otherwise *Lawnston*, is a walled town nigh in compass a mile, but now ruinous. On the north side of the town a castle standing on a high hill with in the said town hath 3 round wards. Part of the castle standing north west is parcel of the wall of the town. There be within this town 3 gates and a postern; also a gate to go out of the castle into the old park. Some gentlemen of *Cornewal* hold their lands by castlegard, that is to say for reparation of this castle and town: and within this castle is a chapel, and a hall for assises and sessions, for a common gaol for all *Cornwayle* is in this castle. Within this town is a market, a mayor and burgesses, with a chapel of Mary Magdalan to their uses.

In a vale at the foot of the hill of the said town, about an arrow shot from the castle northward, is a priory of canons regular dedicate to St Stephan. North east almost half a mile of the said priory is a little village upon a hill, and a parish church of St Stephen in it. The opinion is that the canons first dwelled on this hill, and came thence down to a better and a warmer site. In the Priory churchyard standeth also a parish church. The wall of Duneuet is high, large and strong, and defensably set. By the north side of the priory runneth a little river. In Duneuet be 2 conduits of derived water...

JOHN TAYLOR
of
LONDON, 1649

Mount's Bay, from John Speed's map of Cornwall, 1610

J.O. Halliwell-Phillipps, *The Literature of the Sixteenth and Seventeenth Centuries Illustrated* (1851), reprinted by Frank Graham as *John Taylor's Wandering to see the Wonders of the West* (Newcastle upon Tyne, 1967), 13–25.

Taylor, the 'Water Poet', was a known Royalist and must have had some apprehensions regarding a visit to the South West at the end of the Civil War. Taylor was 69 years old when he visited Cornwall and died only four years later. He was well-travelled and this was only one of many publications.

...I turned my back upon Devonshire, having gone that day fifteen miles to the market town in Cornwall (on the north side of the county) named Stratton. Cornwall is the *Cornucopia*, the complete and replete horn of abundance for high churlish hills, and affable courteous people, they are loving to requite a kindness, placable to remit a wrong, and hardy to retort injuries; the country hath its share of huge stones, mighty rocks, noble, free, gentlemen, bountiful house-keepers, strong and stout men, handsome, beautiful women, and (for any that I know) there is not one Cornish cuckold to be found in the whole county: in brief they are in most plentiful manner happy in the abundance of right and left hand blessings.

It is a wonder that such rugged mountains do produce such fertility of corn, and cattle; for if the happy days and times of peace were once settled, Cornwall might compare with any county in England, for quantity of all necessaries needful, and quality of persons.

The ninth of July I left Stratton, and ambled twenty miles to the town of Camelford, and to a village called Blisland, and there I was taken for the man I was not; for they suspected me to be a bringer of writs and process to serve upon some gentlemen, and to bring men into trouble: But with much ado I escaped a beating, by beating into their beliefs that I was no such creature.

July the tenth, I came to Bodmin, (a market town) and from thence the same day to a village called St Enoder, a part of which parish is called Penhall, there at a smith's house was good lodging, better cheer, and best drink; the smith was lame, his wife was fair and handsome, where if I could have acted the part of *Mars*, there might have been played the comedy of *Vulcan* and *Venus*: that day's travel was eighteen miles.

July eleventh, I progressed to Truro, another market town, which is the Lord Roberts his land; there I bought a fish called a Bream for three pence, it would have served four men; after dinner I went eight miles further to a town called Redruth, in all that day's travels eighteen miles, I saw nothing strange to me but a few Cornish daws (or choughs) with red bills, and legs. They saluted me upon the wing, just in the language of our jack daws about London, *Ka, ka.*

The twelfth of July, I came within two miles of Saint Michael's Mount, to an ancient house called by the name of *Trimineague* [Treveneague]; it hath been, and is the birth place of worthy families, of the noble name of the Godolphins; The right owner and possessor of it now is Francis Godolphin, Esquire, a gentleman endowed with piety, humanity, affability and ability; he hath a heart charitable, a mind bountiful, and a hand liberal; he hath (deservedly) the cordial love of all the county, and would have the enjoyments of earthly contentments, if once these discontented times were quieted; seven days I stayed with him, in which time he was pleased to send a kinsman of his (Mr Anthony Godolphin) with me to see the Mount, which I thus describe. It is about a mile in compass at the foot, and it rises about 700 paces very steep to the top, it is in form like a great haycock or rick, or much like a mountere [sic]; on the top or piramis of it, is a fine church called Saint Michaels, the said church is now for no other use but a well stored magazine with ammunition. From whence (for a relic of remembrance) I brought half a yard of Saint Michael's Mounts monumental match; I went to the top of the church tower seventy steps higher, and in my coming down I viewed the bells (which were five in number) being fair and handsome, they cannot be rung, because the crack rope soldiers have broke all the bell-ropes, insomuch as for any more ringing there, the bells being ropeless, the people are hopeless.

To speak the truth of this so much talked of famous mount; it is lofty, rocky, inaccessible, impregnable not to be taken, or kept, not worth the taking or keeping; it is a barren stony little wen or wart, that with men, ammunition, and victuals is able to defend itself; but if it hath not the sea and land to friend, there is an enemy called hunger (or famine) that will conquer mounts and mountains: it can do no service to the seaward, for the water is so shallow, that no ship can sail within shot of it, and for land service the Town of Market-Jew, stands better for defence: the Mount is an island, and no island, twice in every 24 hours: for when the sea is up, boats must be used to go to it, but upon the ebb, troopers may ride to it forty in rank: Market-Jew is about two flight shoot of it, the Mayor whereof (one Mr William Mabb) caused me to dine with him, for which I return him a few printed thanks.

In the mount I saw a craggy rugged seat, of rocky upholstery, which the old fabulous rumour calls St Michael's Chair: and a well I saw there, which twice in 24 hours is fresh water, and salt water: this mount had a garrison within it; which made the country people to grumble without it; yet the soldiers are pretty civil: and one captain Geary did courteously regard and drink with me at the majors house at Market-Jew. From whence I returned to Mr Godolphin's, and he did persuade me to see the Lands end, fourteen miles further; for which journey on the 16 day of July, he did lend me two horses, with his kinsman to ride with me, where (for his sake) I was welcome by the way, with a good dinner, at one Mr Levale's house, from whence I rode, and went as far as I could ride, go, or creep, for rocks and sea: and there I saw the Island of Scilly, with other smaller Islands, which are said to be 16 or 17 in number. The main Island is held for the Prince, by one Captain (or as some say, a Knight) called Sir John Grenville; it is very strong, with a good safe harbour, and as it is reported there, hath a good fleet of ships in it: some do call it a second Algiers, for there cannot a ship or vessel pass by it, but they do make out upon them, whereby they have great riches, with all necessaries: it was eight leagues at least from me, insomuch that I could but only see it dimly, and two ships I perceived that lay at road (perdue) to give notice (as I conjectured) of the appearance of any shipping that sailed within their ken: I did cut my name four inches deep in a small patch of earth amongst the rocks, at the Lands end, and I am sure no man can go thither and set his name or foot, half a foot before me.

The same day I returned to one Mr Jones his house a mile thence, in the farthest western parish of the county of Cornwall, called Sennen; there I had good entertainment all night, by the gentleman's and his wife's free welcome, which was out of their own courteous disposition; but chiefly for Mr Godolphin's sake, to whom at *Triminaegue* I returned, on the 17th on July, where I rested one day: and on the 18th day I took my leave, having received seven days' hospitality in plenty, with many other courtesies in money and other necessaries which I wanted; besides he sent his kinsman with me to direct me the way to another Francis Godolphin of Godolphin house. That gentleman is the chief of that noble name; his house a stately ancient palace, and my cheer and welcome at dinner, most freely bountiful. After dinner he walked with me, where (in my way) I saw his mines of tin, and a house where his workmen were refining and melting of tin, which is a rich commodity. So at my taking leave of him, he put ten shillings in my hand, which came to me in an acceptable time.

From thence I jogged three miles further, to a house called Clowance in the parish of Crowan where dwells one Mr John Sentabin, he is son-in-law to the first Godolphin I came to, whose daughter he married (a virtuous and beautiful gentlewoman) where I took a welcome, a supper and a bed, till the next morning, being July 19th, he sent a man with me eight miles to a sister of his, named Mrs Gertrude, to her I was so welcome, that after I thought she had been weary of me, she would fain have had me to stay two days more, which I (with thanks refusing) she lent me a mare (and a man to bring her home again) which mare I rode to a town called Penny-come-quick, within a mile of Pendennis Castle, which Castle I looked on afar off, but I durst not attempt to offer to go into it, for fears and jealousies might have mistaken me for a spy; for at all places of Garrison, there is very strict examinations of persons, and at every town's end, in all the sea towns of part of Cornwall, Devonshire, Dorsetshire, and every shire, no traveller could pass without catechizing words: *As what is your name, whence came you, where dwell you, whither go you, what is your business, and wherefore came you hither?* Now he that cannot answer these particular demands punctually, is to be had before governors, captains, commanders, mayors, or constables, where if a man do chance to be suffered to pass freely from them, yet it is a hazard of the loss of a traveller's liberty by either their unbelief or misprison, and at the best it is a hindrance to a man's journey and loss of time.

These considerations made me doubtful to presume to look into Pendennis Castle, or any other garrison or place of defence: this Castle is seated very high, and it stands very defensive for the famous haven of Falmouth (one of the best harbours for shipping in the world): it was built by King Henry the eight, it is impregnable, and as long as it is well manned, ammunitioned, and victualled, it is thought to be invincible, and there is an end of that point.

That day I passed a ferry call King Harry's Passage, (but why it is so named few men know) there I lodged at the ferryman's house, and the next morning being 21 of July, I travelled twelve miles to a fisher town called Mevagissey; that town hath in it two taverns, and six ale-houses, to every one of which I went for lodging, and not any one would harbour me, then I sought for a constable to help me, but no constable was to be found; the people all wondering at me, as if I had been some strange beast, or monster brought out of Africa; at which most uncivil and barbarous usage, I began to be angry, and I perceiving that nobody cared for my anger, I discreetly went into the house where I first demanded lodging; where the hostess being very willing to give me the courteous entertainment of *Jack Drum*, commanded me very kindly to get me out of doors, for there was no room for me to lodge in. I told her that I would honestly pay for what I took, and that if I could not have a bed, yet I was sure of a house over my head, and I would not out till the morning: with that a young saucy knave told me that if I would not go out, he would throw me out, at which words my choler grew high, my indignation hot, and my fury fiery, so that I arose from a bench, went to the youth, and dared to the combat; whereat the hostess (with fear and trembling) desired me to be quiet, and I should have a bed, at which words my wrath was appeased, and my ire assuaged.

But straightaways another storm seemed to appear; for an ancient gentleman came suddenly out of another room (who had heard all the former friendly passages,) and he told me that I should not lodge there, for though I had sought and not found a constable, yet I should know that I had found a Justice of Peace before I sought him: and that he would see me safely lodged: I was somewhat amazed at his words, and answered him, let him do his pleasure, for I submitted myself to his disposal.

To which he replied, that I should go but half a mile with him to his house, which I did, and there his good wife and he did entertain me courteously, with sure fare and lodging, as might have accommodated any gentleman of more worth and better quality than one that had been ten times in degree before me: there I stayed the Saturday, and all the Sunday, where I found more Protestant religion in two days, than I had in five years before. The gentleman's name is Mr John Carew, a gentleman of noble and ancient descent, and a worthy Justice of the Peace in those parts.

I was certified, that in that little town of Mevagissey, there are 44 fisher boats, which do fish for pilchards, that every boat hath 6 men, and that every 2 boats have one net between them: they do call the 2 boats a seine; so there are 22 seines, and 22 nets: every Cornish bushel is in measure 2 bushels and a half of our measure at London: every 2 boats (or seine) do spend 250 bushels of salt (Cornish measure) to salt pilchards only; every seine do use 100 hogsheads to pickle the said pilchards in yearly. So that this one little town, doth spend by God's blessing, and the means of those small fishes, every year,

Of salt, 22 times 250 Cornish bushels, which is in the
  number of our bushels, 14,000,350.
Of hogsheads, or cask, 2,200.
Of men for 44 boats, 6 men for each, 264.

These men with their families (being many in number) are all maintained by pilchard catching; but this is not all, for there are other greater towns in that county, which do every one of them use the same trade of fishing, with more and greater numbers of men, boats, nets, cask, and much more quantity of salt; some of the other towns are St *Kevern*, *Foye* [Fowey], Looe, with others which I cannot recite.

This infinite number of pilchards, being salted and put up in cask, are brought a main by the Spanish, French, Dutch, Italian, and other merchants, and by them they are either eaten or sold, and transported to many other people and nations: And now I hope I have filled my readers' bellies with pilchards, without cloying or offending their stomachs; if any one be queasy, or do feel a wambling in the gizzard; let them call for a cup of sack, drink it, and pay for it.

The 23 of July I came to *Foye*, and to Looe (or *Low*) twenty miles; this town of Looe, is divided in two parts, or two towns together, two mayors, two churches, two governors, and more than two religions; all that I can say of either of the Looes, is, that there was soldiers and swordmen, strong beer and dagger ale, land flesh and sea fish in plenty.

On the 24 of July, I turned my back upon Cornwall, and went from Looe to Plymouth...

AN UNKNOWN MALE TRAVELLER
from
NANSWHYDEN NEAR NEWQUAY, 1741

Launceston, 1810

Devon Record Office, 64/12/29/1/13

The account is from the papers of the Quicke family of
Newton House, Newton St Cyres, near Exeter. Sometime
after 1756 Jane Hoblyn, the widow of Robert Hoblyn,
married William Quicke and it may be through this connection that the travel account came into the family papers.
The unknown traveller, most likely a male, was on a journey
to Bath from Nanswhyden, home of the Hoblyn family,

between Newquay and St Columb Major. He was part of a
large party.

Set out from Nanswhyden October the 24th 1741 Saturday Morn.
Mrs M Hoblyn, Mrs Winslow, & Miss Percival on horseback. Mr
Bagwell, Mr Dunn, Mr Beverige went with us to the nine maids on St
Brege [Breage] downs. Stop at *Warbrige*, ate of our loaf. Miss Paget in
the Coach. I on horse. There a good pleasant country but deep dirty
lanes. Got to Camelford about 6 which was about 22 mile, played at
cribbage before & after supper. Bed between 9 & 10.

Sunday very wet, set [out] about 9. Mrs W[inslow] on horseback,
met Frank Veran who went with her another way. Rained very hard
about one, ate of our loaf, after 2 got to *Lanceston* at the White Hart
dined about 4 then came Sir John Chichester & Mr Berry who stayed
a hour, then we went to Mr Vivian at Matford which almost [is] joined
to the Inn. Found Sir William Moris there, a very pretty house. Had
wine, tea and fruit tarts, bread and cheese for supper. Stayed till ten.

Next morn before breakfast walk[ed] about the town. A very good
church & a pleasant place. It is on the top of a high hill & a terrible
steep hill up to it. 4 good gates & several good houses. Miss Chichester
breakfasted with us & about ten set out. Miss P[ercivall] on horseback.
Polson Bridge divide[s] Cornwall and Devon. A pretty prospect till
we got to *Dart More*. Met Mr Prideax & Son & Mr Guy coming from
Haink. At a loss for the loaf which the dog ate at *Lanceston* ...

GRACE VYVYAN
of
TRELOWARREN, 1760

Pendarves, 1758

Devon Record Office, 64/12/29/1/43

Grace Vyvyan, of Trelowarren in the parish of Mawgan-in-Meneage, was the daughter of Sir Francis Vyvyan and Grace Hoblyn, heir to the Reverend Carew Hoblyn of Nanswhyden. She wrote to Mrs Quicke at Nanswhyden regarding her visit to the Percival family at Pendarves in Camborne and to the Bassets at Tehidy.

Trelowarren, June 26th 1760
Dear Madam,

Very many thanks wait on you, and Mr Quicke for the great civilities received at Nanswhyden as well as the other many favours you have been pleased to confer on us (which believe us, we know how much better how to value than deserve) permit us to return our most grateful acknowledgements and begin to fear you will think us unmindful in our thanks, by not having already received them, as indeed you ought, but hope your goodness will look upon the omission, to proceed from the real cause, the opportunity of writing, which I have not been backward in endeavouring after, but engagements unsought for, has till now prevented it – the most unpleasant weather we surely have, that can be for the time of year, you must have recourse to indoor amusement, as you must suspend the use of your paddle till the weather bears a milder aspect. Master I suppose does not much brook confinement, however [I] hope he continues well and merry, and that you are quite so again will give us pleasure to hear.

We got to Pendarves a considerable time after the family had dined, owing in some measure to our being retarded, above an half hour, on Coswarth Hill, by a carriage of furze coming up the road, which was obliged to be unloaded, before we could proceed. However, to our joy they did not stay dinner, but carefully provided a hot joint of mutton against our arrival; Mrs Percivall appears greatly elated upon being returned to Pendarves and at present finds, after so long an absent [sic] many material repairs, absolutely necessary to be done to her house, and particularly, the essential one of new roofing it, as the rooms in some parts of the house receives the water in; this job she chooseth to inspect the doing of, and which she says will detain her home; but with her compliments to you & Mr Quicke, shall take it as a great favour to see you soon at Pendarves; will accommodate you in the best manner that place will afford and can promise you a dry apartment; the little Dear Boy she wishes to see with you. I gave her no reason to hope it, by saying you would not be fond of its going from home; as the child is young, you judged that, the properest place for him – your coming to Pendarves we flatter ourselves will induce you and Mr Quicke to visit Trelowarren, before your return from thence, that pleasure we shall greatly desire. We went to *Tehiddy* the day Mrs B: Hoblyn intimated we were to go, Mr [?William] Borlase, his Lady, and Miss Petre, came that day to dine with Mrs Percivall. They added to our number and went with us, that really we were a large company of ourselves, without their family which were increased by their relations being with them, as Mr, Mrs Archer, Mr Ennis and his daughter all were there, Mr Bassett behaved with the utmost complaisance, Mrs Basset and her sister we ever liked, their behaviour elegant & easy; after dinner the child appeared; obligingly favoured me by sitting on my lap, she is a sweet little creature, the express image of her mother, and tho' two years old, does not in forwardness exceed your little boy, as Papa & Mama is the utmost of her performance, this surely will make you think your child has the advantage, which certainly is the case.

We did not return from Pendarves till Saturday Evening, much missed poor Mr Percivall's Company. My brother & sister join with me in compliments to you, Mr Quicke & Mrs Betty Hoblyn, and our love to the dear little boy if we are so happy to be remembered by him; excuse a bad scrawl and many imperfections from one whoever esteems it and honour to subscribe herself,

Dear Madam, your grateful humble servant, Grace Vyvyan

AN UNKNOWN VISITOR
of
NANSWHYDEN NEAR NEWQUAY, 1764

Fowey harbour, 1803

Devon Record Office, 64/12/29/1/43

The female writer was probably a member of the Hoblyn family at Nanswhyden or possibly of the Quicke family from whose papers the letter is derived. She was on a visit to Fowey to see the Coryton family and in particular the widow of Peter Goodall, whose grandmother had been Elizabeth Coryton. He had been her heir, changed his name from Goodall to Coryton on his inheritance and died some ten years before this visit. The unknown traveller also spent considerable time with, and attention to, the Rashleigh family at Menabilly. Only the first part of the letter survives.

3 December

My dear Sister,

I hope you received my little letter from *Foye*, there I could not help wishing with us yourself, the Doctor & Jane, as I think every one of you would have been as delighted as we were with the finest harbour I ever saw, had a full view of it from our bed chamber window. *Foye* is almost inaccessible by land & a carriage can not go into the town. We were obliged to walk a quarter of a mile from ours to the House of Harmony, I would to the Desert of Arabia to be with people so worthy as the family of the Corytons. The mother I believe is at most fifty-five, she is well grown, has a good face, is very nimble, has good teeth, quite an East Country dialect, & a sensible manner of expressing herself. She has been a widow eleven years, must have been I am satisfied very happy in a married state, & has acted like a Christian since she lost the man she loved by wholly attendance to the Welfare and Happiness of those he left. One daughter she lost at eighteen, was much afraid another of the same age would have been taken from her appears to have the same complaints. Consulting Doctor Huxom on her case, & its being his opinion Bath was proper for her, away she went last May & is happy in the success of her journey. She is by no means stupid but was so engaged on the errand that carried her to Bath, that she did not see the Circus or go to any Diversion but one Concert for which Lord Edgcombe gave her a Ticket. She has been at *Foye* six & twenty years never farther west than six miles & that was to see if the Turnpike was more like what she was used to. Lived when single at Kensington, is the daughter of a Clergyman whose name is Cox. Menabilly is about the distance from *Foye* that this place is from St Columb.

A great friendship has subsisted between the possessors of that finely situated place, the family of the Rashleighs, & the Corytons. When the head of the last named was taken from his Worthy Wife, Mrs Rashleigh offered & performed all kind offices, his son settled some years at Menabilly has outdone his Father in friendly offices: introduced Mr [John] Coryton into proper company for which his mother is overcome with gratitude & obligingly acknowledged Mr Rashleigh's goodness she called it increasing the acquaintance which Mrs R took very kindly our returning her daughter's visit, said had she made any visits would certainly come here, seemed sorry when, on finding her fearless in a carriage & entirely cheerful in her polite attendance on us to Menabilly & to a fishing scheme, I appeared to expect my visit returned on pain of future. She said she should esteem it a prodigious favour if I would excuse her; If I would not she certainly would come to Nanswhyden. You may assure yourself after this I did not press it.

Thursday was their Assembly supported by the two Mr Corytons whose great good nature induce them to do everything that is sociable, there were fourteen couples. The room is the Town Hall not the worst I ever saw. Mrs Coryton accompanied me, and was almost as great a stranger, not having been there but twice before. She spoke obligingly to everybody & everybody seemed to feel themselves obliged by her notice. The Eldest Brother danced with my sister, the youngest, who is exceedingly amiable & is designed for the Gown, danced with Miss Sanford. Mr Kirkham came to us Wednesday, he danced with Miss Coryton. Wednesday morning Mrs Coryton & Miss, Mrs A Quicke & I went to Menabilly, Jack on horseback to wait on Miss Rashleigh prevailed on her to accompany us to dinner, to stay all night she did not dare for she was only on a Visit to her Brother for [a] Change of Air being much indisposed. Her home is a little way from Menabilly with an Aunt, her father's sister Mrs Hawkins of Pencoite one of the ladies Mr Thomas Hawkins pays. She is a particular woman, a great collector of curiosities for which she spares no cost or pains. She has another Lady who is related to her that lives with her, Mrs Hawkins more periodically dines early, constantly takes a solemn airing in an old coach a few miles after dinner & then to cards, Quadrille with the Dead Man if there happens no other company till Supper which is served at seven, & to bed they go at nine. It is, Mrs Coryton says, impossible for a person to be fonder of another than Mrs Hawkins is of Miss Rashleigh, but so fearful is the young lady of disobliging that she lives in a sort of fright, has tender spirits & a great dislike of Cards. She is in appearance vastly agreeable, received us with great politeness, is well made, I think pretty, & Miss Coryton says composed of sweetness, is very ingenious, makes flowers vastly well. She nets the best I ever saw. I should be vastly glad to have her the wife of Mr Coryton as I should be to have Mr Rashleigh whose character is irreproachable, take Miss Coryton who appears vastly good natured, is quite useful & would I dare say make an excellent wife. Expressing something of the kind to Mrs Coryton she said it was her opinion Mr Rashleigh had long ago seen the woman he preferred to all others. Mr Rashleigh is situated between two Aunts, the before mentioned Mrs Hawkins on one side, who is exceedingly fond of him & on the other a Maiden aunt whose disposition is widely different from her sisters. She has also a niece with her whose name is Pool, who by all accounts lives a much happier life than her cousin Rashleigh.

Wednesday night an express called Mr Rashleigh from us to his dying father [Jonathan] near London. The next day arrived another express with an account of his death. The pleasing effect it had on the family we were with has increased our opinion of their merit. The eldest gentleman almost fainted & afterwards poured forth his gratitude for the many kindnesses he had received when at his house in holiday time from Eton, which calls for my gratefully acknowledgement to you & the Doctor with regard to Bob. We ordered him by last post to set out for Bath where my Aunt kindly received my mention of his spending these holidays. Shall write to him to acquaint him with your goodness & order him to come to you for part of the time. I was fearful of his being troublesome to good Mrs Roberts or should have proposed his coming to you. As I know your constant readiness to serve & oblige me I enclose his last letter, wherein you will observe he does not in the least lament spending his holidays at Eton as he thought he was to do, he is an easy tempered boy & I hope will pass a happy life. I fully designed writing very fully to you Saturday sevenight when I came home on errand, not the least to see Thom who I found vastly happy with his Nancy. Playing with him & doing my little matters quite excluded the pleasure I proposed of holding a long conversation with you.

Sunday morning Jack & I set out by eight o'clock, reached *Egleshaille* half after ten, were kindly received by Mr & Mrs Peers, by eleven came our family & Mr Kirkham's from *Croan*. Mr Peers gave us excellent advice from the words of the wisest man Rejoice Young Man in Thy Youth &c. We all dined with the Worthy Clergyman. After evening prayer we went to Mr Kirkhams & Monday by the help of Mr Kirkham's horses had an agreeable drive to *Foye*, much more agreeable than our journey from *Foye* Saturday, when we hired a pair of horses from Lostwithiel seven miles from *Foye*. We had a delightful walk before we came away, saw a number of vessels & a fine ship full sail from a pretty rise above the town, which is excessive romantic. We had such a stupid driver on our hired horses that some miles this side *Foye*, Mr Quicke made him mount Robin's horse & we found when he became postillion we went on a much better pace tho' we did not get home till after [the remainder of the letter is lost]...

Mrs Hawkins
of
Trewinnard, mid-eighteenth century

Clowance, 1758

Devon Record Office, 64/12/29/1/43

The following letter was written by Mrs Hawkins of Trewin-nard near Hayle in the parish of St Erth probably to a member of the Hoblyn family. She was visiting, as part of a small party, the St Aubyn family at Clowance between Camborne and Helston in the parish of Crowan. They may have travelled in their coach which is now housed in the Royal Cornwall Museum.

November 17 Trewinnard

My Dear Madam,

A few hours after I wrote to you last Saturday, I received your obliging favour, you are exceedingly kind or in other Words <u>Quite Your-Self</u> to be so solitious about what you think would be agreeable to your friend. I had not the least difficulty in obeying you for having on my first expressing an inclination to go my own choice, I went accompanied by my Brother and Mr & Miss Collins whom we called on for that purpose, Mr Collins was pure Chatty consequently very entertaining all the way. About 2 we arrived at Clowance for not having that impatient man, Doctor Turner, here to hasten us so, we found most of the company there before us, doors & windows doubly & trebly lined as we drove up. Was quite the thing for those that love to be stared at when out pops our principal Beau in his broad brimmed hat and great coat and with all imaginable expedition. Miss Terry & her namesake follows, whips through the hall and into the drawing room in a trice (I'll name the Company when I come to the Dancers) in about 5 minutes after we had been seated 'Your Servant Mrs Basset & Mrs Hawkins this was an honour we could not expect &c &c' and behold they entered a few more ceremonies & 'Dinner Waits'. After a very handsome entertainment of about thirty dishes (without any cook) we retired into the Dining Room where we drank tea and began dancing about five o'clock, supper at ten and broke up at four the next morning. After which we drank tea and to bed immediately.

If I can recollect it, I'll give you the list of dancers in the order we were called out for twas all ordained, as we say in Cornwall, how it should be without either drawing or choosing.

Miss St Aubyn	Mr Hawkins
Mrs Bassett	Mr Richard Sandys
Miss Vyvyan	Doctor Tonkin
Miss Grace	Mr Richard Pinnick
Miss Mary	Mr Stephens
W.H.	Mr Sandys (Reverend)
Miss Polly Johns	Mr Churchill
Miss Glyn	Mr William Sandys
Miss Peggy	Mr Treweek
Miss Collins	Mr Arundle
Miss Bab:	Mr Johns
Miss Bla: Sandys	Mr Williams (Reverend)

Twelve couples were too, too many for the room, so that some were always obliged to sit down which made it rather more agreeable as we danced so many hours. Miss Collins was at first the worst off but as I spared her my partner now & then (who was a very good Dancer) she was well pleased. Captain Lyn danced two minuets which was all that was danced. Sir John played at cards, he never does dances (it seems) upon these occasions. There was a great deal of other company but I believe you would scarce thank me for particularizing them. We brought back Miss Jenny with us Wednesday even[ing] who has been with us ever since. And now (as Miss Grace says) what shall I say more of the Ball? I think I have been vastly particular, I fear I have tired you as well as myself. I apprehend they all (the St Aubyn family) begin their journey Monday morning next, dine with Mr Williams and lye at Nanswhyden as proposed, today they have promised to dine with us.

THE REVEREND WILLIAM GILPIN
of
BOLDRE, NEAR LYMINGTON,
HAMPSHIRE, 1775

Launceston Castle, 1775

William Gilpin, *Observations on the Western Parts of England,
relative chiefly to Picturesque Beauty* (1808), 190–202, 215–
219, 230–241.

Gilpin's *Observations on the River Wye* of 1770 opened up
the debate on the Picturesque in Britain. Shortly afterwards
he published other descriptions of the country, including
the Lake District, Hampshire, Sussex, Kent and Scotland,

but he waited twenty-three years to publish his visit to Cornwall. Gilpin noted that during the years in which the tour
was in manuscript he had been able to improve it and wrote
that 'how variously Nature works up the same modes of
scenery in different parts of the world'. Gilpin was about 51
years old when he visited Cornwall and died in 1804.

... The road soon brought us to Launceston, the capital of Cornwall,
which is a handsome town. The castle was formerly esteemed one of
the strongest fortresses of the west, as we may suppose at least from
its bearing the name of *Castle-terrible*. During the civil wars of Charles
I it continued among the last supports of the royal cause in those
parts: though it has suffered great dilapidations since that time, its
remains are still respectable; and, what is more to the purpose at
present, they are picturesque. The great gate and road up to it, and
the towers that adorn it, make a good picture. The stately citadel
makes a still better. It is raised on a lofty eminence, and consists of a
round tower, encompassed by the ruins of a circular wall; in which,
through a wide breach, you discover the internal structure to more
advantage. The construction of this whole fortress is thought to have
been curious; and they who wish to have a full account of it, may be
gratified in Borlase's *History of Cornwall*.

A little to the north of Launceston lies Werrington, an estate
belonging to the Duke of Northumberland. The park contains many
beautiful scenes, consisting of hanging lawns and woods, with a
considerable stream, the Aire, running through it. In some parts,
where the ground is high, the views are extensive. Many antiquarians
suppose this to have been the feat of Orgar, Earl of Devonshire, whose
beautiful daughter, Elfrida, is the subject of one of the most affecting
stories in the English history, and one of the purest dramatic compo-
sitions in the English language.

Somewhere in this neighbourhood lived Thomasine Percival; at
what time, I find not; but the story of this extraordinary woman is
still current in the country. She was originally a poor girl, and being
beautiful, had the fortune to marry a rich clothier, who dying early,
left her a well-jointured widow. A second advantageous match, and a
second widowhood, increased her jointure. Being yet in the bloom
of youth and beauty, her third husband was Sir John Percival, a wealthy
merchant of London, of which he was Lord Mayor. He also left her a

widow with a large accession of fortune. Possessed of this accumulated property she retired to her native country, where she spent her time and fortune altogether in works of generosity and charity. She repaired roads, built bridges, pensioned poor people, and portioned poor girls, setting an example, which should never be forgotten among the extraordinary things of this country.

From Launceston we travelled as far into Cornwall as Bodmin, through a coarse naked country, and in all respects as uninteresting as can well be conceived. Of wood, in every shape, it was utterly destitute.

Having heard that the country beyond Bodmin was exactly like what we had already passed, we resolved to travel no farther in Cornwall; and instead of visiting the Land's-end, as we had intended, we took the road to *Lescard* [Liskeard] proposing to visit Plymouth in our return.

An antiquarian, it is probable, might find more amusement in Cornwall than in almost any county in England. Even along the road we saw stones, and other objects, which seemed to bear marks both of curiosity and antiquity. Some of the stones appear plainly to be monumental: the famous *Hurlers* we did not see.

The naturalist also, the botanist, and the fossilist, especially the last, might equally find Cornwall a country full of interesting objects. Here his search would be rewarded by a great variety of metals, fossils, stones, pebbles, and earths.

Here too the historian might trace the various scenes of Druid rites, and of Roman and Danish power. Here also he might investigate some of the capital actions of the civil wars of the last century; and follow the footsteps of Fairfax, Sir Beville Grenville, Lord Hopton, and other great commanders in the west. The battle of Stratton, in which the last of those generals commanded, was an action masterly enough to have added laurels to Cæsar, or the King of Prussia. Indeed we could have wished to have gone a few miles farther to the north of this country, to have investigated the scene of this action. Lord Clarendon has described it so accurately, that it can hardly be mistaken. It was a hill, steep on all sides, bordering, if I understand him rightly, on a sandy common. On the top were encamped a body of 5,400 of the parliament forces, with thirteen pieces of cannon, under the Earl of Stamford. At five o'clock in the morning, on the 16th of May 1642, the royalists attacked them with very inferior force, in four divisions, who mounted four different parts of the hill at once. After a well-fought day, they all met about three in the afternoon at the top, and congratulated each other on having cleared the hill of the enemy, and taken their camp, baggage, ammunition, and cannon. The scene of so notable an exploit may be still perhaps pointed out by the inhabitants of the country. From Lord Clarendon's description, however, it may certainly be found.

It is probable also that, in a picturesque light, many of the castles of this country might have deserved attention; many of the coasts might have amused us with elegant sweeping lines, and many of the bays might have been nobly hung with rockey scenery. We should have wished also to have heard the winds howl among the bleak promontories of the Land's-end; to have seen, through a clear evening, the light fall indistinctly on the distant isles of Scilly; and to have viewed the waves beating round the rocks of that singular situation, Mount St Michael. The loss of this last scene we regretted more than any thing else. But to travel over desarts of dreariness in quest of two or three objects seemed to be buying them at too high a price; especially as it is possible they might have disappointed us in the end. Many a time has the credulous traveller gone in quest of scenes on the information of others, and has found (such is the difference of opinions) that what gave his informant pleasure, has given him disgust.

In returning from Bodmin, we passed over that part of Bradoc-downs, where Lord Hopton's prowess was again shewn in giving a considerable check to the parliament's forces in those parts. This wild heath, and much of the neighbouring country, is in the same style of dreary landscape, with that we had found between Launceston and Bodmin. So very undisciplined the country still is, that the wild stags of nature, in many parts, claim it as their own. We did not see any of them; but we were told, they sometimes shew themselves on the high moors about Bodmin and *Lescard* [Liskeard].

And yet these are the lands, wild as they are, that are the richest of the country. They bear little corn, it is true; but it is very immaterial what the surface produces: the harvest lies beneath. In this neighbourhood some of the richest of the Cornish mines are found; and *Lescard*, where we now were, is one of the Coinage-towns, as they are called. Of these towns there are five, which are scattered about the different parts of Cornwall, where mines are most frequent. After the tin is pounded, and washed from the impurities of the mine, it is melted, separated from its dross, and run into large square blocks, containing each about three hundred pounds weight. In this form it is conveyed to the Coinage-town, where it is assayed and stamped. This stamp makes it a saleable commodity.

We had not, however, the curiosity to enter any of these mines.

Our business was only on the surface. Great part of this country, it is true, is in a state of nature, which in general is a state of picturesque beauty; but here it was otherwise. Our views not only wanted the most necessary appendages of landscape, wood, and water, but even *form*. We might, perhaps, have seen this part of Cornwall in an unfavourable light; as the sweeping lines of a country depend much for their beauty on the light under which they are seen; but to us they appeared heavy, unbroken, and unaccommodating. In the wild parts of Scotland, where this dreariness of landscape often occurred, we had still a distance to make amends for the fore-grounds. It was rarely that we had not a flowing line of blue mountains which gave a grandeur and dignity even to an impoverished scene. But in these wild parts of Cornwall we sometimes saw a face of country, (which is rather uncommon in the wildest scenes of nature,) without a single beauty to recommend it.

This dreariness, however, had begun to improve before we arrived at *Lescard*. Plantations, though meagre only, arose in various parts; and the country assumed somewhat of a more pleasing air; particularly on the right towards *Lestwithiel*. The high grounds formed intersections; something like a castle appeared on one of them, and the woody decorations of landscape in some degree took place.

As we left *Lescard*, the country still improved. Extensive sides of hills, covered with wood, arose among the fore-grounds, and ranging in noble sweeps, retired into distance. These bursts of sylvan scenery appeared with particular beauty at a place called Brown's-woods. Here too we entertained with an *incidental beauty*. The whole sky in front was hung with dark clouds to the very skirts of the horizon. Behind us shone the brightest ray of an evening sun, not yet indeed setting, but very splendid: and all this splendor was received by the tops of trees, which rose directly in front, and being opposed to the gloomy tint behind them, made a most brilliant appearance. This is among the most beautiful effects of an evening-sun. These effects are indeed as various as the forms of landscape which receive them; but nothing is more *richly* enlightened than the tufted foliage of a wood.

We now approached the sea, at least the river *Tamer*, which is near its estuary; and as this coast is perhaps one of the most broken and irregular of the whole island, we had several views of little creeks and bays, which being surrounded with wood, are often beautiful. But they are beautiful at full-sea only: at the ebb of the tide, each lake becomes an oozy channel.

The picturesque beauty of a scene of this kind once cost a poor traveller dear. He had long been in quest of a situation for a house, and found one at length offered to sale, exactly suited to his taste. It was a lake scene, in which a little peninsula, sloping gently into the water, presented from its eminence a pleasing view of the whole. Charmed with what he had seen, he ruminated in his way home on the various improvements it might admit; and fearing a disappointment, entered, without farther scrutiny, into an agreement with the owner, for a considerable sum. But what was his astonishment, when, on taking possession, his lake was gone, and in its room, a bed of filthy ooze! How did he accuse his rashness, and blame his precipitate folly! In vain he wished to retract his bargain. In vain he pleaded, that he had been deceived; that he had bought a lake; and that, in fact, the object of his purchase was gone. "You might have examined it better," cried the unfeeling gentlemen of the law: "What have we to do with your ideas of picturesque beauty? We sold you an estate, and if you imposed upon yourself, you have nobody else to blame."

From the road, as we passed, we had a view of Trematon-castle, where a stannery court is still kept, which had formerly very extensive privileges. *Trematon-law* is almost to this day an object of reverence among the common people of Cornwall.

Soon after, Saltash-bay opened on the left, and on the right, Hamoaz[e] harbour, with many a gallant ship of war at anchor upon its ample bosom. Beyond the *Hamoaz* rose the hanging lawns and woods of Mount *Edgcomb*, forming a noble back-ground to the scene.

At Saltash we had good views of the river Tamer, both above and below the town. A sweeping bay is formed on each side, in many places at least a mile in breadth. In both directions the banks are high, and the water retires beautifully behind jutting promontories.

Having crossed the *Tamer* at Saltash, we had four miles farther to Plymouth. Through the whole way we had various views of the sound, Mount *Edgcomb*, Plymouth harbour, *Hamoaz*, Plymouth town, and Plymouth dock. From all these views together we were able to collect a clear geographical idea of this celebrated harbour.

Two rivers, the *Tamer* and the Plym, (the first of which is considerable,) meeting the sea at the distance of about three miles asunder, form at their separate mouths too [sic] indented bays. These two bays open into a third, which is the receptacle of both, and larger than either. The bay formed by the *Tamer*, is called the *Hamoaz*; that formed by the Plym is called Plymouth Harbour; and the large bay, into which they both open, is called the Sound. At the bottom of the Sound, where the two bays communicate with it, lies St Nicolas, a large island, fortified with a castle and strong works; which are intended to defend the entrance into both these inlets. The entrance into *Hamoaz* is very intricate; for the island can be passed only at that end next Plymouth; which makes the passage narrow and winding. The entrance at the other end is wide and direct; but is defended by a dangerous shelf of hidden rocks; the situation of which appears plainly at low-water from the ripling of the tide above them. The Cornish side of *Hamoaz* is formed by Mount *Edgcomb* ...

Our curiosity having been gratified among the dock-yards at Plymouth, led us next to visit Mount *Edgcomb*.

The promontory of Mount *Edgcomb* running a considerable way into the sea, forms, as was just observed, one of the cheeks of the entrance of *Hamoaz*-harbour, which is here half a mile across. The whole promontory is four or five miles long, and three broad. In shape it is a perfect *dorsum*, high in the middle, and sloping gradually on both sides towards the sea; in some places it is rocky and abrupt.

Lord Edgcomb's house stands half way up the ascent, on the Plymouth side, in the midst of a park, containing an intermixture of wood and lawn. It makes a handsome appearance with a tower at each corner; but pretends only to be a comfortable dwelling.

The great object of Mount *Edgcomb* is the grandeur of the views. As we advanced towards the summit of the promontory, we saw, in various exhibitions, on one side, all the intricacies and creeks, which form the harbour of Plymouth; with an extensive country spreading beyond it into very remote distance; and scattered with a variety of objects; among which we distinguished the well-known features of Brentor.

The other side of the promontory overlooks the Sound, which is the great rendezvous of the fleets fitted out at Plymouth; though sea-men speak very indifferently of its anchorage. One of the boundaries of this extensive bay is a reach of land running out into pointed rocks; the other is a lofty smooth promontory, called the Ram's-head. The top of this promontory is adorned with a tower, from which notice is given at Plymouth, by a variety of signals, of the number of ships and their quality, that appear in the offing.

Between the *Ram*'s-head and Mount *Edgcomb* is formed a smaller inlet, called *Causand* [Cawsand] bay, at the head of which lies Kingston. Before this little town rode a large fleet of which appeared to be fishing boats; but we were informed that most of them were smuggling vessels.

The simplicity of the few objects which form the Sound on one side, made a pleasing contrast with the intricacies of the Plymouth-coast on the other.

At the distance of about three leagues from the *Ram*'s-head, stands the Eddystone lighthouse. We could just discern it, as it caught a gleam of light, like a distant sail.

Having viewed from the higher grounds of Mount *Edgcomb* this immense landscape, which is, on both sides, a mere map of the country, and has little *picturesque beauty*, especially on the Plymouth side, we descended the promontory, and were carried on a lower stage round its utmost limits.

The grounds here are profusely planted. On that side which overlooks *Causand*-bay, the plantations are only young; but on the other, which consists of at least half the promontory, they are well-grown, and form the most pleasing scenes about Mount *Edgcomb*. That immense map, as it lay before the eye *in one view* from the higher grounds, and appeared variously broken and scattered, was now divided into portions, and set off by good foregrounds. Some of these views are pleasing; but in general they are not picturesque. A large piece of water full of moving objects, makes a part of them all; and this will always present at least an amusing scene.

The trees, both evergreens and deciduous, are wonderfully fine, considering their sea-aspect. But chiefly the pine-race seems to thrive; and among these the pinaster, which, one should imagine, from its hardy appearance, to be indigenous to the soil. The woodman would dislike that great abundance of hoary moss, which bedecks both it and most of the other plants of this marine scenery, but to the picturesque eye, the vegetation seems perfect; and the moss a beauty. It is moss of a peculiar form, at least of an unusual growth. Its hue is generally cerulean, with a strong touch here and there of Naples-yellow, mixed with other pleasing tints, which being scattered profusely about the whole plantation, give it an uncommon richness. In these woods the arbutus grows in great perfection, and many other shrubs, which are generally found only in sheltered situations.

Besides a luxuriance of wood, a variety of rocky scenery embellished our walk, especially about the vertical point of the promontory. It is a well-coloured brown rock; which appears in all forms. Nor is it bald and naked, but everywhere garnished with twisting boles and hanging shrubs.

Upon the whole, though there are many formalities about Mount *Edgcomb*, terraces particularly, and vistas near the house, a few puerilities also, and too little advantage taken everywhere of the circumstances which nature has pointed out; yet it is certainly a noble situation, and very well worth the attention of a traveller...

At Plymouth we heard much of the scenery upon the Tamer, of

which we had had a little specimen at Axworthy. We resolved therefore to navigate that river as far as the Weir, which is about twenty-two miles above Plymouth, and as far as we could have the advantage of the tide. Procuring therefore a good boat, and four stout hands from the *Ocean* man of war, then lying in the *Hamoaz*, we set sail with a flowing tide.

The river *Tamer* rises from the mountains of Hartland, near Barnstaple-bay, in the north of Devonshire, and, taking its course almost due south, divides that county from Cornwall. No river can be a more complete boundary. As it approaches Plymouth, it becomes a noble estuary. The *Hamoaz* is esteemed, after Portsmouth, the best station for ships of war upon the British coast. This grand bay, which was the first scene we investigated on the *Tamer*, is about a mile in breadth, and seven miles in length; though the larger ships we observed seldom to anchor above a league from the sea. Its banks on each side, though rather low, are by no means flat. They are generally cultivated; and the shore is finished by a narrow edging of rock.

The next view we had of any consequence, was the opening towards St German's on the left. This is a creek about three leagues in length. The woods of *Anthony* occupy one side of the opening; and a house which appeared at a distance in the centre, is Ince, a seat of the Killigrews.

Soon after, we came in sight of Saltash, which stands high, but affords no very picturesque appearance. When we crossed the ferry the day before, the views of the creek from the hill presented a beautiful scene, both above and below the town; but when the eye is stationed *upon* the water, the retiring reaches of the river are lost, and the landscape is much impaired.

Our next scene was the opening of the Tavey into the *Tamer*. Sir Harry Trelawney's house was one of the principal objects of this view. The distance was composed chiefly of the *Dartmore* hills. The banks of the *Tamer* were still low, and cultivated; and bore no proportion to the extent of the water, which did not begin to contract itself, nor the banks to swell, till we had proceeded nine or ten miles up the river.

The first scene, which in any degree engaged our attention, was composed of the woods of *Pentilly*, on the Cornish side. The house too is a good object, and a building at the bottom of the bank has a picturesque appearance; though its dignity was degraded when we learned it was only a lime-kiln. Lime is the chief commodity of trade on this river, employing many large boats in transporting it; and the lime-kilns, which we see in many places on its banks, are of such noble dimensions, that they may, at a little distance, be mistaken for castles, without any imputation on the understanding. They are among the greatest ornaments of the river. The background of the scenery of *Pentilly*, is a lofty bank adorned with a tower, to which belongs a history.

Mr Tilly, once the owner of *Pentilly*-house, was a celebrated atheist of the last age. He was a man of wit, and had by rote all the ribaldry and common-place jests against religion and scripture; which are well suited to display pertness and folly, and to unsettle a giddy mind, but are offensive to men of sense, whatever their opinions may be, and are neither intended nor adapted to investigate truth. The brilliancy of Mr Tilly's wit, however, carried him a degree farther than we often meet with in the annals of prophaneness. In general the witty atheist is satisfied with entertaining his *contemporaries*; but Mr Tilly wished to have his sprightliness known to *posterity*. With this view, in ridicule of the resurrection, he obliged his executors to place his dead body, in his usual garb, and in his elbow-chair, upon the top of a hill, and to arrange, on a table before him, bottles, glasses, pipes and tobacco. In this situation he ordered himself to be immured in a tower of such dimensions, as he prescribed; where he proposed, he said, patiently to wait the event. All this was done, and the tower, still inclosing its tenant, remains as a monument of his impiety and prophaneness. The country people shudder as they go near it:

— Religio pavidos terrebat agrestes
Dira loci: – sylvam, saxumque tremebant.

As we sailed farther up the river, we came in view of the rocks and woods of *Coteil* [Cotehele], which are still on the Cornish side, and afford some beautiful scenery. Here we had grand sweeping hills, covered with wood. At the bottom of one of them stands a noble lime-kiln-castle, which is relieved by a lofty background.

Near the bottom of another stands a small Gothic ruin, situated, with much picturesque beauty, in a woody recess. It was formerly a votive chapel, built by a chief of the Coteil family; though some say by one of the Edgcombs. Its founder had engaged on the unsuccessful side, during one of the periods of the dubious wars of York and Lancaster. His party being beaten, he fled for his life; and as he was a man of consequence, was closely pursued. The *Tamer* opposed his flight. He made a short vow to the Virgin May, threw himself into the river, and swam safe to the promontory, before which we now lay on our oars. His upper garment, which he had thrown off, floated down the stream; and giving occasion to believe he had perished, checked the ardour of pursuit. In the mean time *Coteil* lurked in his own woods, till a happier moment; and in the day of security raised this chapel to the holy Virgin, his protectress, who had the full honour of his escape.

We have the story sometimes told otherwise, and given to the times of Charles I; but a story of so late a date, one should imagine, might have been better ascertained, than this seems to be; and if the chapel have any connection with the story, it is much more credible, that a votive-chapel should have been erected in the 15th century, when we know they were common, than in the 17th, when such structures were never heard of.

At *Coteil* [Cotehele] house we landed, which is entirely surrounded with wood, and shut out from the river. If it were a little opened, it might both see and be seen to advantage. To the river particularly it would present a good object; as it stands on a bold knoll, and is built in the form of a castle. But it is a deserted mansion, and occupied only as a farm-house. Here we refreshed ourselves with tea, and larded our bread, after the fashion of the country, with clouted cream.

Round this old mansion grew some noble trees; and among them the Spanish chestnut, fully grown, and spread out in huge massy limbs. We thought these chestnuts scarce inferior in grandeur to the proudest oaks. The chestnut, on which Salvator Rosa has hung Edipus, is exactly one of them.

We had now sailed a considerable way up the *Tamer*, and, during the whole voyage, had been almost solely obliged to the Cornish shores for amusement. But the Devonshire coast, as if only collecting its strength, burst out upon us at Calstock, in a grander display of lofty banks, adorned with wood and rock, than any we had yet seen, and continued without interruption through the space of a league.

But it is impossible to describe scenes, which, though *strongly marked*, have no *peculiar* features. In Nature these lofty banks are infinitely varied. The face of each rock is different; it projects differently: it is naked, or it is adorned; or, if adorned, its ornaments are of different kinds. In short, Nature's variations are as infinite on the face of a rock, as in the face of a man. Each requires a distinct portrait to characterize it justly; while languge can no more give you a full idea of one, than it can of the other.

With the views of Calstock we finished our voyage up the *Tamer*; and though the banks of the river were diversified both with rocks and woods, with open and contracted country; yet, considering the space through which we had sailed, and the high commendations we had heard of this river, it was, on the whole, less a scene of amusement, than we had expected to find it. We had a few grand views; but in general the navigators of the Tamer find only some of the common charcteristics of a river:

— *Longos superant flexus, variisque teguntur*
Arboribus; viridesque secant placido æquore sylvas.

All is beautiful, sylvan, and highly pleasing; but if you ask what we saw, we can only say *in general*, that we saw rocks, trees, groves, and woods. In short, the whole is amusing, but not picturesque; it is not sufficiently divided into portions adapted to the pencil.

The scenery itself, on the banks of the *Tamer*, is certainly good; but had it even been better, the form of the river could not have shewn it to much picturesque advantage. The reaches are commonly too long, and admit little winding. We rarely trace the course of the river by the perspective of one screen behind another; which in river-views is often a beautiful circumstance: and yet, if one of the banks be lofty, broken into large parts, and falling away in good perspective, the length of the reach may possibly be an advantage. In some parts of the *Tamer* we had this grand lengthened view; but in other parts we wished to have had its continued reaches more contracted.

These remarks, however, it must be observed, affect a river only in *navigating* it. When we are thus on a *level* with its surface, we have rarely more than a fore-ground; at most we have only a first distance. But when we take a higher stand, and view a remote river, lofty banks become then an incumbrance; and instead of discovering, they hide its winding course. When the distance becomes still more remote, the valley through which the river winds should be open, and the country flat, to produce the most pleasing effect.

In the immense rivers that traverse continents, these ideas are all lost. As you sail up such a vast surface of water, as the Mississippi, for instance, the first striking observation is, that perspective views are entirely out of the question. If you wish to examine either of its shores, you must desert the main channel; and, knowing that you are in a river, make to one side or the other.

As you approach within half a league of one of the sides, you will perhaps see stretches of sand-banks, or islands covered with wood, extending along the shore, beyond the reach of the eye, which have been formed by depredations made on the coast by the river; for when the winds rage, this vast surface of water is agitated like a sea; and has the same power over its shores. As the trees of these regions are in as grand a style as the rivers themselves, you sometimes see vast excavations, where the water has undermined the banks, in which immense roots are laid bare, and, being washed clean from the soil, appear twisted into various forms, like the gates of a cathedral.

Though the banks of the Mississipi, we are told, are generally flat, you frequently see beautiful scenery upon them. Among the vast woods which adorn them, are many groves of cypresses; to which a creeping plant, called the Liane, is often attached. What kind of flower it bears, I have not heard; but if it be not too profuse, it must be very ornamental: hanging from tree to tree, and connecting a whole cypress-grove together with rich festoons.

These woods are interspersed also with lawns, where you see the wild deer of the country feeding in herds. As they espy the vessel gliding past, they all raise their heads at once, and standing a moment with pricked ears, in amazement, they turn suddenly round, and darting across the plain, hide themselves in the woods.

From scenes of this kind, as you coast the river, you come perhaps to low marshy grounds; where swamps, overgrown with reeds and rushes, but of enormous growth, extend through endless tracts, which a day's sailing cannot leave behind. In these marshes the alligator is often seen basking near the edge of the river, into which he instantly plunges on the least alarm; or perhaps you descry his hideous form creeping along the sedges, sometimes hid, and sometimes discovered, as he moves through a closer, or more open path.

Contrasts, like these, between the *Tamer* and the Mississippi, are amusing, and set each scene off to more advantage. The *Tamer* may be called a noble river; but what is it in point of grandeur, when compared with the Mississippi, which, at the distance of two thousand miles from the sea, is a wider stream than the *Tamer*, where it falls into it? On the other hand, though the Mississippi, no doubt, has its beauty; yet as a river, it loses as much in this respect, when compared with the *Tamer*, as it gained in point of grandeur. In the Mississippi you seek in vain for the rocky banks and winding shores which adorn the *Tamer*, and are the glory of river-scenery.

To these contrasts I shall just add one more. As Lord Macartney and his suit, in their way to Canton, sailed down one of the rivers of China, they passed under a rock of grey marble, which arose from the water to the amazing perpendicular height of six hundred feet. It was shagged with wood, and continued varying its form, but still preserving its immensity, through the space of at least two miles. In some parts its summit beetled frightfully over the river, and gave an involuntary shudder to the passenger, as he passed under its tremendous shade...

AN UNKNOWN GENTLEMAN
from
HAMBLE, HAMPSHIRE, 1793

Looe, 1825

The journal of this unknown traveller is part of the papers of the Wilder family of Suhlum near Reading in Berkshire and it may be that he was a member of that family or associated with them. He sailed in the *Friendship*, a lobster smack from Hampshire, which was carrying a cargo of barrel hoops to Falmouth, on 13 August 1793. His travels appear to have been undertaken as an adventure. He left on 13

August with some regrets that 'we then took a last view of Hamble, & I cannot but own, that however willingly I undertook our little voyage, & however great might be the pleasures I expected to receive from it, I begun to feel that I had left my own home, & wished for those I had left behind – not that I had the least desire to return, but I had that sort of feeling which I always experience at leaving anyplace where I have parted with my own family or my friends'. They then sailed west along the coast to Plymouth. When he returned, only a month later, he wrote that 'Here I finished my little voyage and if I should ever happen to read this at any future time, I am sure I shall recollect it with the greatest pleasure, tho' I am free to confess there were times during the excursion when I could have wished myself in a different situation form what I was. At the same time I shall always say that the pleasure I received so far out balanced the pain which attended it that I should willingly embark again on the same terms & with the same prospects'.

Wednesday August 28
We went ashore to breakfast at Plymouth – the town dirty & disagreeable, the houses very old & badly built & the streets very narrow, in shore quite a seaport town. After breakfast we went to Mount Edgcumbe, in our way we passed through the village of Stonehouse & the town of Dock, this is much such another town as Plymouth, & seems to be the chief resort of the Navy. Here is the Hamoaze, which is the grand dock for his Majesty's shipping, having very lately seen the Dock Yard at Portsmouth, & having but little time to spare, we did not go to look at it, but crossed over the water to Mount *Edgecumb* where we were highly pleased & satisfied. Here are some of the most beautiful groves of trees I ever saw & these flourishing in great perfection down to the very edge of the sea & what renders this the more surprising is that the whole of the grounds are upon the solid rock, which in many places has but about 4 inches of earth to cover it, the views of the sea from it are very charming & from the highest part of the ground you have a beautiful view of the country round Plymouth. There was very little appearance of wood, tho' the country in general seemed to be fruitful & well cultivated. On the top of the hill is Maker Church, from the tower of which balls are hung out as

signals of the arrival of any ships in the harbour. We went up to the top of the tower & from it had a most extensive view both of the land & sea, which together with the beauty of Mount Edgcumbe made the scene highly interesting & pleasing. The towns of Plymouth & dock, which we before thought in the highest degree disagreeable also appeared to very great advantage & there were many villages which we saw, which appeared equally pleasing. Here, as in Guernsey, the misfortunes of a war had made considerable alterations, camps & fortresses were to be seen everywhere around us, besides many Men of War in the Sound & near it. To the West of the Sound is a very good harbour called Cawsand Bay & at the end of it the village of *Causand* – in this bay were many merchantmen & some few ships of war, after dinner we took a walk up to the garrison, which is an exceedingly strong fortress, which not only commands the whole of the Sound, but every part around it. A charming view of Mount Edgcumbe & the adjoining country from the battlements, we were here again pleasingly put in mind of Guernsey, by the band of the regiment, who were exercising there. We returned onboard at 9 o'clock expecting to sail in about 2 hours.

Thursday August 29
There was no wind at all & we did not sail till 8 o'clock this morning. A disagreeable accident however had nearly prevented our sailing at all, for we were all awakened about 5 o'clock by a great noise alongside our vessel, & a very great bustle was heard on the deck. On looking out of the cabin we found that the Press Gang had boarded us – all our men but one were protected & he poor fellow had no other means of escape than by concealing himself & the only place he could do this was where I slept – he had but that instant come in & shut the door when the banditti entered the cabin to search for him. I felt for the poor fellow, & wished I could have assisted him, the only thing we had to do was to lie as still as possible, after they searched all round the cabin, they came to the door where we were & tried to open it, at this moment I am sure the man's feelings could not be greater than mine were for him, but we had fastened the door on the inside & they fancied there was no opening, & after searching all the other parts of our vessel, they left us. I know nothing of the policy of manning our ships of war, I can only say that if it be a necessity it is a very cruel one, not many days since an East Indiaman came into this harbour on her return from a long voyage, she had nearly 100 men onboard, many of them had families, & probably all of them friends whom they were in hopes of seeing again on their

return. But they scarcely cast anchor in the Sound when the Press Gang were alongside of them & took away above 90 of their men. I am sure I shall always hate a press gang as long as I live.

We were in hopes to have found some wind when we came out into the Sound, but not a breath of air was stirring & we were obliged to throw out our anchor again, it was a glorious fine morning & we had a sweet view of Mount Edgcumbe from the Sound. It was amusing to see the porpoises rolling over in water & it was so calm that we could see many other smaller fish playing round our vessel. To an interested beholder nothing can be a more pleasing sight than a calm sea, or a more horrible one than a storm. A nice breeze opening up about 10 o'clock & soon carried us out of the Sound. But we were scarcely round Penlee Point when we spied a Man of War's boat making signals to us to lie to, which we did immediately & they soon came up with us. It was no other than the Press Gang come again, suspecting that we had deceived them in the morning. But our man had the good fortune to escape them a 2nd time. For after asking a few questions & seeing not one on board to answer their purpose, they left us in pursuit of more prey.

The next point of land we passed was the Rame Head, I should suppose so called from its having that appearance at a distance. We were now on the coast of Cornwall & at a distance from the shore, we could discern but little difference in the face of the country, the appearance of in general barren without any wood, tho' in some few places there seemed some arable. Round the Rame Head is Wrinkle Bay, & in the midst of it the village of Wrinkle. The shore all the way very full of rocks. We now came in sight of the cliffs of Rocky Seaton. I cannot tell why but I expected to be much pleased with a view of this place, but it is barren & naked, with not a tree near it. The village, if it may so be called, consists of two or three houses, which are the habitations of fishermen. We called here to take in lobsters but did not go ashore.

About 3 miles west of this place lies the town of Looe, it is situated in a bottom between two rocks & as you pass it is a very romantic & pleasing object, the coast between here & Seaton is remarkable for the beauty of its rocks, which in some places are tinged with a variety of beautiful hues, & in others covered with grass & shrubs, so as to look like the ruins of an old castle overgrown with ivy. Opposite to the town of Looe is Looe Island, where we called again for lobsters. I had the curiosity to go ashore & look at it. There is only one house on the island, which is inhabited by an old man of 70, & his family, consisting of 8 including some grand children, it is about a mile round & is cultivated by the old man who rents it. We came in the midst of harvest & saw them taking in their corn. I called at the house & the old lady regaled me with some barley cakes & some cider. I was welcome, she said, to the best her house would afford, the old man said he kept a horse & 2 cows & told me he thought there were about 12 acres of culpable land in the island. After leaving this island it was soon dark & the weather began to look very thick & unfavourable. We could discern the light from the Eddystone lighthouse, the appearance of the sea was very beautiful as it sparkled like so many diamonds round our vessel. I know not if the sailors look upon this as a presage of bad weather, but it was not long before it blew such a gale & rain so violently that we were obliged to lay to & reef our sails. I looked out of my cabin about 2 o'clock in the morning, for so great was the motion of the vessel that it was impossible to sleep, & the sea ran very high indeed. How thankful was I at this moment that those whom I wished for at other times were not with us.

Friday August 30
The gale continued for about two hours, & when I came upon deck in the morning the wind was abated & we were in Mevagissey Bay, in the night we had passed by Polperro & the town of Fowey. In the middle of Mevagissey Bay is a town of that name where there is a harbour & a good Pier. Passing from hence round Chapel Point you come to the village of Gorran Haven inhabited merely by fishermen. Off Chapel Point is a rock called the Black Rock – there are no rocks between this &the main land but there is plenty of water between them for sloops or smaller vessels. The wind continued this morning as it had done the day before SW, which was directly against us. To the west of Gorran Haven is the Point of the Deadman [sic]. Round this point is the little fishing village of Portholland. To the west of this is the Greyhead & rather to the East of it off in the Sea in the Gull Rock but there is water enough for a man of war to go between it & the main land. After passing this you come to a spacious bay in which is situated the village of Gerrans. At the western extremity of this bay is St Anthony's head or Falmouth, very little variety is to be seen down this part of the coast. The villages are generally situated in a deep valley with a small beach towards the sea, chiefly the habitations of fishermen. The appearance of the country barren, naked & uncomfortable, not a tree to be seen anywhere. Round St Anthony's head you open Falmouth. You enter a very spacious bay, which is defended by the castle of St Mawes on one side & Pendennis

Falmouth castle on the other. On our right hand we had the town & harbour of St Mawes which tho' a borough town is mostly inhabited by fishermen. Beyond this is the river which leads up to Truro, on the other side we approached Falmouth, & at about 2 miles distance you have a view of Penny. Falmouth is situated upon a rising ground & from the harbour appears to be a large & well built town. Here we anchored our vessel & went ashore. The houses are tolerably good & the streets clean. Our vessel was loaded with hoops for this place & we were to have returned home as soon as we had unloaded them, but unfortunately the Capt. could not sell them & was obliged to go further to the West for that purpose.

And the next morning, Saturday August 31, we set sail for Penzance, but we had not long left Falmouth before it blew a heavy gale of wind & we obliged to put into Helford Haven. The wind increased very much, & came in squalls & we began to be afraid of such another day as we had at Swanage Bay, but towards the middle of the day the gales abated & we went ashore. This haven is situated about 2 leagues west of Falmouth, it is up a broad river & sheltered on almost every side. Helford is a little fishing village, & is famous for the oysters which are caught there. The houses in it, or rather huts, are very wretched & bad, we walked across the country to a little village called Manaccan, which is much such another. We went into one of the cottages & found it equally miserable with its inhabitants. We saw a very few trees, & there seemed to be some tolerable corn. We all went ashore in our jackets & trousers, & I suppose it was on this account that in the course of our walk that we were taken by the country people for Frenchmen, & having heard that the inhabitants of Cornwall are not famed for their politeness towards strangers, we thought they might suspect us to be Frenchmen come out of prison. On our return to the village we were met by our Captain who with joy in his countenance told he had by accident disposed of his hoops & that he should unload them & set sail homewards on Monday morning. This was a piece of news which rejoiced us much, as we were all beginning to grow tired and wished to return, for we had already been out nearly a week longer that we intended when we left Hamble.

Sunday September 1

It rained & blew very violently but our harbour was so sheltered that we felt but little inconvenience, at least so as to apprehend any danger & we thought ourselves fortunate that we had not proceeded any farther on our voyage. About 12 o'clock we were able to go ashore but it still continued to rain so very fast that it was impossible for us to walk out or to enjoy ourselves, so we went to a very decent clean public house in the village where we amused ourselves by reading all the landlady's library would afford us. The weather in the afternoon was nearly as unfavourable as in the morning, & we went to our vessel at night tired & fatigued with doing literally nothing.

Monday September 2

A tolerably find [day] for all who were onshore but the wind too much to be enjoyed on board. We breakfasted at the little public [house] at Helford & afterwards walked into the country but our walk afforded us very little variety & nothing interesting. The country consists entirely of hill & valley. In the valleys we sometimes met with a little wood & some few trees. But on the hills the same naked appearance which we had observed everywhere in this country. The method of baking bread here was to us very singular. After the loaf is made they put it upon an iron plate & cover it over with an iron kettle. Upon this kettle they make a fire of furze, which they continue till the loaf is sufficiently baked. In the afternoon the sky looked very heavy & began to threaten us & by the time we went on board it blew very hard indeed & the wind increased till the middle of the night, when there came on a very violent gale. As I lay in my hammock I heard the wind roar most tremendously from my heart I did pity those who were at sea, & was sincerely thankful that we were in so safe [a] harbour.

Tuesday September 3

The gale lasted but two or three hours & about 4 o'clock in the morning the horizon looked clear & we had a very fresh & pleasant breeze from NW. We soon weighed anchor & very shortly found ourselves out of harbour in our way towards the East we called at St Mawes to take in fish, but did not stay there. The day continued to be very favourable & a fair wind soon brought us to the Deadman point to the east of which is Mevagissey Bay, the situation of the town, which had some beautiful rocks on each side of it, makes it appear a pleasing object from the sea at a distance, but as you come near to it all its beauty ceases. We had occasion to call here, & we went ashore for a few minutes. There is a very good pier in the front of the town, this indeed is the case with all the towns in the West of England, even the little fishing places which consist perhaps but of two or three huts, have generally a little pier for the safety of their boats, for the wind is sometime so violent in the winter that without some shelter of this kind their boats must be driven against the rocks & lost. After looking at the pier at Mevagissey, we went into the town, but of all the places I ever was in this is the most wretched & disagreeable. In the whole town there seemed to be scarcely a habitation fit for a human being to dwell in. The streets were all nauseous & offensive to a great degree. For this was the season of the year for catching pilchards, & during the operation of curing the fish, a very fetid oil arises from them. This constitutes a considerable part of the employment, as well as of the riches, of the inhabitants of this part of Cornwall at this season of the year, & it is almost incredible the quantities that are [caught] & I was told that it is not uncommon or a thousand hogsheads of these fish to be caught at once in an account I read of this fishery it is asserted that 4000 barrels, each barrel containing 400 fish have been known to be have been taken at one time. About 4 o'clock in the afternoon we arrived off Polperro here I took leave of our vessel & went ashore not to return on board anymore. However sorry I was to leave my companions, I cannot but own that it gave me much pleasure to set my foot on *Terra Firma* again. Notwithstanding the many inconveniences we met with at sea, I cannot but say that on the whole I was well pleased with my excursion & it fully answered the end that I intended besides that during the three weeks I had been out, I had seen what it is to be obliged to follow a seafaring life. I had seen how much was the pain & how little the pleasure that could be derived from it, & it taught this useful lesson, to be contented with the comforts of our own country, & the society of my own family & friends & not to wish to part from them. The situation & appearance of Polperro as you look at it from the sea gives a very pretty variety to this part of the coast of Cornwall. You enter it by a river or Bay, on each side of which are some rocks, as romantic as they are beautiful. In the village the houses are in general mean, dirty & disagreeable & the inhabitants rude, stupid & uncivilized. I was shown a wretched looking house, which they called an inn, here I enquired if I could have a horse to carry me to Plymouth. Their dialect is uncouth & the answers I received were almost as unintelligible as they were dis-satisfactory. I did at last however procure a little horse, or at least a part of one, for the poor creature looked so miserable & half starved, that I quite hurt to ride him. Its owner also I hired to show me the way to Plymouth, he was obliged to walk, indeed I walked a great part of the way myself for the hills were so high & so steep & the road so bad that it was impossible to ride. From Polperro to Plymouth I was told that it was about 17 or 18 miles, but we were obliged to go so slowly that it was near midnight when we arrived at a place called Torpoint which is on the opposite side of the water from the town of Dock. I now thought it too late to proceed to Plymouth & awakened the people at a public house there, where I procured a bed...

THE REVEREND
THOMAS RACKETT
of
SPETTISBURY, DORSET, 1794

Truro, 1802

Dorset Record Office, D/RAC:81. See H.S.L. Dewar (ed.),
The Thomas Rackett Papers, 17th – 19th centuries (Dorset
Record Society, III, 1964).

Rackett was rector of Spettisbury for more than sixty years.
He was on a tour through Devon to Cornwall, accompanied
by Charles Hatchett, a chemist who later wrote *Analysis of
the Magnetical Pyrites*, and by William George Maton who
later wrote his account of their travels in *Observations relative
chiefly to the natural history, picturesque scenery and antiquities of*

the Western Counties of England, made in the years 1794 and 1796. The following three letters were part of a series of correspondence from Rackett to his wife. At Plymouth Rackett had promised his wife that he would not descend into a mine and wrote that one of his companions 'will take care not to lead us into any danger'. He was thirty-seven years old on this first visit to Cornwall.

─────────────

Fowey August 24th

My dear love,

I have just received yours written by my mother & directed to this place, & have just time to say that we are all well, & have reached the place where Mr Hatchett was to see his friend Mr Rashleigh, he went to him last night & having learned that we accompanied him Mr Rashleigh means to call on us tomorrow morning to invite us to his House, about a mile distant from hence – as I cannot exactly tell when we shall set out from hence, your next had better be directed to Post House, Marazion, Cornwall which place we shall certainly visit.

Fowey is one of the most beautiful situations that can be imagined, it being surrounded with high hills covered with wood, down to the rocks which rise out of the sea, we came from Plymouth thro' Saltash & St Germans, to Looe a very romantic spot indeed & the farther we travel the more we have to admire, Capt. Barlow resides with his family in this town, he is not here at present but I shall leave my Name at his House.

The bank note which was found, if a ten pound note, is most unquestionably mine & the note which I told you I missed. Which you supposed a 5 guinea one but was in fact a ten pound note, of course you will give the boy or his family a handsome reward for finding it.

I find the post does not go out on Tuesday so shall send this tonight.

Pray let the gardener be told to sow a bed of Welsh onions to stand the winter.

We have been entertained with the manner of catching & curing the pilchards, a fish which abounds here, they are salted & put into hogsheads.

Pray give my love to Mother, Father and Dorothea, I am yours affectionately, T. Rackett

Maton desires his compliments.

Truro August 29th

My dear love,

I have just time to tell you a little of our proceedings, Mr Rashleigh called to invite us to his house on Monday where we stayed till this day. He has shown us great civility & attended us to everything curious in the country, on Tuesday we went to some tin mines where the whole operation was explained to us, the engines put in motion for extracting the water from the mines &c &c & we dined at St Austell with a Society of Gentlemen concerned in the business, yesterday we went to a most remarkable place called *Roach* Rock, it is a chapel built upon the pinnacle of a most stupendous Rock but some miles distant from the sea, Mr Hatchett is quite in his element as he is very inquisitive about mines. I do not intend to descend any of them as I am not fond of going down ladders. This sort of scene is quite novel, & very amusing, the face of the County alters very often, & we have generally something to admire, it will be a day or two before I get to Marazion where your lettter is to be directed. & I hardly know where to desire you to direct again as we shall move every day but as I shall like to hear I think I shall get a letter if you direct to Post House, St Agnes, Cornwall. I have sent a paper parcel by the Coach, which when you receive pray take care of it; Charles Hatchett & Maton desire their complements the former is smoking his pipe, we're now in Truro, a pretty neat town today we dined with Mr Tremaine & several captains of the mines, who are to show Mr Hatchett the different products of the mines, Maton has collected many plants. We have sent a letter to the Doctor this evening. Give my love to all and kiss my Dorothea for me. I am your affectionately, TR

PS Have nothing to write to Mother but hope she has made some Devonshire Cream.

Camborne, September 3rd

My dear love,

Since I wrote last we have proceeded to Falmouth, the Lizard, & Marazion where I got a letter. We have been much entertained with the country particularly St Michael's Mount near Marazion which is a most striking object. We surveyed it for some time & were very sorry to leave so charming a spot.

From thence we proceeded to Penzance, a considerable town, & yesterday we arrived at the Land's End, having seen everything worthy of notice in that part of the country, such as Druidical monuments, ancient British castles, a tin mine under the sea, &c &c. We slept at St Ives last night, from which place I procured a riddle for Dorothea, see the next page, & today we have been to view some copper works, where we have seen the whole process of working copper from the ore to the formation of copper sheets on plates fit to make saucepans &c, all which is very curious.

I shall reach St Agnes tomorrow, & hope to find a letter there, pray direct yours next to Plymouth & Maton desires to have his enclosed, so you may get a frank if you can. Tell Dorothea that I have got a pretty box for her with St Michael's Mount on it if she is very good.

As to the bank note it cannot possibly be mine if it was clean when it was picked up & fresh lost, as mine must have lain some time there & I had rather let the finder have the advantage of it than pretend that it was mine if I had any doubts upon the subject, give my love to all, as the post is not very regular here I don't know when you will get this, we are now on our return home but as we may never see Cornwall again we are unwilling to omit viewing all that is curious & Mr Hatchett is now in his element among some very remarkable mines. I shall leave to make the cream I told you of before I leave this country, we have it everywhere. I am yours affectionately, TR

A riddle for Dorothea to find out

> As I was going to St Ives
> I met seven wives
> Each wife had seven sacks
> Each sack had seven cats
> Each cat had seven kits
> Kits, cats, sacks & wives,
> How many were going to St Ives?

Dr Maton: I shall make some little drawings of certain remarkable places we see to show you & Dorothea & her mama. Tell Dorothea Hatchett cannot find out the riddle on the other side.

MRS PARRY PRICE
of
CHESTER, 1805

Mount Edgcumbe, 1860

Berkshire Record Office, D/EEg/Z1. See Todd Gray, 'The Travels of Mrs Parry Price through Devon in 1805', *Transactions of the Devonshire Association* (vol. 128, 1996), 65–89.

Mrs Price, a widow and grandmother, was in Plymouth for a christening and travelled with a female servant whom she referred to as 'Jones'. Mrs Price resided in Stanley Place in Chester.

Monday 27th

Went in two of the *Salvador del Munda*'s boats, with a large party to Mount *Edgecombe* where all the beauties of nature are collected together; Hill & Dale, most luxuriant woods, fine lawns, with Wilderness & variety of beautiful buildings & a most extensive view of the sea; with an innumerable quantity of vessels of all descriptions, amongst which were several Men of War, some of them first rates; with a most extensive land prospect of the counties of Devon & Cornwall; commanding a view of ten towns & villages, Lord Borringdon's & several other fine seats; but did not go into Lord Mount Edgcumbe's house as it is not esteemed worth seeing but is a large stone Gothic building & makes a good figure from the grounds & I apprehended would be much more respected were it not for the fine new modern house of Lord Borringdon's which is so near it, & is built in the Grecian style of architecture. We took cold meats and liquor with us & dined in the white seat, which stands on an eminence & commands one of the finest views. One of the Woods is chiefly composed of the Arbutuss, which here grows into fine trees; there are also several Myrtle & Cork Trees, & a very fine magnolia tree & several tulip trees. We returned to Dock between six & 7 o'clock...

LOUIS SIMOND
of
FRANCE, 1809–10

Pendennis Castle, Falmouth, *c*.1750

Louis Simond, *Journal of a Tour and Residence in Great Britain during the years 1810 and 1811, by a French Traveller with remarks on the country, its arts, literature, and politics and on the manners and customs of its inhabitants* (Edinburgh, 1815), 1–11.

Simond wrote in his preface that he had originally prepared his manuscript for publication in France but that circumstances made that impossible. He noted in the journal that he made no mention of Napoleon Bonaparte who at that time was of particular interest to English readers. Simond arrived in Cornwall after a voyage from the United States where he had lived for some twenty years and was married to an English woman. His observations as a Frenchman are intruiging, even on English cooking ('an English cook only boils and roasts') and the perceived lack of taste of Cornish apples.

———

24th December 1809. – We found ourselves, on waking this morning early, anchored in the harbour of Falmouth, where we had arrived in the night, after a speedy and prosperous passage of twenty-one days from America, without a single storm to describe, or any extraordinary occurrence. This harbour is a small basin, surrounded with gentle hills. Looking round, we saw green fields, with cattle grazing, – a grove of trees, – some pines, and many green tufts like laurels. The town of Falmouth, – little, old, and ugly, – was seen on our left, and another assemblage of little old houses on our right, (Flushing); Pendennis Castle behind us, on a mound near the entrance of the harbour. The air was calm and mild, – the sky of a very pale blue, – a light mist hung over the landscape, – and the general impression was peaceful and agreeable: on the surface of the water twenty or thirty ships, mostly packets, and two or three Dutch vessels with licenses, – a strange sort of trade! The custom-house officers mustered in crowds about the ship, ransacking every corner:– Barrels and bags, boxes and hampers of half-consomeed provisions, empty bottles and full ones, musty straw and papers, and all that the dampness of a ship, pitch and tallow, and the human species confined in a narrow space, can produce of offensive sights and smells, were exposed to open day. These custom-house officers have seized a certain surplus of stores beyond what a ship is allowed to bring in port, whether the voyage has been long or short. I overheard the head seizer asking the Captain whether he preferred having his wine or his spirits seized; and the Captain seemed to take the proposal in very good part, and told me afterwards the man was very *friendly* to him. In this general confusion no breakfast could be expected; and permission being procured for the passengers to land, with their baggage, every one was eager to make his escape. I went on shore to reconnoitre, and to secure comfortable quarters, and brought back hot rolls, – the olive-branch to the ark.

The houses, in a confused heap, crowd on the water; the tide washes their foundation; a black wall, built of rough stones, that stand on end, to facilitate the draining of the water, and steps, overgrown with sea-weeds, to ascend to the doors. Through one of these odd entrances I introduced my companions to the hotel, – a strange, old, low building, extremely neat inside, with a tempting larder full in view, displaying, on shelves of tiles, fish of all sorts, fat fowls, &c. Well-dressed servants, civil and attentive, wait our commands. We are put in possession of a sitting room and two bed-rooms. Our windows overlook two or three diminutive streets without footpaths, – too narrow, indeed, for any, – all up and down, and crooked. It is Sunday. The men are, many of them, in volunteer uniforms, and look well enough for citizen-soldiers; the women highly dressed, or rather highly undressed, in extremely thin draperies, move about with an elastic gait on the light fantastic patten, making a universal clatter of iron on the pavement. Ruddy countenances, and *embonpoint*, are very general and striking. C.'s young astonishment was awakened at the sight of a sedan-chair, vibrating along on two poles. A monstrous carriage turned the corner of a street, overladen with passengers, – a dozen, at least, on the top, before, and behind; all this resting on four high slender wheels, drawn along full speed on a rough unequal pavement. We observed some men, in old-fashioned cocked-hats with silver lace, compelling a Quaker to shut his shop; – which was opened again the moment they were gone. An elegant post-chaise and four stopped at the door. A young man, fat and fair, with the face and figure of a baby, six feet high, alighted from it; it was the Marquis of St [blank] the first man of quality we had seen in England. He goes, we are told, to lounge away his *ennui* and his idleness beyond seas, – a premature attack of the *maladie du pays*. The English *maladie du pays* is of a peculiar character; it is not merely the result of extreme regrets when they have left their country, and of that perpetual longing to return, felt by other people, but an equal longing to leave it, and a sense of weariness and satiety all the time they are at home.

Dinner announced, suspended our observations; it was served in our own apartments. We had three small dishes, dressed very inartificially (an English cook only boils and roasts), otherwise very good. The table-linen and glass, and servants, remarkably neat, and in good order. At the dessert apples no bigger than walnuts, and without taste, which are said to be the best the country produces.

December 25. – I have been this morning to the custom house, with the other passengers, to get our passports. They obtained their without difficulty, but I must write to London for mine. Twenty-two years of absence have not expiated the original sin of being born in France: but I have no right to complain, – an Englishman would be worse off in France.

We have on our arrival a double allowance of news; those which were coming over to us when we left America, and what has occurred since; an accumulation of about three months. The first thing we have learnt was an Imperial repudiation and an expected Imperial marriage, which seems to be a great stroke of policy. Political news are no longer what they were formerly; they come home to every man's concerns, and state affairs are become family affairs.

December 26. – I have been introduced to several respectable citizens of Falmouth; they all live in very small, old habitations, of which the apartments resemble the cabins of vessels. A new house is a phenomenon. The manners of this remote corner of England have retained a sort of primitive simplicity. I have seen nothing here of the luxury and pride which I expected to find everywhere in this warlike and commercial country. There is much despondency about Spain, and but one voice against the Walcheren expedition and against the ministers, who are not expected to withstand the shock of such general dissatisfaction.

We have left our hotel, to take furnished lodgings in an elevated part of the town, – a kind of terrace, – looking down upon the beautiful little harbour, and surrounding country. This apartment, composed of very small, neat rooms, costs only a guinea and a half a week, and the people of the house cook, and wait on us. This would cost more in the smallest town in America, or in fact could not be had. Domestics are here not only more obliging and industrious, but, what is remarkable, look better pleased and happier.

December 30. – The weather has been singularly mild since we landed; the sky cloudy and misty, without absolute rain; a little, and very little sun, seen every day. Fahrenheit's thermometer about 50°.

December 31. – We left Falmouth this morning, in a post-chaise, fairly on our way to London. The country is an extensive moor, covered with furze (a low, thorny bush), evergreen, nipped by a few goats and sheep; not a fourth part of the surface is inclosed and cultivated. The total absence of wood is particularly striking to us, who have just arrived from a world of forests. It gives, however, a vastness to the prospect, and opens distances of great beauty; hills behind hills, clothed in brown and green, in an endless undulating line. The roads very narrow, crooked, and dirty; continually up and down. The horses we get are by no means good, and draw us with difficulty at the rate of five miles an hour. We change carriages as well as horses at every post-house; they are on four wheels, light and easy, and large enough for three persons. The post-boy sits on a cross bar of wood between the front springs, or rather rests against it. This is safer, and more convenient both for men and horses, but does not look well; and, as far as we have seen, English post-horses and postillions do not seem to deserve their reputation. This country (Cornwall,) abounds in mines, which we have not time to visit. There is a singular sort of secondary mine, called *stream-tin*; the metal is found in very small particles, mixed in horizontal beds of clay.

January 1 1810. – From Bodmin, where we slept last night, travelling all day, we have gone only 32 miles, through a very hilly, unpleasant country; a thick fog hid many a fine view from us. The furze is in full blossom about the hedges; much holly, with rich varnished foliage and bright red berries, and ivy, in wild luxuriance, mantling over cottages and stems of trees. No new houses to be seen; very few young trees; all is old, and mouldering into picturesque forms and colours. The trees are uniformly covered with moss, even to the smallest branches, owing to the prevailing moisture of the climate. We have no creeping plants in North America which preserve their verdure in winter, and the effect of this profusion of ivy is very striking. The mildness of the climate is truly astonishing; geraniums, and other greenhouse-plants, require only shelter, without fire, in winter, and wall-flowers are now in full bloom out of doors. We have seen to-day several gentlemen's houses at a distance, spreading wide and low over fine lawns, with dark back-grounds of pines, and clumps of arbutus and laurel, as green as in spring. Near dusk, we crossed the bay to Plymouth Dock, amidst its floating castles, one of them bearing 90 guns. To-morrow we go to Mount Edgecumbe, if the weather permits. This place struck us as very like Philadelphia, and not the modern part of it. The inhabitants, however, do not look much like Quakers, being mostly army and navy.

January 2. – Armed with umbrellas and greatcoats, we set out this morning for Mount Edgecumbe, in the midst of a drizzling rain. Crossed the bay at Crimble passage; landed on a strand of firm pebbly sand, near the porter's lodge. It was not the day of admittance, and we were told it was necessary to write to Lord M.E. A note was dispatched, and word returned that we were welcome, and a key given to us, opening all gates, with directions to find our way, and no guides to overlook us, which is a refinement of politeness. A gentle ascent of lawn, skirted with old chestnut trees and elms, leads to the house; a plain edifice, half gothic, of a greyish white, with a fine background of trees upon the hill behind. The grounds, which I should judge not to exceed five or six hundred acres, form a sort of headland on the bay. A gravel walk, eight or ten feet wide, leads from the lodge to the house, and, turning round it, through the wood behind, brings you to an open lawn, (A) sloping abruptly to the water. A small gothic ruin stands there, of modern erection, near which the walk divides; a branch descending to the sea-side, another keeping along the high grounds, and, after plunging again into the shade of a dark wood, and passing through groves of evergreen trees and shrubs, advances along the precipitous heights, (B) where the sight, unchecked by any trees, and from an elevation of two or three hundred feet, embraces at once the ocean on the right; in front, on the other side of the bay, at about one mile distance, a line of buildings, like an immense town, broken and diversified by fortifications, arsenals, batteries, &c. so as not to look like a mere field of roofs and chimneys; and in bird's-eye view, line-of-battle ships and frigates passing under your feet with as little ceremony as boats on a river. Thence the walk, turning to the right, ascends higher grounds still, to a plain on the top, where an old gothic church stands, (C) with a tower serving for signals. A path along the heights, and across a wood, brings you back to the place of beginning, – a walk of two or three miles, which took us something less than three hours.

There is nothing done at Mount *Edgecumbe* which a gentleman of moderate fortune could not perform; and nature herself has been at no great expense of bold rocks or mountains; it is a lump of earth sloping to the water, more or less abruptly, but with great variety, and deeply indented with bays. The great charm is the contrast of the loneliness and retirement of the objects near you, with the lively scene and richness, and immensity, bursting on the river here and there; and, upon the whole, this comes nearer to my ideas of beauty, than any spot I ever saw. The green walk, particularly, I shall ever recollect. Laurels of such bright verdure, with large shining leaves; the arbutus, and laurustinus, covered with blossoms; another evergreen tree, resembling the wild cherry of America, (Portugal laurel we are told); then such draperies of ivy, in ample folds over the rocks and trees; such pines with moss of all colours, along the trunk and branches; and on the ground turf as vivid as in the spring, with daisies and periwinkles in flower, and fern, and furze with papilionaceous blossoms. Then through the trees, far below, the surf breaking in measured time, and spreading its white foam among the black rocks of the shore.

The sun had no share in the splendour of the scene, for it was not visible, nor any part of the sky; a misty, drizzly something, like rain, drove along in the blast, and made us tolerably wet; particularly as some deceitful appearances of fair weather, and the heat, had induced us to leave our umbrellas and great coats at the lodge...

JOSEPH FARINGTON
of
LONDON, 1810

Joseph Farington

James Greig (ed.), *The Farington Diary* (1926), VI, 110–145.

Joseph Farington, landscape painter and member of the Royal Academy, was on an extended visit to the West Country. He was 53 years old on his tour of Cornwall.

August 29 After breakfast we crossed the Hamoaze river to Mount Edgcumbe. At the Park Gate Lodge we entered our names in a book kept for that purpose. We also wrote a note to Lord Edgcumbe requesting permission to walk through the grounds. The weather was favorable, and we saw this celebrated situation to the greatest advantage. We were nearly 5 Hours in viewing the scenery from different points. From the highest point of the Mount we had the wide expanse of the Ocean, with the *Edystone* [Eddystone] light House perceptible on the Horizon, and the new-stone rock at the entrance of Plymouth Sound on our left, and high rock with the village of Cawsand seated under them on our right. We had before seen the view from the White Seat from whence Plymouth and all that is connected with it or in its vicinity, was in a long line spread before us. From these Heights we descended to a level walk which forms a belt round a considerable part of the whole of Mount Edgcumbe.

I saw only one instance of bad taste at Mount Edgcumbe, which was a building erected to appear as a ruin. The form of it is bad; and the situation of it worse. It interrupts a view where nothing should be seen that would not be consistent with this splendid display of the power and prosperity of this happy country.

At 4 oClock we left Mount Edgcumbe and recrossed the water, and at 5 oClock dined at our Inn where we found the accommodation good, and the people civil. My Brother informed me that yesterday Mr Tucker, Master Attendant in Plymouth Dock yard showed Him an extraordinary proof of the power of the Sun operating by reflection. The *Culloden* Man of War being at Her station in the East Indies happened to have Her stern placed in such a direction that the rays of the sun which struck the water were reflected upon the Cabin windows. A ray was thus reflected with such heat as instantly to decompose and shatter the glass which it struck. Many pieces of the glass in this state were brought to England and are in Mr Tucker's posession.

August 30 At Liskeard I immediately applied for Horses & a guide to conduct me to the *Cheese-Wring*, a collection of stones of vast size piled upon each other in an extraordinary manner; whether by nature, or by art, seems to be conjectural. After some delay William Moone, a Barber, who said he had often followed the Hounds in that direction undertook to be my guide. Some said the distance we should have to go would be 9 miles; Moone said not more than Six miles, & I believe he was right. At 3 oClock in the afternoon we set off and reached the Cheese-Wring at ½ past 4. It is situated on the side of a small Hill of a conical form, the surface of it studded with pieces of rock. When we arrived at the foot of the Hill my guide told me we could go no farther on Horseback; but having been more accustomed to travel in mountainous countries than had been his lot, I showed Him the way & ascended without danger or difficulty.

The Cheese-wring is a very singular object. It consists of 6 or 7 stones placed one above another. The upper stones of prodigious size resting upon smaller ones below. The general form of the whole has somewhat of a circular appearance which accounts for the name given to it which implies as here meant "Cheese upon Cheese". The height of this pile is said to be 34 feet, but being foreshortened to those who stand to view it where they can see its parts it does not appear to be so high raised. Were the Cheese-wring placed like Stone Henge in a situation far removed from anything of its own quality or were it more insulated than it is, the mind would probably with little hesitation consider it to be a stupendous work of human labour; but here it is surrounded by rocks & stones exhibiting an infinite variety of forms, & some of them both in figure and size so singular and large as almost to claim equal attention. My conjecture therefore could only be that the Cheese-wring with all that accompanies it is an operation of nature. Having made a careful sketch of this curious pile I returned to Liskeard, & on my way made another sketch of a collection of large stones bearing one of greater size which forms a roof over the other stones. The had much the appearance of a Druid-ical erection. It is called "The Trevathy Stone." At 8 oClock I got to Liskeard and dined.

August 31 I should have noticed in my account of yesterday that on my way to the Cheese-wring I passed the Hurlers a line of stones which have the appearance of a regular arrangement. The superstitious tradition respecting them is that they were men turned to stones as a punishment for having played at the game of hurling on a Sunday.

After breakfast I took a Chaise to East Looe, 9 miles distant, and left Liskeard which is a Borough town & returns two members to Parliament.

Being desirous of reaching *Polperrow* [Polperro] this evening I applied for a Boat for that purpose; and having the last year passed a day at East Looe I had nothing to detain me; but to one unacquainted with its situation & pleasing scenery, I should recommend a short stay which would be well rewarded.

At ½ past one oClock I entered the Boat I had hired; and the wind

& tide being unfavourable the Boatmen proceeded with oars only. They were Father & Son in Law; the former told me he had been blind 34 years, caused by his having struck one of his eyes with a needle whilst mending a sail. He said he did not suffer much pain. "It was like the touch of a fly upon his eye," but he lost the sight of it, and in two years the sight of the other eye. Yet, in this apparently helpless state, this industrious man continued his occupations; went out to fish; and placed his nets with more judgment than most of those who were so employed; could mend sails, and in short seemed scarcely to want eyesight. He brought up a large family of children, five of whom he told me he never saw; and never had assistance or applied for relief. This he modestly expressed, but with seeming satisfaction. I met Him walking alone in the town, and when he was recommended to me I objected to him on account of his unfitness; but I was assured I could not employ a better man, & so it proved.

Soon after leaving the harbour of Looe we approached Looe Island, a rock in the Sea, covered with a fine green pasturage, and of sufficient size to have two or three small dwellings upon it which are inhabited by those who look after the sheep & cattle which are upon it. This Island belongs to Sir Harry Trelawny. After leaving Looe Island there was nothing to engage the attention till the Boat approached the harbour of *Polperrow*, when a scene singularly romantic and picturesque open'd to the view. *Polperrow* is a small fishing port almost wholly inhabited by fishermen. It consists of a number of houses clustered together which cover the lower part of a steep Hill which is the boundary of the head of the harbour. They were built of stone or of mortar of various colours. The roofs are of slate. Everything that comes into the view has a character of simplicity, and is in perfect unison. It is formed for the Landscape Painter.

Here I took up my lodging for the night, & dismissed the Boatmen. Their charge was six shillings, and with this and a little Beer they were well satisfied. The distance we had come was not more than five miles, but they had rowed against wind and tide. We were two Hours on our passage.

Some peculiarities of the Cornish people I had before & did now notice. They speak in a singing tone; and, as "Yes sure" is always in the mouth of a Devonshire man, so when a Cornish Man, in this part of the country at least, answers in the negative he does it with this repitition "No, No Sir. No.'"

The evening was dull with misty rain, which caused me to remain in my Inn, The Ship, kept by a widow, a woman of some property. I was treated with civility, and in a very small House had all the accommodation I could reasonably desire.

September 1 After breakfast I went to the rocks at the entrance of the harbour and being favoured by the weather passed several Hours in tinting a sketch of *Polperrow*. At half past 3 I dined. Having recollected that Jefferies, the Seaman, who was put on shore on a desert Island in the West Indies by his Commander, the Honble. Captn. Lake, was said to be a native of this place I was induced to ask some questions respecting Him, which led to my being told that his mother continued to reside at *Polperrow*, and that I might see Her. All of those I spoke to believed Jefferies to be dead, and that all the reports to the contrary were published by the friends of Captn. Lake hoping thereby to prevent any further discussion of this subject which so greatly agitated the public mind.

September 2 Mrs Coade, mother to Jefferies, the Seaman, called upon me, a woman of very respectable appearance. The account she gave me was as follows, "The name of my first Husband was Jefferies. We lived at Fowey & had several children, Robert Jefferies, the unfortunate young man spoken of was the eldest. We was born at Fowey; but whilst he was an infant we removed to *Polperrow* where my Husband died. The name of my second Husband is Coade. He is a Blacksmith, & brought up my son Robert Jeffries to this trade. About three years ago when very young he went out in a Privateer, as Armourer, and from that Ship was pressed into the King's service, & so came under the command of Captn. Lake: at Christmas next, my son, if living, would be 21 years old. When Captn. Lake put him on Shore he was not 18 years old. Another Man of the name of Lecky went from *Polperrow*, was pressed, and saw my son put on shore but was not in the boat with Him. Whilst the case of my son was before the Parliament, Mr Whitbread, M.P., wrote a letter to my Husband, Coade, which I have now in my house."

She then went to Her House for the letter which I read. It was dated Cardington, April 23rd, 1810, & stated that he had communicated the answer which he had received from Mr Job (a very respectable & wealthy inhabitant of *Polperrow*) to Sir Francis Burdett, and to the Admiralty, who had ordered Lecky & another Seaman to be sent for. That Coade's loss of his son's service could not be acted upon unless his death was certain, and in that case Mr Whitbread feared that Coade's situation would be lost in consideration of the crime of Capt. Lake towards the public. He concluded that Coade might write again to him if he saw occasion for it. Mrs Coade told me they had not again written to Mr Whitbread, but intended it, to request his opinion of the reports which had been circulated of Robert Jeffries being alive. I endeavoured to comfort Her by saying, That there had appeared in the Newspapers accounts of Her son being well & settled in America, & that they did seem to be authentic.

The Church to which the people of *Polperrow* go is two or three miles distant from the Port. My desire was to get to Fowey, 6 miles distant, in time for morning service, & I rose early for that purpose, and had hired a horse and guide but I was not able to leave *Polperrow* till past nine oClock. We went but slowly and a longer time passed while we were upon the road than I had reckoned upon; not on account of any objects to be seen for excepting the pillar which stands 120 feet high erected to the memory of the first Lord Chatham at Boconnoc, the late Lord Camelford's which appeared at the distance of many miles, I saw nothing to remark.

Whilst we were on our way my guide gave me the following information. In *Polperrow* there are about 1400 inhabitants. Whilst the smuggling trade was carried on money was plentiful, but that being over the condition of the people is much changed; but they live and are healthy, & few of the children that are born die. Not so in Plymouth said He, where a large proportion die very young. The Fishermen & their families live upon Fish, bread & Potatoes, and never think of eating animal food, but on Sundays, & they are then the worse for it. The life of a Fisherman is not a life of hard labour, otherwise they would require animal food. The gains of a Fisherman are of course uncertain, but may be averaged at 60 to 70 pounds a year.

The men & women marry at a very early age, & generally signs of connexion make it necessary for the credit of the female. But when this sign does appear the men are very faithful; and [when] a marriage has been solemnized there is no after reproach. A considerable proportion of the inhabitants of Polperrow are methodists. They assemble together to the number of perhaps one hundred on Sundays at 7 in the morning, sing Psalms, and several will rise in succession and make extempore prayers, they having no Methodist preacher at their morning meetings; but at their meetings in the evening of Sundays, they have one, persons of this description going as my Guide said, like Excisemen from place to place to officiate in this capacity. He added that these Methodist meetings do not affect the people with respect to the *Church*, to which they go regularly.

He spoke of the high value of the land adjoining *Polperrow* on which cows graze which lets for eight guineas an acre. He informed me that Mr Job who has larger property and greater influence than any other inhabitant of *Polperrow*, is a native of Penzance & came from thence without a shilling. He said Mr Job is King of the place, and held in much respect for his good qualities, & his clerk is one of the best of men.

When we arrived at the Ferry where we had the river to cross to Fowey I found it was too late for morning service, which had begun before I could reach the Inn. I stopped at the Ship Inn kept by two young women of the name of Hoals. At one oClock it was proposed to me to dine at the Ordinary which I agreed to, and found there two young men only, who from their conversation I learnt travelled for orders in some mercantile line. I found them very good humoured and communicative, & I obtained from them much useful information respecting the Inns & roads in Cornwall, & Devonshire. One of them told me that he had in the last fourteen years travelled through these counties twice in each year.

At 3 oClock I went to Fowey Church to Divine Service which was very thinly attended. In this Church there is not an Organ & there was no singing.

September 2 Between four & five oClock I took a Boat to carry me to Lostwithiel six miles from Fowey. The tide was at the best point, and the evening being fine, the passage up the river Fowey was delightful. In an hour & thirty five minutes I was at Lostwithiel having used oars only. I paid for the boatmen four shillings & sixpence. Much of this passage was through Scenery very like that of a Lake. *Pennyquite*, which formerly belonged to Mr Rashleigh and now to Mr Tremayne Junr on the left of the river is a beautiful situation. On the right St Winnow posessed by the Revd Mr [Robert] Walker, seems almost to rival it. My companions at dinner availed themselves of my going up the river to accompany me & I was glad to oblige them with the opportunity. They told me that Mr Walker has lately had a contest with *Finden*, publisher of the Cornwall newspaper, who from having been a very violent partizan against the present government has now become their supporter. After the battle of Corunna & death of Sir John Moore he put his paper in mourning & exhibited something of the Gibbet kind on the margin to signify what was due to the administration.

When he changed from holding these sentiments to the opposite it gave great offence to many & in some way Mr Walker came into contact with him on this account. The result of Finden's conduct has been the establishing of another Newspaper which it is expected will have a serious effect upon this property of Finden. At Lostwithiel I went to the Talbot Inn, Mrs Roberts, where there is good accommodation. She informed me that she is Godmother to [John Bryant] Lane a Student of the Royal Academy, a promising young artist much patronised by Lord de Dunstanville. She said Lane was born at *Polperrow* at a small House opposite to the Inn she then kept in that place.

September 4 At 9 I went to *Kirclaise* tin mine, two miles distant, and made a sketch of the interior of the mine, it being an open mine, a vast chasm, in which mining is carried on, and the machinery used adds to the interest & to the variety of the scene. The depth of the Chasm is very considerable; but the walk to the bottom is made easy by forming the path in an angular manner. When [I] arrived there the view upwards on every side is sublime. The mind has an awful feeling of the vastness of the whole, and contemplating immensity, admires the singularity of many of the parts, which, in spiral forms, shoot up like the much reported glaciers in Switzerland, those pointed masses of Ice which excite in the traveller surprise and admiration. The resemblance is brought nearer by the rocks of this mine being of the colour of chalk, and wanting only transparency to make the similitude complete.

This was my second visit to this mine, in which I made a drawing in October last. Having fixed upon another situation for the same purpose I sat down & commenced a sketch under very unfavourable circumstances. I had to endure a cold North wind, with the apprehension of rain. In this predicament I experienced great kindness & respect from those of the miners who were working near me. One of them threw his Thick waistcoat over me to protect me against the cold; another held my umbrella over me, and thus I was enabled to remain a considerable time, but at last my fear of the cold which had chilled me much got the better of my desire to proceed, & I took my leave of my kind assistants sooner than I would willingly have done.

Kirclaise tin mine may be viewed without the least difficulty by those who being at St Austell may be disposed to ride or walk the short distance of two miles. A Horse may advance to almost the edge of the mine, & the length, and width, and depth of this excavation may be fully seen, with the machinery, & the miners who appear like spots below. *Kirclaise* tin mine is the largest *open* tin mine in Cornwall.

On my return to St Austell I was informed that the Tides were now favourable for seeing objects upon the Sea Coast which cannot be approached but at low waters. I therefore resolved to postpone what I had to do in the vicinity of St Austell, and after dinner proceeded in the Mail Coach to Truro, and arrived there before 8 oClock, at the Hotel, an excellent House for a country town, with beds such as I do not recollect to have seen in any other Inn, and a Chambermaid who attended to everything that could be required. This material point was very satisfactory, but there was too much noise & bustle in the House for me to approve it equally in other respects.

September 5 Took a Chaise to Helston 18 miles before breakfast. I lost no time in ordering a Chaise to carry me to Kynance Cove, 10 miles distant, this being a point upon the coast which had been particularly recommended to my notice. Everything favoured my purpose. I arrived there soon after 12 oClock at the right time of the tide, the water then admitting my walking upon the sand to the Cove which cannot be done at high water.

On approaching this part of the Coast which is about two miles west of the Lizard point, the eye is struck with the appearance of a rock shooting up like a tower to great height about the center of a vast mass of insulated rock. The road then winds down to the beach, which is a flat of the finest sand and so dry and hard that the foot step makes no impression. Here I found a Cart with Boys who were employed in collecting sand; and one of them became my guide for explanation. He first took me into the Cove which is entered through two or three apertures, but one of them opens directly into it. The Cove is an excavation made by the Sea which has perforated the rock in such a way as to give it somewhat the appearance of a rude work of art. The principal entrance to the Cove would admit a Horse & probably a man upon it. The interior of it is a large apartment formed by nature the floor of fine light sand, and the walls and arched ceiling, of dark rock. Having seen excavations upon a much greater scale I was not much affected with the appearance of Kynance Cove, but other parts of this scenery I surveyed with admiration, particularly an insulated rock near the Cove. This vast mass reared on and towered to a height which made the people at the foot of it appear so small that I could not use them as a scale to calculate its size. This pile standing, as it appears to the eye, in the center of a circle of immense rocks forms a very picturesque arrangement, which I endeavoured to represent in a sketch.

I next ascended high rocks by which I got nearer to the tower-like rock which I first saw, and having gratified myself with looking in every direction I sat down on my way back, to contemplate the scene before me. In a short time I was alarmed by a roaring sound and the issuing of a body of water which was discharged from a crevice in a rock near me with the force of a piece of artillery. Finding that the spray reached me I shifted my situation & waited for a repetition of this singular effect. In a few minutes it was repeated with greater force. It happens at a certain time of tide, and the country people give it the name of "The Devil's bellows". This collision of air & water is a curious exhibition of the force of the former.

Having passed several Hours at Kynance Cove I reascended the Hill above it, and on the grass took some refreshment which I had brought from Helston, & cheered the spirits of my driver & guide with their full proportion of it. From this spot the view was sublime & beautiful. The Sun was declining & gave a deeper colour and broader shadows to the mass of rocks which in various forms stood far into the Sea, and the wide extended ocean filled up the scene to the Horizon.

I had now to go to the Lizard point, which being the Southernmost extremity of England my curiosity led me to it. The distance being short I was soon there, and finding nothing to notice but two large light Houses which are illuminated every evening, & having little time to give to contemplation, I could only remark that the situation is solitary & uninteresting: that a single small House is placed near the light Houses; that there is a little village near it which has the meanest appearance of [any of] those to be found in England, and that the road from the Lizard point to Helston is in nearly a right line of 12 miles through a country open and little cultivated.

September 6. Having been informed that Mr Rogers of Penrose near Helston, Brother-in-law to Lord De Dunstanville, was in town, I went to Him and delivered a letter of introduction from his Lordship. He immediately offered to ride with me to the *Looe* [Loe] Pool, and to show me what had been noticed in this neighboroud, to which he added an invitation to dine with Him. He first took me to the Church yard which being an elevated situation I could from thence see much of the country including the *Looe* Pool which appears like a small Lake. It seemed to be about a mile in length, and is a fresh water Pool. At the South end it is separated from the Sea by a Bar of Sand. It frequently happens that the water of the Pool is much increased in quantity from streams flowing into it after heavy rains, that being overcharged it stops the Mills, & produces other inconveniences. It is then necessary to cut through the bed of Sand to allow the water of the pool to flow into the Sea.

On granting leave to have the Bar cut, Mr Rogers receives each time 2 leather purses with three half pence in each purse. Mr Rogers proposed that we should ride to the Bar of Sand, and make a circuit to his House which stands on the west side of the Pool which we attempted but repeated showers prevented us from accomplishing our purpose.

It was on this Bar of Sand that the *Anson* Frigate was lost & the Commander, Captn. [Lydiard] was drowned, he having resolutely persevered in remaining in the ship till it was too late to save Him. In the same season, a little before the period of this melancholy accident, a transport with Cavalry troops was lost about a mile and ½ from the Bar. The Vessel struck in the night, & the country people who had seen Her distressed situation immediately went to the short to give assistance even at the risk of their lives. The tide was for sometime favorable and there being several Ladies passengers on board, they were seated one after another, in a Cabin Chair, and let down into the Sea, & were dragged through the Surf by the people on shore who had been able to fasten a rope to the Chair.

After the Ladies, all the Officers were got on shore in the same manner. Unfortunately much time was lost in repeating this for each person singly. The consequence was that the tide flowed in before it was possible to bring off the soldiers, and the Surf ran so high that all attempts made for the purpose failed. These unfortunate men had forbore from making any exertion to save themselves, and with a perfect submission to the authority of the Officers saw all but themselves carried off from their perilous situation. Mr Rogers told me he saw these gallant men, standing on the wreck, scarcely 100 yards from the Shore, waiting their fate. The only hope left was that the vessel might hold together against the heavy billows brought up by the tide.

It was now daylight, & extreme anxiety filled every breast. Suddenly the ship broke in two under the weight of the waves; and a rolling Sea overwhelming that part of the ship on which the men stood, a violent cry was heard, and the whole of them were instantly buried in the surf; not a man of them escaped; & thirty-six bodies of fine young men in the flower of life, were afterwards taken from their watery grave & placed in a row on the shore previous to their being interred together near the spot.

In the ship when she struck was a young lady, the widow of an officer who was killed at Buenos *Ayres*. She was left without a husband, & without means of support. When she was let down from the ship her mind was in such a state of distress as to leave her without a wish to be preserved. She was brought on shore a stranger, without a friend or any being to whom she could have recourse. She was a native of Ireland, & knew none out of her own country. Thus miserable & forlorn Providence had in its goodness to ordered that here where she had given herself up to despair she found all the benefits which could arise from humanity. Mr Rogers took her under his protection; comforted her in every way in his power; and by active exertions, and a strong representation of her case, procured for her a subscription to the amount of eight hundred pounds; accompanied her to London; and there, by his interest, obtained a pension for her & some other advantages, and enabled her to return to her own country easy in her circumstances & grateful for the blessings bestowed upon her.

Being now within less than 30 miles of the Land's-end, the most western part of England, I remarked to Mr Rogers that I was rather surprised to see much wheat still standing, as I had concluded that the Harvest would be over in this part of the Island. He said "In this country we have Spring throughout the year; In the Winter we have not severe cold; and the Heat of our Summers is temperate. The glass (The Thermometer) at 75 is considered to be a high point. In the Midland Counties there is more heat and great vigour of vegetation; and the produce of the earth sooner ripens."

Penrose, the House of Mr Rogers, is situated at the Head of a Valley on rising ground above the *Looe* Pool, & being surrounded with woods of full growth has a singularly rich appearance, all without it being wild and barren. A walk of a mile reaches to the sea. The Pool is well stored with Fish, and a Boat is placed for the purpose of sailing or fishing. It is about a mile and Half long.

At 4 oClock we dined at Penrose. I was very kindly recd. by Mrs Rogers, Sister of Lord De Dunstanville. Mr & Mrs Rogers have 17 children living, & have buried one. Their two elder Sons are Clergymen, one has the living or Redruth, the other [The Revd John Rogers], that of Mawnan, 5 miles from Falmouth. They have a Son in the East Indies; and one in the Navy; the remainder are daughters. One of them married to Mr [Thomas] Hartley, a gentleman of Yorkshire now a resident [at Bonython] near Marazion. Mr [Francis] Wills & Mr [Thomas] Grylls, are agents to Mr Rogers. We had some conversation respecting the Climate of Cornwall; and I wished to know whether in this mild atmosphere people are remarked to live longer than they do in the Northern parts. There was some hesitation in replying to me, but it was observed by them that there are many instances of women living to a great age. Mr Grylls concurred in opinion with Mr Rogers in regard to vegetation.

At tea Mrs Rogers spoke of a tour she made in Westmorland and Cumberland 19 years ago. She remarked that the people in Westmorland, particularly have more simplicity than those in Cornwall.

September 7 At 9 left Helston in a chaise and proceeded to Marazion 10 miles. On my way I walked to Pengersick Castle Half a mile from the road. I found it a ruin of a building which had nothing interesting in its appearance either from its size or its form. It belonged to the Godolphin family, & in now the property of the Duke of Leeds.

At Marazion I went to the Star Inn, which stands upon the shore facing St Michael's Mount, & perhaps from no [other] point does the rock & Castle appear to greater advantage. Here I found accommodations that were quite satisfactory to one disposed to be contented. Having made my arrangements with Mrs Clements, the Landlady, I went and with the advantage of the finest weather, began to make a drawing, an East view of the Mount. On my return to the Inn in the afternoon I was informed that Lord de Dunstanville with a party, was gone to dine at the Mount, where Sir Thomas Dacre Leonard, Brother in Law to Sir John St Aubyn, owner of the Island, was with his family. I wrote a note to his Lordship, & soon after I had dined, saw him with his party walking across the neck of land which at low water unites the Island with the main land. He called upon me & then set off for Tehidy, 12 or 14 miles from the Mount. It had been fixed by Mr Rogers that I should meet his Lordship at Penrose on Monday.

September 8 Before breakfast made a finished sketch of St Michael's Mount from the Star Inn. I next hired a Boat with two Fishermen to take me round the Island, which they undertook to do and to allow me time for making sketches, for a reward of four shillings. The weather was very fine, & the sea sufficiently smooth to enable them to keep the boat nearly stationary wherever I chose to remain. This rock, with its Castle, is a noble subject for a painter. The west front of it which faces the Ocean is the most rugged & precipitous. The form & the Colour of it is beautiful, & all the parts are so much in unison; the Castle is in all respects in such harmony with the rock upon which it stands, as almost to seem a natural part of it. The general colour of the rock is grey of various degrees; such also is that of the

Castle; but in both there is a mixture of other tints which by their opposition give greater effect to the whole. The Herbage which forms a part of the surface is of a mild and subdued colour, well agreeing with the grave hue of the castle & rock.

The Bass rock at the mouth of the Firth of Forth, and the rock of Dumbarton in the Clyde, are famed features of nature in their respective situations; but cannot either of them be compared with St Michael's Mount, which far exceeds them in elegance of form & picturesque beauty.

I passed a considerable time in contemplating the Island from various points & in sketching; & my Boatmen being satisfied with the bargain they had made, and being young and chearful, they sung, while I pursued my purpose. They told me they were engaged six weeks ago by a person of property in the neighbourhood, at the rate of fourteen shillings each per week, to fish for pilchards; that they had hitherto been unsuccessful, the pilchards not having appeared; & that the Season would soon be over, & that they have no further interest in this speculation beyond their weekly pay, the profit or loss falling upon their employer. The time of their going out to fish I understood to be in the earliest part of the afternoon, & they continue out till about 8 oClock at night. In the night the pilchards sink low in the water, too deep for the nets.

September 9 At Marazion there is a small Church, but I was informed it is seldom used. A Methodist meeting House is the place to which the inhabitants go; it is used in the interval between the morning & evening meetings as a Sunday School. There is also a Baptist meeting House which is frequented.

In the evening at 5 oClock, the Mail Coach from Penzance passed through Marazion, in which I returned to Helston. In the Coach I found a genteel young man who told me he left Mogador, in Barbary, about a month ago. He went there in January last, and soon found the heat of that climate too powerful for his constitution. He had fevers repeatedly, & was to reduced as to leave no hope of his being able to live in that Country. Mogador is situated upon sand, waste and unproductive, but the interior of the country is fruitful. The town is large, but dismal to behold. The windows of the Houses look into the Courts round which they are built. Women are scarcely seen. The natives hold those who come to their country in great contempt. They are not admitted to the Mosques. All business done with them is in the streets. Yet with all this they have a high idea of the power of England & France which, they say command all other countries. The

French have Consuls at Mogador, who take much pains to prevent supplies of provisions from being carried to Gibraltar, but have not succeeded.

He said he left Barbary in a Ship richly laden with gums &c., and had proceeded almost to the Irish Coast when on Monday last they were attacked by a French Schooner from St Malo. Having no means of defence they surrendered immediately. The French men who first boarded the ship had a Lieutenant at their head, and behaved very roughly; but upon being addressed in *French* by some of those on hoard, they became civil, & treated their prisoners with respect. The Captain of the Schooner had then an American vessel in his possession, & he agreed to let the Captn. of the English vessel, with my companion and others who were on board, go to England in the American ship, taking their promise to endeavour to obtain the release of as many French prisoners as their number amounted to. The motive for this act they concluded to be an unwillingness to burden Himself with so many men as he otherwise must have done, or to have lessened his number by sending part of his Crew with this vessel to France. When they left the French Schooner the Captain allowed them to bring several necessaries with them. Their trunks were opened on the decks to show to the Frenchmen what they contained; this the Captain said must be done to satisfy them as to what was given up.

All letters found were detained. The Captain declaring that the Seals were *not* to be broken, but the letters were to be delivered sealed to a public office at their port. Having taken leave of the French Captain they made the best of their way to England, and soon arrived at Penzance. In this instance was shown the advantage of being able to speak the French language; and of the Social feeling which is excited when there can be communication in language familiar to the parties who are thus brought together. Here it caused Barbarous outrage to be softened even into liberality.

September 10 In the afternoon, I walked to Penrose to dinner, and found the family party assembled. We dined soon after 4 oClock.

Before dinner on my looking at a picture of the late Mr Bassett, father of Lord de Dunstanville, It led to a conversation respecting his reconnoitre with the late General Johnson at the Opera House, which was much spoken of at the period when it happened. Mr Bassett being one of many gentlemen who according to the Custom of that time stood upon the stage near the Scenes, was grossly insulted by Johnson, who ridiculing Mr Bassett's small figure, treated Him otherways with contempt. Johnson was celebrated for his skill in fencing & being a tall man had every advantage; but on this occasion nearly lost his life; for Mr Bassett drew his sword & attacked him with such spirit as nearly to have run Him through the body. They were instantly separated, but his Majesty, George 2nd, happening to be at the Theatre that night, the bustle occasioned by this affray caused Him to inquire into the occasion of it. He was informed that it was Major Johnson who had given the offence, on which his Majesty said "And *Major* Johnson he shall remain." Lord de Dunstanville told me that Johnson's promotion at that time was He believed stopped, that is, during the old King's reign. He said that when Johnson was advanced in years he knew Him, and had conversation with Him on this subject. Johnson said, "That he on this as he believed he had on many other occasions acted very improperly; and with the inconsiderateness and impertinence of a vain unthinking young man." Lord de Dunstanville remarked to me that whatever improprieties he might have been guilty of he was punished for all by his marriage with Lady Cecilia, a perfect termagant in disposition, who as far as she was capable of doing it made Him miserable.

Lord de Dunstanville mentioned the cause of the death of De Cort, the Landscape painter from Antwerp. On a day when he was very warm with walking he went to Lord Grosvenor's to see the Collection of pictures and there for the purpose of cooling Himself sat opposite to an open window. This caused Him in a very short time to be affected with an inflammation in his chest, and he became so ill as to require the attendance of a Physician, but his disorder increased; he became delirious & in a very few days dies. Having no relation in England, the care of his property fell into the hands of a person named Bellchambers, who keeps the Cambridge Coffee House in Newman Street. It was in consequence of Bellchambers having a Son who was a pupil of De Cort that he came forward with the pretension of managing the affairs of the deceased. De Cort had stated Himself to be of a respectable family at Antwerp, & that his family had the office of Sheriff of that City hereditary in it.

He told Lord de Dunstanville that till he was 40 years of age he never practised painting as a profession; but his situation and that of his family having been much changed by political causes which operated upon the property of many in the country, he was necessitated to fix upon some mode of procuring a livelihood; and having had recourse to his pencil he came to England about the year 1790 or 91. He said he has been so successful in his practise that should he live to finish commissions which he had from Mr Henry

Hope, Mr Philip Hope, and another gentleman amounting together to eight pictures at about 150 guineas each. He should then be independent. He had two or three Sons who have not followed the industrious example set by their father; but have lived in a dissipated manner, & have subjected Him to much expence to discharge debts incurred by them. One of them was in England in the King's Bench prison for debt; but they are now at Antwerp. Lord de Dunstanville said De Cort had read a good deal, & had much anecdote, but with some good humour, had a considerable share of petulance. His Lordship had five pictures painted by Him; & he recommended Him to Lord Digby who employed Him to paint two views of *Sherborn* Castle. He also recommended Him to other persons. Dr Manners, the present Archbishop of Canterbury, employed him to paint a large view of Canterbury Cathedral.

I could have told his Lordship that from what I have heard no Artist could have practised more cunning and address in soliciting employment and putting himself in a way to be employed than De Cort; and that his modes of obtaining notice for this purpose had been such as to cause him to be thought of with little respect by those artists who felt for the credit of their profession, and would not acknowledge in their rank a man who showed so little respect for Himself.

In the course of our conversation this evening, I asked Lord de Dunstanville why the number of Parliamentary Boroughs in Cornwall so far exceeded that of any other county. He said the only cause he knew of was, that in Cornwall the Royal Domains being extensive so as to give the Crown considerably authority & influence at former periods; it was exercised in this county in making up parliaments, where to return members, was considered a grievance on account of the expence attending it – the Borough which sent a member being required to make Him an allowance to defray his expences. The requisition to return members being on this acct. disliked, the Crown looked most to that part of the Kingdom which was likely to receive it with the least objection, and thus the number of Boroughs in Cornwall became great above all proportion. Some of the Cornish Boroughs were after a time relieved from this obligation as they considered it. Marazion, & another Borough, on their petitioning were disfranchised. It occurred to me that there might be an additional motive for the Crown to increase the number of Cornish Boroughs; as it might be supposed that members coming to Parliament from a County in which there was so much Royal influence would be most likely to act in obedience to the wishes & views of the

Crown, which even in despotic times must have been convenient & agreeable.

Mr Rogers told me that for some time he was one of the Members returned by Helston; and that it was remarkable that at one period (in Mr Rogers's time) there were only *two Electors*, the number having been diminished by deaths. The number of Electors is now 16, of which Mr Rogers is one.

After our walk we had tea, & I then had a pleasant ride to Helston by moonlight. It was Helston fair, and there were still so many people, and Cattle, and Canvass standings for the Show of goods, &c., that it looked by night like an encampment.

September 11 With [Mr Heath] the Collector I had some conversation respecting the climate of Cornwall. He said the mildness of the weather in the winter Season is such that for 4 or 5 years past there had been no ice strong enough to bear skating upon it. In the bleak moorish part of the country about Bodmin it might, he believed, be otherwise.

Having leisure to look over my Diary continued thus far, I now make the following addition to the account given me by the young man from Barbary. He said that though the government of that country is perfectly despotic, no apprehension is or need to be entertained unless by those who are distinguished for their great property. There are many Greeks who are held in contempt & subjection; and abundance of Jews who carry on trade to a great extent.

September 12 At ½ past 9, I left Helston, [and] proceeded in a Chaise to Tehidy, Lord de Dunstanville's, about 12 miles but charged 14 miles, through an open country, & much of it rugged heath, and in some places the machinery of mines showed their situation.

When I got to Tehidy I found that Lord de Dunstanville was not returned from his excursion but would be at home at dinner-time; and I employed myself during the interval in regulating my drawings.

Before 5 oClock Lord and Lady de Dunstanville & Miss[es] Bassett returned and we dined. After dinner our conversation turned upon the character of the Cornish people. I observed that the impression on the minds of those who inhabit other parts of this kingdom is, that the Cornish miner has something of a savage character; but that I had on the contrary found them civil & obliging and not at all of the description supposed. Lord de Dunstanville said when assembled in bodies they are rough when moved by some occasion, but individually are sufficiently peaceable. At one period during the French Revolution a very bad spirit had got among them, as it had in other parts of the Kingdom. I think he said it was in the year 1795 that an insubordinate disposition rose to such a height in this part of the county of Cornwall as to cause a body of men to assemble & by threats to oblige Millers and Dealers in grain to do their business at certain prices fixed by these rioters. This happened whilst Lord de Dunstanville was in London, and when his Lordship returned to Tehidy no opposition had been made to their demands, the Magistrates being afraid to act.

He, however, told them he would show what could be done, & finding their timid disposition, he had recourse to his Brother in Law Mr Rogers of Penrose only, who, at his Lordships's request came over to Tehidy, and after taking the depositions of the Millers they immediately swore in 80 Constables, who, according to a plan formed, proceeded to take up from their beds at 2 oClock in the morning 50 of the most noted of the rioters, who were without delay conveyed to Bodmin Gaol. At the Assizes which followed this period, they were tried and three of them were condemned to die, some were ordered to be transported, and others sentenced to be imprisoned. After the trials were over Lord de Dunstanville had a private conversation with the Judge, who remarked to Him that the execution of one of the three who were sentenced to die might have a sufficient effect & that the punishment of the other two might be mitigated. In this his Lordship fully concurred, and there being one more vicious & profligate than the rest he was left for execution.

In carrying on this business so necessary for the public security Lord de Dunstanville complained of having been put in a very disagreeable predicament by the magistrates in addition to their former want of resolution. After the trials were over & sentence had been passed they addressed his Lordship to obtain a remission of the punishment. He replied that they had done that which was very painful to Him, for that in refusing to make the application they wished Him to do, it would seem to be fixing upon Him the death of anyone who might suffer. He added that notwithstanding this disagreeable reflection, he should do what he believed to be his duty, and would not prevent an example being made which was highly necessary for the benefit of Society.

The effect of this resolute conduct was soon visible throughout the country, and the manners of the people were suddenly changed from rudeness & disrespect to proper obedience. For a very short time there was some agitation, and the body of the man who had been executed was brought to *Camborn* about 4 miles from Tehidy, attended by a thousand persons to witness the funeral & show their respect. It happened that at the time when they were thus assembled Lord de Dunstanville having occasion to go that way passed through the place & stopped at the House of a Clergyman there who warned Him of his danger. To this he replied loud enough to be heard by many of the Mob that the danger would be with them if they acted improperly. No attempt was made to molest Him, & the people dispersed quietly after which order was generally restored. Thus by the prudent & manly exertions of his Lordship the evil spirit of the time caused by revolutionary notions was effectually banished from a district where he had a power of acting for the public good.

After speaking upon this subject Lord de Dunstanville adverting to the late Mr Burke, said in his predictions respecting the French Revolution he spoke & wrote in the spirit of Prophecy. All he foretold has been realised; he had the largest comprehension and was the most extraordinary man of his time. Mr Pitt on the contrary was slow in believing that a bad spirit was rising in this Country from the example set in France; but being at length persuaded of it, he was prompt and vigorous in preventing the growing effects; and by the *Sedition Bill* which he brought into parliament and carried he saved this country.

We talked of Old families in Cornwall. Lord de Dunstanville said that when Carew wrote his account of this county towards the end of the reign of Elizabeth there were then 20 families existing in Cornwall whose ancestors came into England at the *Conquest*, of which only 3 or 4 now remain. Sir John St Aubyn's & his Lordship's families are included in this number. Lord Falmouth's family is comparatively of modern date; & Sir William Lemon's grandfather was a miner without a shilling, but by industry and good luck acquired £200,000. Mr Gwatkins' maternal grandfather was Captain Lovel who had a packet at Falmouth & made a pretty fortune.

Miss Mary Bassett spoke of De Cort; said he was hot in his temper, & when his drawings were said to be *pretty* would cry out "That is a term for Milliner's work & such trifles." he had made a very large number of drawings but never sold any or gave them away. He painted 3 views of Haarlem House in Holland, for Mr Henry Hope, it having been his residence, a subject as little picturesque as possible.

Being without company today the family lived thus: After a few glasses of wine Coffee was brought, to the dinner table, & in a little time the Ladies walked out, before tea which was had at 8 oClock. Lord de Dunstanville also walked out, saying he had a weak stomach

& the open air was necessary for him. We retired to bed at Eleven oClock.

September 13 At breakfast brought us the News papers which contained an account of the death of Sir Francis Baring on the 11th inst. at his House at Lee in Kent. Lord de Dunstanville spoke of this event with much regret great friendship having subsisted between them. He said Sir Francis was the true English merchant; had large and liberal principles & no unreasonable ambition. According to his own account given to Lord de Dunstanville he began the world with a fortune of £10,000, of this he had expended £9,000 and part of his last thousand before he acquired anything but a knowledge of trade & Commerce. In the expending his original fortune he had committed no act of extravagance but it gradually wasted while he was learning the business of a merchant. His Lordship then gave an instance of the great liberality of Sir Francis.

A family possessed of an estate at or near Lee in Kent from a change in their circumstances found it necessary to dispose of it, & it being offered for sale Sir Francis became the purchaser. After the bargain was completed he found the purchase had been made at a low rate, upon which in addition to what he had paid he presented the family with a gift of ten thousand pounds, thereby rendering the sale of the estate an advantage to them beyond any expectation they could have formed.

Lord de Dunstanville read part of a letter he had received from Lord Sidmouth, who he said had entertained but faint hopes of what might be done in Spain and Portugal to resist the French, but now began to think more favourably, and to believe it not improbable but that those countries might maintain their independence.

Mr Pitt being mentioned Lord de Dunstanville said that at one period he had a good deal of intercourse with him, and had in conversation remarked upon the vast weight of business which must press upon his mind. To this Mr Pitt replied, that however much engaged he might be in the daytime he never carried care to his pillow, but that with his cloaths he put off all consideration of business, and being satisfied with having done the best he could he went to rest with a free and easy mind. I observed to his Lordship that notwithstanding this reasonable reflection it showed great firmness of nerve to be able to compose his mind so fully after such exertions as he was frequently obliged to make.

After breakfast I rode with Lord de Dunstanville to about four miles from Tehidy. It being low water we were enabled to ride along the coast, upon the sands to a sublime piece of scenery, a natural arch not less than one hundred feet high through a rock of vast size which stood out to the Sea. This arch is called "Tabbins Hole." The rock is completely perforated, and on both sides, for we walked through the arch, presents the most magnificent appearance of the kind that I recollect to have seen. Here I made a sketch, and his Lordship standing under the arch served to show the vast scale upon which this scene is formed.

This being the public day at Tehidy, and company expected, we returned to dinner, which was served before 4 oClock. Every Thursday is appointed for this purpose & the dinner hour is early for the convenience of those who return home. Mr Steevens is one of the Members for St Ives, & resides near that place. Dr [John] Luke, a Physician, of much reputation, residing near Helston, but wishing to change his situation, and to practise in London, though towards fifty years of age, is now keeping terms at one of the Universities to enable Him to effect this agreeably to what is required by the College of Physicians. One of his objections to continuing to reside in the Country is the being frequently required to ride long distances to visit patients. Mr J. Rogers is the eldest Son of Mr Rogers of Penrose and has the living of Mawnan five miles from Falmouth. Mr [Thomas] Leonard is the eldest Son of Sir Thomas Leonard, who married a Sister of Sir John St Aubyn.

Lord de Dunstanville told me that Mr Steevens was born at or near St Ives and is but of low origin. When he offered himself a Candidate to represent St Ives an opposing Candidate reproached him with this circumstance which, however, Mr Steevens very judiciously turned to his own advantage. In his reply he acknowledged that he sprung from the lower order of the people, but that he could boast of having a very considerable number of the Electors in the list of his relations, & hoped to have the gratification of being returned Member by near connexions. This retort had its effect & he was elected. He married a Lady who brought Him a fortune said to be £100,000. The evening was passed as usual; tea, cards & books for those who chose them.

September 14 Towards noon I rode to Redruth Rectory, with Mr J. Rogers. There I saw his Brother, the Rector, and Mr Rogers of Penrose who had brought over two of his daughters. From hence I ascended Carn Brea Hill with Mr J. Rogers & there made a drawing of Carn Brae Castle, including the town of Redruth. The top of Carn Brea Hill is a long ridge upon which there are several Druidical monuments, one of them supposed to have been an Altar of Sacrifice. The Castle which is situated at the east end of the ridge, is considered to be of Roman foundation. What remains is a single tower founded upon a rock which serves as a base to the building & seems to form a part of it. Here Mr J. Rogers who is much inclined to the study of antiquities employed Himself in sketching parts of the Castle.

This evening Lord de Dunstanville told me that when he was a very young man, 19 or 20 years old, he was in Germany & passed sometime with the Prussian Army which was then in the field contending respecting the Bavarian Succession. It was commanded by Prince Henry of Prussia. At this time his Lordship was much acquainted with Prince Leopold of Brunswick. One morning while they were at breakfast in a Mill, the Prince was apprised of the approach of 5000 Cossacks, a force he was not in sufficient force to resist. Seeing his danger he urged Lord de Dunstanville to go off while there was time to escape, but this he would not do, & placed himself in the ranks. Many were killed; the brains of a Serjeant struck Him. Fortunately two Prussian regiments of Cavalry came up, charge & brook the enemy & took 2000 prisoners. He said the Prussian army at that time was made up of people of various countries & had in it also many deserters. There was no sentiment of love of country among them; no patriotism. Prince Leopold of Brunswick was of a very amiable disposition. He was drowned in the Danube at a time of a great overflow of that river while he was endeavouring to assist those whose habitations were swept away by the force of the water. Northcote painted a picture of this subject from which an engraving was executed.

Lord de Dunstanville had some intercourse with the Father of Buonaparte, & brought a letter from Him to General [Pasquele de] Paoli, which was intrusted to his Lordship from the confidence the other had in him as an Englishman, as had it been discovered that he held correspondence with Paoli it might have been fatal to Him. This circumstance caused an acquaintance to commence between his Lordship & Paoli which continued till the death of the latter. Notwithstanding the wonderful success of Buonaparte from all that is known of both, Lucien Buonapart has an abler mind than the French Emperor.

September 15 At noon I rode with Lord de Dunstanville to Polnatha rock scenery upon the coast a mile from Tehidy, & there sketched his Lordship sitting upon the grass by me.

Something which caused the late Lord Camelford to be mentioned led to speaking of his death. [Everard] Home, the surgeon being applied to by Lord Camelford to attend the duel, was desired to go to his Lordship's house for some purpose, & was directed to bring his Lordship's pistols with him. This part of his commission home forgot, & when the combatants met Mr Best's pistols were used by both. Mr Best has since said that when they took their ground he concluded Lord Camelford would not fire at him with an intention to kill him but would turn his pistol so as to show that not to be his intention. But Lord Camelford took the best aim he could & the ball he fired passed near the ear of Mr Best, who, according to his own account knowing that if Lord Camelford should again fire at Him he would certainly kill him then took aim & shot him.

Lord de Dunstanville after having mentioned these circumstances reprobated the practise of those who endeavour to become what are called "good pistol shots" & said that if it depended upon Him he would hang any man who being so prepared should shoot another. In this conversation he never alluded to the Duel he lately had with Sir Christopher Hawkins. Something having passed respecting politics I asked Him whether he believed that the question of relieving the Irish Catholics was really the cause of Mr Pitt retiring from the government in 1801. He said he had no doubt of it.

After dinner we had some conversation respecting the French Revolution. His Lordship [said] it was principally caused by the French Nobility, who were generally speaking in a state of great profligacy. Religion was ridiculed by them, and morality had very little effect. The word liberty was taken up by them and used without any discretion; and the free intercourse they had with their servants who heard their sentiments propagated the most dangerous opinions. At table his Lordship said he had heard such immoral things said as were shocking, but were smiled at or unnoticed. The part the French took respecting America also greatly contributed to the revolution. The writings of Voltaire, Rousseau &c. had also made a large preparation for a change.

September 16 At Eleven I went to Illogan Church one mile distant in the carriage with Lady de Dunstanville. The two Misses Bassett had gone before in order to inspect a Sunday School established by the Hon: Miss Bassett. After Divine Service I went with the Ladies to Portreath where they have a Cottage delightfully situated under rocks near the sea side. Here they have everything for a breakfast or a repast, with books to amuse those who would read & admire the prospect. Near this place in Baths formed in the rocks Miss Bassett frequently comes to bathe, & this in such scenery as would be quite poetical. Here we had some refreshment then walked to the top of the Hill above the Cottage where we were taken up by the Carriage and proceeded home.

Lord de Dunstanville dined with a few principal farmers who assembled to adjudge prizes to such tenants of his Lordship, holders of Cottages with a small piece of ground attached to them, as should have shown the best husbandry & Management of their respective dwellings & ground. This encouragement given excites emulation that has a very good effect. In the evening he walked to the chapel of ease which he has built one mile or more from Tehidy, which he makes a point to do as an example to the people.

In the evening the Revd Mr [James Jenkin] Keigwin, curate of Illogan, came and at nine oClock read prayers in the Chapel in one of the wings of the House, in which there is a neat Altar & Altar picture painted by the Honble. Miss Bassett. At prayers the whole family of servants attended. On acct. of Mr Keigwin there was a light supper.

In conversation the Buonapart family was spoken of. Lord de Dunstanville said that Joseph Buonapart is a Drunkard, & much given to women, and in this is followed by Louis Buonapart who however is a man of more humane disposition than his other Brothers, & better intentions.

September 17 We dined at 5, & had tea at 8 after which Cards while I was engaged in reading the Diary of the late Bubb Doddington, Lord Melcombe, an extraordinary exhibition of Political insincerity, selfishness, & meanness. That such a record of his own conduct should have been left by a man proves how much the mind may be vitiated by long habits of intrigue & servility for ambitious purposes.

September 18 At breakfast Lord de Dunstanville said that Dr Lecke had given his opinion that all medicines have some effect upon the constitution so as to render taking them habitually not a matter of indifference, he included Magnesia, reckoned the most innocent, in this objection; at the same [time] he allowed that certain constitutions required such aid & relief as certain medicines would give taken habitually.

Style of living was a subject of conversation. The late [third] Duke of Portland was ostentatious in this respect, and gave the best dinners in his time. I mentioned that I had been told the dinners given by Mr Henry Hope of Cavendish Square were magnificent. Lord de

Dunstanville said he had dined there but did not think so; there was expense enough, but a Dutch clumsiness prevailed in the manner of conducting the entertainment, Sir Francis Baring's dinners were in a better style. His Lordship then spoke of making up parties; & said he would not for social intercourse wish to see more than seven at table. When company is increased to more than that number they get into committees, and for his own part when there are more than seven he cares not if there be forty.

September 19 The mining concerns of Cornwall were spoken of. These are carried [on] by bodies of men united for the purpose who share the profit or loss. Lord de Dunstanville remarked that they had frequently justified what he believed to be a truth, that whatever they may be individually considered, bodies of men are never liberal.

The conversation today was not interesting. After tea Lord de Dunstanville spoke to me of Ruythson, a Fleming, who had given lessons in drawing to Miss Bassett, and in the Summer Season, had twice come down from London to Tehidy Park. He is a well-behaved, good-natured liberal man. Lord de Dunstanville having paid him money, offered him more, which he would not accept. Unlike many foreigners he affects to be nothing more than he is in reality. He spoke of his Father being a miller, and that by some means he was able to go to Rome where he studied seven years. He is about fifty five years old, and is much employed in London in giving lessons in drawing, which he does in a singular manner.

September 20 At breakfast [James] Redhead Yorke, the political newspaper writer was spoken of. During the French Revolution he was a violent Democrat, & for his proceedings was thrown into Gaol by a sentence of the Court of King's Bench, where, & since his confinement expired, his political sentiments have undergone a total change, & he is now an active opposer of those who maintain Revolutionary principles. He is believed to be sincere, & that is now the opinion of the Attorney General respecting him.

This being the public day at Tehidy Park, we dined at Half past three oClock. Mr Sandys told me he went to Rome in 1771; that he was acquainted with Jacob More, the Landscape Painter, who having got a prize at Edinburgh for painting, left Scotland, and for a while resided in London, from whence he was carried to France by a Mr Alexander, and to Italy, where he remained till his death. His reputation for Landscape painting was very high, and his employment was in proportion; but he lessened the respect in which he would have been held by forming a Connexion with an artful woman altogether unworthy of his attention.

More passed the three first years of his residence in Italy without painting anything, being entirely occupied in collecting matter for study, and subjects for painting. Mr Sandys returned to England in 1774, being then 30 years old and in 1777 again went to Italy with Lord de Dunstanville (then Sir Francis Bassett) and was absent with him about a year and a Half, Lord de Dunstanville being of age in 1778. After tea the Ladies were employed in Musick & in working at a social round table.

September 21 Mr Sandys resides at Minver near Padstow. The parish of which he is Minister, is wholly or nearly so, his own property. He is a widower without children and has a handsome income, which enables him to live very comfortably & agreeably to his taste.

Lord de Dunstanville spoke of the Borough of Bodmin of which he is the Recorder. There are only thirty four Electors. Through the interest of his Lordship Mr Davies Giddy is one of the Members. His father is a clergyman and resides near Marazion. Mr Giddy married a Lady with whom he will eventually probably have £100,000. He is devoted to the business of Parliament, and is becoming so well informed in all that relates to it, that it is not improbable but that he may at some period [be] the Speaker. He is a good Mathematician, & habitually a man who seeks to acquire knowledge. Such was Lord de Dunstanville's account of Him; & from what I saw of him was pleased with his unassumin manners.

Lord de Dunstanville spoke of [James] Christie, the Auctioneer & expressed his surprise that a man who had been educated at *Eaton* School, & had been there distinguished for his classical acquirements should have submitted, or rather by choice should have chosen to be in the line of life in which he is now established. After tea, we talked of the late James Barry, formerly Professor of Painting in the Royal Academy, & Lord de Dunstanville showed me a criticism on his life & works published in the Edinburgh review for August 1810. It was written by Mr Richard Payne Knight. It contained much just observation mixed with superficial remarks on art, and want of liberality to Artists.

September 22 At 7 Left Tehidy and went to Green Bank, Falmouth. After breakfast I crossed the Ferry at Green Bank to Flushing the distance about the third of a mile. Half the profits of the Ferry belong to Lord Wodehouse. Beautiful views from the heights above Flushing commanding the harbour and town of Falmouth &c. The situation of Flushing most favourable for consumptive invalids on account of the mildness of the atmosphere in this part, protected by hills from the east & the north and fronting the South and West. It has been called the Montpellier of England. The scenery has much of the *Lake* character.

September 23 The morning wet. I walked to Falmouth Church, three quarters of a mile, the organ and singing very good, female voices with those of men. Curtains drawn before the female singers who are placed in the front of a gallery. I observed that the people *sat* during the singing and that many men as well as women sat during the prayers. Revd Mr Hitchins, the Curate, officiated; which office he had filled 16 or 17 years. He preached *extempore* about 40 minutes. His charitable disposition, attention to the poor, and the pains he takes to regulate & educate children have rendered him very popular. Having a small independent income, and being a bachelor, he can afford assistance to many and does it to the extent of much of his income. The name of the Rector, a non-resident, is [the Revd Mr] Wilbraham ...

An Unidentified
Young Woman
1836

Penzance, *c.*1855

Bodleian Library, Ms Don. c.166, folios 245–8

The unidentified writer was most probably a young woman. She had travelled from Bristol by boat with her father and this appears to have been her first visit to West Cornwall. They stayed at Poltair, just outside Penzance.

June 1836
25th

Ill at intervals, excellent spirits between whiles, 2nd day every soul on board ill except Captain Vivian (great consolation that), 2nd night just the same, nearly pitched out of my berth by the heavy seas on my side, the Vessel arrived at Hayle after 37 hours voyage, very glad to put my foot on shore, arrived at Poltair 6 o'clock on Sunday morning, had breakfast and glad enough to get to bed.

26th

Quite an idle day regularly tired, glad to see it rain all day.

27th

Mrs Graham, Miss Vaughan & self went in the Phaeton into Penzance in my [?] a little dirty town. Miss V a most tiresome, undecided person to go shopping with, saw Mrs Marsh, a very odd looking person decidedly primitive in appearance. Mrs Cox called, a self-opinionated person. After dinner walked to Madron, a pretty village and lovely view of the Bay. Danced in the evening, all good Valterers though they never valter with the Guts (no fun that).

28th

Mrs G. Papa, self & old Mrs G. drove just to Penzance, called on Mr & Mrs Moyle, pleasant people, also on Mrs Marsh & Miss Lee, Capt Marsh rather an odd looking man, but very kind, promised to take us to the Lizard Point in his Cutter. Went on by Marazion, the Madeira of England, to Ludgvan, Graham's rectory, the most lovely spot the imagination can possibly paint or even fancy, quite beyond description. The sky without a cloud, the lovely bay, the brightest blue, St Michael's Mount from the terrace an imposing object, mines in every direction (should love to go down one but mustn't think of it), hill & dale, wood & water myrtles as large as the Guilder Rose with us. Roger randoms large enough to be cut up for firewood, high ranges equally large as laurels with us & the lichens that we give a high price for as common as grass. Gladiolas common in every cottage garden, Gates made of bars of iron, not lathes as with us & supported with granite pillars sparkling in the sun. Mr Rodd dined with us ...

29th

Papa took me to call on Mrs Giddy, a pleasant sort of person, received me much more as an old acquaintance than as a stranger, gave me a feast of the best strawberries I have seen, her garden small but very tastefully laid out, fuchsias as large as a sweet briar bush with us, the Spanish double, purple larkspur, very beautiful. Captain Giddy and Mr Cox dined with us – a Mrs & Miss Ley of Penzance called.

30th
We all went to the Levant Mine, the richest in Cornwall, Machinery stupendous, most of us clambered down to the mouth of the mine. Tremendous to look either up or down, singular to hear the mines hammering below, you get some beautiful specimens of ore, went on to the Lands End – to attempt description perfectly useless. Three of us stood on the last stone, some few hundred feet over the Sea, the green coral rocks the most splendid colours I have ever seen, yet one in particular appeared quite transparent, saw for the first time the celebrated Cornish Chough, the roar of the sea from the Lands End awful, and the shriek of the cormorants, the plaintive cry of the other sea fowl under the spot melancholy and romantic. I remained there some time, there you forget the world and feel indeed alone. I returned home with Capt. Giddy which I enjoyed much, he is a most intellectual companion, showed me the famous Lanyon cromlech or the Giants Quoit, 3 unshapen pillars supporting a large table stone – supposed to be the burial place of some distinguished person, the direction nearly north & south. The Flat stone 47 feet in girt, 12 in length, the height sufficient for a man on horseback to pass under. By the sea I had almost forgotten to mention the Longships lighthouse, something like the Eddystone, almost inaccessible, we went through St Just and returned by Sancreed one of the most enjoyable days I ever spent.

July 1
Quite a lazy day, all glad of rest.

2nd
My Birthday. After dinner all the party who are walkers went down to Penzance, saw some of the best part of the Town, rather changed my opinion. Saw some very good houses, went along the shore, made up my mind if practicable to bathe, saw the new church, a very pretty building though they have made a small mistake as not a window will open very much, like going into a hot house, not pleasant in a church, came home soundly tired.

3rd
Walked to Madron Church twice, no joke in a broiling sun, Mr Cox

very much like a ranting Methodist preacher, Mr Rodd came to dinner, he improves on acquaintance.

4th

Papa, I, Miss Paxton, Mr Graham & Harry went in the *Sylvia* Revenue Cutter to the Lizard, the rock scenery the wildest I have yet seen. More so then the Land's End. Lieutenant Clayton took Miss Paxton & I to see the Devil's Bellows, which is really wonderful, the water breaks from the rock exactly as if through the nose of the bellows, you first hear a noise like thunder then the hissing and spray through the rock. Mullion Island and Kynance look very lovely. Did not forget to observe the soap rock, returned and drank tea at St Michael's Mount, went over the Castle and to the top of it, the rooms are very beautiful, particularly the Chevy Chaise or Dining Room, and the Drawing Room, the roof of the Dining Room is magnificently carved oak and the furniture all corresponds, the Drawing Room is blue, the vases on either side the door exquisite. There are a few good paintings which are from neglect going fast decay, the bedrooms gave me an idea of suffocation from the bedstead being in recesses they also are of magnificently carved oak turned by time quite black, the chapel is a very elegant one and the view from the top really sublime. They won't allow you to go up with a bonnet on for fear of catching the wind, which is, by the way, an excellent precaution. Returned to Poltair about 11, quite tired. Must not forget to mention the romantic appearance of the Water Carriers with their red pitchers on their heads and some were very pretty girls, also the girls before we left bringing their clothes out to whiten had a pleasing effect as they were scattered about among the rocks, but oh, the smell of the rabbits that really was a sad nuisance.

5th

A day of rest, of which all the party stood in need, Mr Morice dined with us.

6th

All the party after Dinner walked up to Trengwainton ... a lovely view from the terrace which is a magnificently broad one, the House not good enough for the grounds though we should not judge as 30 rooms have just been taken down. Mrs G, Papa and myself went in the Morning to Penzance shopping to see the Geological Rooms where I was very much pleased and bought all the prints of what I had seen.

7th

Papa, I & Harry walked to Penzance on our road, called on Mrs Giddy who had fallen down stairs the evening previous. Walked through the Market, was surprised to see such a large one, particularly the meat, pork weighing 20 score as long as a young bullock, shopping then to the beach where I was tempted to bathe which was delightful, returned home better than I went out, a wet afternoon.

8th

Papa took Mrs G, Miss T & Miss Hicks to see Mount St Michael, the rest of us stayed at home, having seen it previously. Mrs Clayton dined with us.

9th

Miss G took me into Penzance to bathe, she went on to Ludgvan, Papa came down to walk back with me. Mr & Miss Moyle came to dinner, rather a pleasant young woman.

10th

All the party went to Ludgvan for the opening of the National & Sunday Schools, Graham preached a Charity Sermon, did not get home to Dinner till nearly 7 o'clock, quite tired. Mr Rodd came to tea, he improves on acquaintance.

11th

Henry Batten came to Dinner. I stayed at home all day not being very well. Mr Cox came in the evening, talked of nothing but religion and as he could not sing, recited hymns. Saw from the windows a few of the fireworks in commemoration placing the 1rst stone of the new market place.

12th

This day was passed entirely with Papa – see his description of it. Immediately after breakfast drove down to Penzance, the streets were thronged with all the population of the surrounding country & 24 carriages to attend the funeral of Mr Carne, the head of the firm in one of the banks. He was a Wesleyan Methodist and personally acquainted with old John Wesley. He was buried at Gulval, was originally nothing more than a common carpenter & has probably died the richest man in the County. We went down to the Pier & embarked onboard Mr Thomas J. Bolitho's yacht & with a spanking breeze at NW by N passed by Newlyn, Mousehole, down to the Logan

Rock. The day cold not have been finer. The wind could not have been more favourable, the skipper said he had never made the run in so short a space – we were only 3 hours & 5 minutes from the time we left the pier to our making it again. The Yacht's name is the *Wave*, she won the Prize in the last Regatta. We saw the *Sylvia* found a Frenchman, a brig, & tho' they called it a smooth sea yet several times we lost sight of both these vessels. Mousehole so called from a cavern in its Vicinity, the rocks there and at the Logen when seen from the sea underneath are indeed stupendous – Shapes of granite in the most gigantic forms, in some places layers of granite as if hewn & placed by the hand of man in right lines, the varied and diversified strata of earth have a strange & unusual appearance. Miss G, Miss V & self drank tea at Mrs Johnbilles, all very much delighted with Miss Gold's singing particularly her Italian songs. The Miss Johnbells are not bad performers on the Harp & Pianoforto. Papa & Mrs G dined there.

13th
Papa, Catherine & self walked to Penzance to see Fox's gardens, very pleased but returned quite tired.

MRS JANE ALLEN
of
BRIDPORT, DORSET, 1845

Redruth, *c.*1855

Jane Bauden was born in St Day in 1816. In 1845 she married William Allen, a Methodist missionary, returned to Cornwall for this short visit and with her husband moved to Africa. After three years they returned to England and Mrs Allen died ten years later in 1858. She was 28 years old when she wrote the following account.

Wed 3 Sept 1845
At eight we left Bristol for Exeter where we arrived at eleven o'clock. At two took coach for Devonport the distance of forty five miles. We found coach travelling torturous after travelling per rail.

Thursday 4
At half past ten [we] left Devonport for St Day the place of my nativity, the distance of fifty-seven miles where we arrived at seven in the morning. I always feel of late a saddening influence when entering this place. The one I most loved is not now the first to meet me, home has changed but shall I regret her absence? No, for I <u>may</u> go to her. But my feelings were of a particular nature at this time coming to bid my friends adieu perhaps until that time when we shall meet in judgment.

Saturday 6
We drove down to Redruth the distance of four miles from St Day, called on Mr Martin's friend. Saw the grace of Mr Carrie.

Sunday 7
I heard Mr Miller preach this morning and my dear husband in the evening, the chapel much crowded. There was a good feeling and I hope many the slain of the Lord.

Monday 8
Visited Redruth, spent part of the day with Miss G. She effects soon to go into the mission field. In the evening attended the chapel in St Day where Mr A gave them a missionary address, the people appeared interested, may they feel to in the right way.

Thursday 11
We visited Falmouth, the distance of nine miles from St Day. This place is much gone down since the removal of some of the packets, 14 years has made a great change, from thence we went to Redruth.

Friday 12
At nine we left Redruth for Hayle per rail. At one left Hayle for Bristol per steamer.

AN UNKNOWN TRAVELLER
from
WEST BUCKLAND, DEVON, 1855

Cornish fields, *c*.1855

West Buckland Yearbook: an Kalendar, for 1857 (South
Molton, 1857), 84–8.

The unknown writer travelled from Devon through Cornwall
by horseback during the summer of 1855.

If it were my wish it would be quite beyond my power to describe the
scenery, or the historical interest attached to many of the places we

passed in this tour: but hoping that some, when they have read this paper may be inducted to follow our example, I am bold enough to lay before the readers of this work a short account of our ride, asking indulgence for its defects.

We started a party of four in the summer of 1855 for a riding tour of Cornwall, our principal object being to visit the most interesting places on the north coast. Having ridden through some part of the north of Devon we forded the Tamar (here a small stream), and found ourselves in Cornwall. We passed through Stratton, one of the most northern towns in the county, and arrived at Bude Haven, a small but growing watering place beautifully situated amongst the rocks.

The next morning we started betimes, having a long ride before us, saying to each other, in the words of Prince Henry, "Thou and I have thirty miles to ride yet ere dinner time." Our road lay all along the beautiful coast of Widemouth Bay, through that most picturesque little village, Crackington Cove; then through St Gennys, over cliffs more than 700 feet above the sea, till we at last arrived at Boscastle, a small town possessing a most curious harbour, or rather chasm, winding amongst high cliffs, which so shut out the view of the sea from any one standing at the head of the harbour as to give the appearance of a dark mountain lake. There is a very pretty walk along the cliffs, in an easterly direction, at the head of numerous small bays; and the great quantities of sea birds that build here tend much to enliven the scene at this time of the year.

After a ride of about four miles we came to Trevenna, and leaving our horses there, walked down to the old castle of Tintagel, the birthplace and residence of King Arthur. This magnificent rock stands all but insulated, rising perpendicularly on all sides, and is indeed deserving of its celebrity. Suffice it to say, the sea view extends from Hartland to Pentire.

Delabole slate quarries were the first object in our next day's ride. Wonderful quarries they are! affording some of the most valuable slate in England. The slate is brought from the bottom, by aid of machinery worked by steam engines, to platforms at the top, where it is placed on trucks and drawn along tramways to the different workshops. After examining all the different processes to which the slate is subjected, we again continued our journey, passing through Wadebridge to Padstow, and (after a row on the river there) back to St Columb, not having seen anything very remarkable since Delabole; but the scenery, though we had quitted for a time the noble coast, was still of a most pleasing character.

On the following day we visited the nunnery at Lanherne, and were allowed to enter the chapel; the convent is in a prettily wooded situation. We then rode along the sea coast to Newquay, and fording a river near Crantock, arrived at St Cuthbert (pronounced Cubert), and having obtained a shoemaker for a guide, we set off over the sands of Perranzabuloe under a broiling sun in quest of the old church of St Piran. This church is said to be very ancient indeed, and to have been built over the remains of St Piran (who was sent over from Ireland by St Patrick to convert the inhabitants); he died in the fifth century, and this church is supposed to have been in use about two hundred years, and then to have been submerged by the shifting sand. It thus lay hidden and lost for many years until in 1835 it was again disclosed to view in excellent preservation, but has since been much injured by the hands of the too-curious traveller.

Perran Round is also well worth a visit, being one of the most perfect remains of the sort in England. It appears to have been used by the British either as a theatre or as a court of justice.

Leaving the barren sands of Perranzabuloe, and having refreshed ourselves and our horses at Perran Porth, we mounted St Agnes' (pronounced St Anne's) Beacon. A country lay stretched before us, to all appearance as unproductive as those sands we had just passed over; and as to the surface this opinion is not far wrong, but underground lies concealed the great wealth of the county, for now you enter the mining district of Cornwall. Having passed through Portreath, where great quantities of ore are shipped for Wales, we entered Redruth, a town situated in the midst of mines, and suffering this inconvenience from them, namely, that the inhabitants have to fetch water for drinking purposes two miles; for although water runs down by the side of the principal street, yet coming from the mines it is unfit for drinking.

Next day we ascended to Carn Brae, on the summit of which is a British castle and a monument to Lord De Dunstanville, from which, on a fine day, a very extensive view of the surrounding country is obtained, the sea both to north and south being I believe visible; but on the day we were there we could only distinguish it to the south. Our road was now through Camborne to Hayle, and thence to St Ives, one of the principal places for the pilchard fishery. Having rested here awhile, we again started for St Just, but stopped on our way to see Gurnard's Head, and well did it repay us, a magnificent granite promontory sloping away from the mainland, and then again abruptly rising in the deep sea. When we were there the sea, dashing violently against the rocks which bound it on every side, contributed much to the beauty of the view, which is one of an extraordinarily wild and grand character.

Presently we arrived at St Just, and after a good night's rest, walked, on the morrow, to Botallack Mine, which runs out some way under the sea. Being told that it took the miners themselves one hour to come up, and having a good ride before us, we were not tempted to explore this submarine mine. Once more on our horses it was not long before we reached the Land's End, as everybody knows, the westernmost point of England. This gives it an interest without which it might perhaps slightly disappoint the traveller who has visited Tintagel and Gurnard's Head, for they, in the grandeur of their scenery, certainly surpass the Land's End. This promontory is composed of granite; its extreme point is not more than sixty feet above the level of the sea. About a mile and a half from the shore, on a cluster of rocks, a lighthouse is built, called the Longships Lighthouse; and again, thirty miles from shore rise the Scilly Isles, a group of about one hundred and forty islets and rocks. There is a tradition that they were once joined to the main land by a tract of country called the "Lionnesse," which was completely overwhelmed by a sudden inundation. Leaving the Land's End, the next point of interest is the Tol Pedn Penwith, a curious hole in the cliff, growing smaller towards the bottom (not unlike a funnel), and opening to the sea. The cliffs between this and the Land's End are very high and grand. Next we came to the Logan Rock, a block of granite of about sixty tons weight, and of such a shape and so poised on the stones below it, that it is very easily rocked. In the year 1824 a lieutenant in command of a revenue cruiser, with a boat's crew, for his amusement, threw down this stone, but was, by command of the Admiralty, at the remonstrance of the whole county, obliged to replace it. It still rocks, but not now as before, – not "all the king's horses, nor all "the king's men," could restore the broken charm of the old Logan Rock.

Soon after leaving the Logan the change of scenery is very remarkable; we, who since St Columb had been passing through the most barren looking country, with scarce a tree, now found ourselves travelling along an exceedingly pretty road lined with trees, and other roads joining it, lined in the same manner, thus forming the most beautiful avenues, leading to Penzance.

And now having arrived in a country more known and traversed by better roads, any further account of our tour would be useless; but should any one be tempted to follow our example, let him not forget, on his eastward journey, to visit St Michael's Mount, the Lizard, and Kynance Cove, with rocks of every hue and colour; Carclaze, with its china clay, and veins of tin running all through the clay (it is situated about two miles from St Austell); let him go and see Boconnoc, with its fine park and beautiful trees; and, near Liskeard, he should visit the Cheesewring; at St Germans, if an antiquarian, the church will repay him for a visit, if not, the views about Port Eliot; and then he can either proceed to Plymouth by road or water; the latter, in fine weather, is well worth the experiment; he will pass Ince Castle and Trematon Castle on this left hand; on his right, Antony, the woods of which latter place overhang the river with most picturesque effect. Now on his left again he will see the enormous tube of the new railway-bridge at Saltash; all around him the old ships of war laid up in ordinary; before him, Devonport Dockyard and Mount Edgcumbe: but here having tried to describe briefly, a tour which it is possible to make from Bude to the Land's End, and from the Land's End to the Tamar, I must, from the banks of that lovely river, say – Farewell.

MRS ANNE PORTER

of

BIRLINGHAM, WORCESTERSHIRE, 1858

Launceston, *c*.1827

Worcester Record Office, BA3940/64(i)

Mrs Anne Porter was on a tour of north Devon and Cornwall.

Thursday October 21 We left Bideford soon after breakfast this morning for Clovelly. The landlady let us take four horses to Clovelly.

Being in our own carriage we drove through the Hobby to the top of this remarkable little fishing town. The day was lovely & so were the views. We discarded from the carriage at the top of the town & walked to the New Inn, ordered luncheon & then walked down to the Pier, a steep, stony impracticable descent. After admiring the little town hanging in the glen we returned to the Hotel to luncheon & afterwards with the same horses drove on to Bude Haven where we arrived at the Falcon Hotel at about 6 o'clock. 60 fishing boats went out from Clovelly while we were there with their pretty reddish brown sails.

Friday October 22nd We are charmed with Bude Haven it is a wild desolate looking place with a magnificent sea – pure bracing air, fine water, only this one small hotel & very few small lodging houses. The place belongs to Sir Thomas Ackland, no doubt in a few years it will be as large as Ilfracombe as the land is already letting on building leases. We have been distressed here by not having had our letters properly forwarded [word obscured] and were much shocked by our servants having told us they had seen in the newspaper the death of our dear cousin Mrs Jarman on Sunday last the seventeenth.

Saturday, October 23 Still no letters. We walked about Bude today & to the Breakwater where the sea air is most enjoyable.

Monday, October 25 We left Bude Haven this morning about 11 o'clock luncheoned at the Wellington at Boscastle & walked to see the small harbour & rocks from the heights, went on to Treven. Intending to sleep at the Stuart Worthley Arms there but it was full with [there being] a cattle fair in the town & we were obliged to go to Camelford where we got accomodation at the Kings Arms Hotel.

Tuesday, October 26 We had a fly this morning to visit Tintagel & see the remains of the Castle famous as the residence and birthplace of King Arthur. It is on a rock jutting out into the [sea]. The ascent a fearful precipice – Phoebe was panic struck attempting to ascend it & we were all in great danger at the edge of the cliff but thanks to a protecting Providence got down safe. I afterwards walked up to the Land side & saw the fearful ascent to the [top] & the fine sea view. As we returned to the Hotel we got out of the carriage to see the slate quarry.

Thursday, October 28 I walked to see the church this morning. The stonework is curiously carved all over the building. We left Launceston after breakfast & luncheoned at the White Hart Hotel at *Oakhampton* a very dirty Hotel & dull looking town. They made some excuse about the diffficulty of their horses taking us to Exeter – we supposed they wanted us to sleep there. So we went on to Copplestone, rather out of our way, & from thence to Exeter where we did not arrive till near 9 o'clock & dined & slept at the New London Hotel, very comfortable.

Friday October 29 We walked to the cathedral this morning & about the Town & left Exeter by the 2.40 train for Bristol & went to dine & sleep at the Bath Hotel at Clifton.

ALGERNON CHARLES SWINBURNE
of
LONDON, 1864

Etching by William Bell Scott of Algernon Swinburne, 1860

Cecil Y. Lang (ed.), *The Swinburne Letters* (New Haven, 1959), 105–107, 109.

Already an established poet, Swinburne came to Cornwall on a holiday with John William Inchbold, painter, and other unidentified companions. He was twenty-seven years old when he visited Cornwall.

All six letters were written to Mary Gordon, his cousin, who in 1917 edited the following letters and left instructions that after her death the originals were to be destroyed.

[September 2]

I could have wished for [your] company yesterday night when we took out horses, borrowed from a neighbouring farmer, and rode through the dusk and the dark to the adjacent city of Boscastle. This important and flourishing seaport does not exactly boast of a highway to the sea, but it has a path cut or worn in the slope of the down, along which we let our horses (being surefooted Cornish ones who know the nature of their sea and their down ...) feel their way till we came out one after another on a narrow standing place of rocks, breaking sharply down to the sea on both sides. This ridge of rocks shuts in the harbour, and the sea having incautiously poured in through a strait between the ridge and the cliff opposite turns twice at right-angles upon itself and makes a sort of double harbour; one parallel with the outer sea, blocked out by the rocks to which we had ridden; the other running straight up the valley to the houses of the little town as thus:

and as there is no beach or shore of any kind, you can imagine how the sea swings to and fro between the cliffs, foams and swells, beats and baffles itself against the steep faces of rock. I should guess it must be unique in England. Seen from above and on horseback it was very queer, dark grey swollen water, caught as it were in a trap, and heaving with rage against both sides at once, edged with long panting lines of incessant foam that swung and lapped along the deep steep cliffs without breaking, and had not room to roll at ease. My horse was much the pluckier, and made forward as if on a road; would, I believe, have tried to mount the rough rock-hewn steps from this natural platform to a sort of beacon at the mouth of the inlet; but seeing the difficulties of redescending (which was a delicate business as it was) I turned him round after a bit of ascent. It was not unexciting, especially by a grey and glimmering night without moon or star. Had it been on a smuggling expedition it would have been sweet indeed. Having ridden back towards the scattered lights of the town and got on a high road again instead of a cliff path just above the sea, I tried my beast's pace at a gallop, having already tested the goodness of his head and sureness of his feet, in which he matched any possible Alpine mule. He went very well and we tore over the ground in the night at such a rate that we all but banged against late carts in the lanes, and *quite* electrified the stray population. I have bathed twice, but the sea is very treacherous and tiring; no sand, hardly any beach even at low water in the narrow bays, sudden steep banks, shelving rocks, and sea pitching violently in the entrance of the bays; so that where there are rocks to take breath at one can't make for them lest the sea should *stave* one's ribs in against the reefs; and a sea that pitches from side to side without breakers or rollers, and has no resting places except on the high and dry rocks inland, takes it out of one in swimming much more than one thinks. We are twenty-five miles from the nearest railway, and *Clatt* ... is as it were Babylon or Nineveh to *our* post town – Camelford, which is six miles inland. Nothing can be funnier than these villages except the downs and glens in which they are set. The sea-views are, of course, splendid beyond praise. On one headland [Tintagel] (split now into two, divided by a steep isthmus of rock between two gulfs of sea, not wide enough for two to walk abreast across) is the double ruin, one half facing the other, of the old castle or palace of the kings of Cornwall. Opposite on a high down is the old church, black with rain and time and storm, black at least in the tower, and grey in the body. The outer half of the castle, on the headland beyond the isthmus is on the very edge (and partly over the edge and on the slant) of the cliff; and has indescribable views of the double bay, broken cliffs, and outer sea. Practically, the *total* want of beach at any time is a great loss.

October 2
The aforesaid came to see me, who have had an adventure which might have been serious but has only resulted in laming one foot for a day or two, I hope ... I had to run round a point of land which the sea was rising round, *or* be cut off in a bay of which to my cost I had just found the cliffs impracticable; so without boots or stockings I just ran at it and into the water and up or down over some awfully sharp and shell-encrusted rocks which cut my feet to fragments, had twice to plunge again into the sea, which was filling all the coves and swinging and swelling heavily between the rocks; once fell flat in it, and got so thrashed and licked that I might have been [blank] in [blank]'s clutches, ... and at last got over the last reef and down on the sand of a safe bay, a drenched rag, and with feet that just took me home (three-quarters of a mile or so and uphill mainly with stones) half in and half out of the boots which I had just saved with one hand; and then the right foot began to bleed like a pig, and I found a deep cut which was worse than any ever inflicted by a birch to the best of my belief, for it was *no end* bad yesterday, and to-day makes it hopeless to walk except on tiptoe, but as I wouldn't have it dressed or bothered I hope it will soon heal.

H.G.
of
LONDON, 1866

Penzance, 1863

H.G., *A Traveller's Notes in Scotland, Belgium, Devonshire, The Channel Islands, The Mediterranean, France, Somerset-shire, Cornwall, The Scilly Islands, Wilts and Dorsetshire in 1866* (1867), 136–44.

The author, a bachelor identified only by his initials, noted in the preface that 'A very serious illness, resulting from over-work and anxiety, having necessitated a continuous change of air and scene for several months, these notes were made for the amusement of relatives and friends at home, to whom it would have been difficult, or rather impossible, otherwise to have conveyed a succinct narration of my travels. They are now published, almost word for word, from my pencillins by the way, without the smallest pretension to literary merit.' H.G. had travelled from London to Bristol by train and then by steamer to Cornwall.

Friday, 12th October, 1866. – I was awoke by a good shake, administered by the steward, whom I had asked to call me at 6 o'clock. I found that we had passed Ilfracombe, and were entering Bude Bay, the coast of which is very rocky and picturesque, with verdant fields running down to the very edge of the cliffs. The steward gave me a cup of tea, and, one by one, the passengers made their appearance on the Captain's bridge, which is very broad, and was the only part of the ship free from obstruction. I made acquaintance with a young Clergyman, from the neighbourhood of Malden, and his wife, very nice people; a pleasant elderly gentleman, in business at Hayle; and two little girls and a boy, on their way, with their Mamma, to Truro, as I found out. So, what with the fresh air (it was a beautiful morning), the pretty scenery, agreeable conversation, and playing with the children, I was thoroughly happy.

About half-past 8 o'clock the steward gave us a capital breakfast, for which I was quite ready; and then we were on the look out for Trevoise Point, which we rounded, and saw the entrance to Padstow Harbour, about 10. We had still twenty miles to make, and the appearance of the coast changed, hereabouts, from rock to sand, which is thrown up from the sea in high embankments. We had made pretty good speed hitherto, but now the tide was flowing out against us, and it was nearly noon when we anchored in St Ive's Bay, there not being water enough for the steamer to enter Hayle Harbour; so two small boats came alongside, into which we (meaning the passengers generally) were trans-shipped, a breaking sea making the slipping down the steamer's side rather hazardous, and involving considerable display of the ladies' legs. The little ones were rather frightened, and, to comfort them, as they were swung down by the steward, I took one of the girls on each knee and boy between, and soon managed to amuse them. Then we pulled for the shore, and expected to be taken to the landing-place of the town; but after nearly grounding once or twice, the boatmen said the current was so strong, and the load so heavy, that we must land on the sandbank, and walk up.

I had previously arranged with my clerical friend to share a conveyance with him to Marazion, and thence to St Michael's Mount, before going on to Penzance; but we were compelled to alter our plans. There was a heap of luggage to bring up, but we bribed the boatmen to carry ours, and I amused myself by helping the children to find shells for some time; but after a while everybody got very tired, the sand being as soft as mud to walk on, and then we came to a dead halt at a point where we had to cross the water again. This was, however, a very short passage, and, having accomplished it in a ferry-boat, the parson and his wife and I persevered in making our way onwards, over some very rough rocks, towards the hotel, leaving all the others behind us. We were nearly there, having tramped about two miles, when the steward overtook us in a carriage, and gave us a lift the rest of the way, which was very acceptable; and as soon as we reached the hotel, we begged for something to eat and drink, for we were almost famished, from our unexpected mode of transit thither from the steamer. Fortunately, we were just in time for a joint of roast beef, to which we did ample justice, as also to some Burton ale. Hayle is a business-looking but a dull and stupid sort of place, and St Ives, on the other side to the Bay, looked a much more inviting spot for a sojourn. We seemed to like Hayle, however, for we were only just in time to save the train to Penzance, where I parted with my friends, and jumped into the omnibus in attendance at the station, for the "Queen's" Hotel, a first-rate house, situated in the centre of the Bay. Having secured a bedroom there, I was fortunate enough to induce a red-haired chamber-maid to bring me a cold bath, for I felt as dirty as a pig, and having freshened me up, I took counsel with the chief-barmaid how to amuse myself till dinner-time. She advised a row to St Michael's Mount, and accordingly I went, enjoying the pull of three miles immensely, and still more the glorious view of the Bay and surrounding scenery from the summit. I went through the principal rooms of the house, but they, and the Mount generally, are so fully described in the guide-book, that it would be only waste of time to introduce them here. I must mention, however, that the house-maid who was my cicerone, was a very pretty girl. On our way back, we saw a steam yacht steering into the Bay, and it proved to be a Trinity Surveying Vessel, seeking anchorage for the night, a very pretty craft indeed.

I was quite ready for my dinner on reaching the Hotel again (which, by the way, is a most comfortable one), and here I made friends with an old Gentleman, who seemed very inclined to be sociable, but terribly fastidious about his inner man. I spent an hour or more after dinner on the Esplanade, which is quite half-a-mile long, and came to the conclusion that Penzance would be a very nice place to spend a week at; but as I meant to leave it on the morrow, and wanted to see something more of it by daylight, I curtailed my reflections, and went to bed.

Saturday, 13th October, 1866. – The view from the Hotel window whilst I was breakfasting was not promising; a sort of haze seemed to encompass the Bay, and to threaten a thick and deadly calm passage to Scilly; nor were my hopes raised as I sauntered about the town, and observed that it seemed well enough to do, with plenty of good shops, and a busy bustling look. I bought some views, and peeped into the Church, which is a handsome one exteriorly, but very heavy and plainly-fitted internally; and then I made my way down to the pier, whence the steamer to Scilly was to start. Eleven o'clock was the stated time of her departure, but the Mails did not come on board till nearly 12. In the meantime, however, I was amused in watching the embarkation of the cargo, consisting of all sorts, including a ram, a dog, and a pony; each of which strongly objected to the belly-bands which transferred them to the hold. There were not more than seven or eight passengers, among them a gentleman and his wife, with whom I reckoned to make acquaintance on the voyage; and at the last moment, the Captain made his appearance, – a very portly looking fellow, and as I learnt in a few minutes, very much inclined to take things easy. Our boat, the *Little Western*, a slick little screw steamer, slipped her cables, and was off a few minutes afterwards, saddled at starting, with a barque, which she had engaged to tow out of the harbour. Having cast her off, we stood quite close into the shore, which is very rocky and bold, but the land exceeding verdant, and every inch of it cultivated. Amongst the rocks it was curious to observe the innumerable flocks of sea birds; and the coast itself, with its iron cliffs and headlands, and dangerous ground-rocks, reminded me of the Channel Islands. On a prominent headland is the "Logan Stone," a detached piece of rock weighing many tons, but so nicely balanced that it can be moved to and fro by the slightest touch. Farther on, we came to a very dangerous rock, marked by a buoy, and shortly afterwards, we sighted the real "Land's End," with the "Lizard Point," the other extremity of Cornwall, about twenty miles in the offing. The Land's End is high and precipitous, with some low rocks running out in front of it, and at the extremity of them a light-house. Behind, inland, is a small white house, named "the first and last Inn."

We scudded away at a good speed, through a sea almost as

brilliantly lit by the afternoon sunshine, and as calm, as the Mediter-ranean. The Captain allowed me to stand on his bridge, and soon after 2 o'clock, I espied the outline of the Scilly Islands, the Cornish coast being still in view behind. Their first appearance was in the shape of a Maltese Cross, and this was preserved for some time. Then two conspicuous land-marks stood out, one a Martello Tower, and the other a beacon, erected by the Trinity Board. We seemed to be steering for the very centre of the group, which, as we approached it, looked even more like the rock-bound coast of the Channel Islands than the Land's End had done. The water was very smooth, and we turned into St Mary's Bay as quietly as into a pond.

The chief town of the Islands (St Mary's) lies round a headland, at the point of which we met the Governor (a jolly looking fellow), who had come out to meet us in his boat, and the steamer was stopped to hand him his Letter Pouch and sundry parcels and packages. Then we made for the pier, and were soon ashore on the far-famed Scilly Isles. I had been told before starting, that the Captain of the steamer was the proprietor of the principal Inn at St Mary's (to call it an Hotel would be nonsense), and I accordingly intimated to him my wish to avail myself of his hospitality. He called a man to take my luggage, and accompanied by the lady and gentleman I have already mentioned, and who proved very agreeable people, we followed Mr Porter to the house, and of all the queer places I have put up at, this was certainly the queerest; a sort of village farmhouse with a long garden in front, and when you got inside it, exceedingly low and stuffy rooms, and reeking with the smell of tobacco and gin, for it is the head-quarters of the ship Captains who put into the Bay during contrary winds, or in stress of weather. The Captain's daughter, a very pleasant-spoken and good-looking woman (it would be absurd to call her young, though I don't believe she is more than thirty), showed me upstairs to a double-bedded room, and invited me to choose whichever of the two beds I preferred, but having a horror of sharing a room with anyone else (till I get a wife), I intimated that I should infinitely prefer even a closet to a fellow lodger, and she accordingly led the way to the pokiest little bed-room I ever occupied, and, after the grand room I had had at the "Clifton Down," it was anything but an agreeable contrast. However, the only way was to make the best of it, and having arranged to dine with the lady and gentleman in an hour's time, I started for a stroll about the place. I bent my way up a very step hill, at the top of which, I found myself at the gate of the "Fort," bearing Queen Elizabeth's monogram, and the date 1590. A sailor passing told me there was free access, and on opening the gate, a bright-eyed little boy ran out of the Guard House and said, "you must go all round, and it is very pretty", which proved to be quite true, for the Fort stands on the highest ground in St Mary's, and commands a view of all the other 50 odd Islands, only five of which, however, are inhabited or cultivatable.

I was quite ready for my dinner, which consisted of beef steak and onions, on my return; and there being no evening amusements in the Islands, I endeavoured to entertain the lady and gentleman, with whom I had got on very sociable terms, with the views I had collected, and in chatting generally, until he announced that he had got a sore throat, and began to look so seedy, that when his wife proposed his going to bed I quite agreed it was the best thing he could do, and I very soon followed them.

Sunday, 14th October, 1866. – Almost in despair of accomplishing my object, I had asked the chambermaid (or, to describe her more correctly, the serious-looking young woman, who was evidently either crossed in love, or the perpetrator of some horrible mis-deed) to give me a bath in the morning, and she said she would; and soon after daylight I heard a sort of snorting outside my door, which I presently learnt was caused by her blowing into the interstices of an india-rubber contrivance which produces the identical thing, a circular flat-bottomed boat, that she handed into my room with two kilderkin-looking receptacles of water, – and I was soon enjoying the luxury of a thorough wetting. I was then very much disposed for a walk, which I again took right round the Fort, and came in with a famous appetite for breakfast, having discovered the said Fort is at present manned by *one* sergeant of artillery and *three* old washer-women, whom I saw ironing up (Sunday morning though it was) through the windows of the fortress. I could not catch the name of my married couple, so I must still call them the lady and gentleman: I was sorry to learn from her that her better-half had been very sick all night, and was still poorly and in bed; so she and I took breakfast together, one of the dishes at which was broiled slices of a fish called (as it sounded) "H." Then I had a walk through the village, and over some fields, to the remains of a very old churchyard and church, of which only one transept remains, the pathway to which is covered with sand, but so bright and brilliant, that the ground seemed studded with diamond dust; just as the pattern on the ripple of the waves during our passage over seemed the exact design of the sands over which we landed at Hayle, – as though the sun sketched the pattern on the top of the water, and the sands caught the idea and imitated it below.

At 10.30, I walked through the village, which contains about 1,500 inhabitants, and looks very neat and clean – the houses being all built of granite, to the Church, which was erected by Old King Billy in 1837. It is also of granite, with some very pretty National Schools close by, and fitted in very good taste, but plainly. The long narrow windows on either side contain clear-coloured glass of the different shades of the rainbow, and, consequently the sun shifts his rays from one to the other, a different tone of light – green, red, orange, and blue, in succession – pervades the interior, and has a very singular effect. The service was very reverently performed by a very priestly clergyman, who wore a *mauve* hood, and preached a very plain practical sermon. The singing and organ-playing were also very respectable; and Monk's Hymns, Ancient and Modern, have found their way even to these far off Islands, and seem to be duly appreciated. The congregation consisted of about 200, and I was surprised to see so many well-dressed people among them. Their hands showed that they mostly belonged to the industrial class, but they are sufficiently well-off to indulge in London fashions. Many of the girls were very smart; but, to their credit be it said, that they have the good taste not to indulge in "chignons." I dined alone in the drawing room (or, to call it after its prevailing colour, the "Green Room,") at 1 o'clock, as the nautical gentry, who, with the Captain, in his shirt sleeves, as their chairman, had commenced pipes and grog immediately after breakfast, and had elected to have their *ordinary* later, and I had ordered a boat at 2 o'clock to take me across to Tresco, another of the Islands two miles off, where the Lord of the Manor, Mr Augustus Smith, resides.

At 2 o'clock, however, the boatman came to say, it was blowing so hard that we had better have a third hand, if I did not mind the expense; and whilst he was getting him, I had to amuse myself at the piano for half-an-hour. Then the Lady and Gentleman came to see me off, – he looking as white as a ghost, and although the weather was superb, the sea was decidedly rough; and we had a tremendously stiff pull over, against wind and tide. But when I landed I was amply rewarded. Mr Smith's house stands close to the water (though we had to take a circuitous road to reach it), and is surrounded by six acres of the most lovely garden ground imaginable.

The climate is so temperate (Jack Frost being almost unknown in the Islands) that fuschias, geraniums, and myrtles, grow almost wild, in most beautiful luxuriance; and several kinds of tropical plants and trees have quite naturalized themselves there. In one part of the grounds are the ruins of a very old Abbey, covered with ivy and flowering creepers; and in another is an Italian terrace, most tastefully arranged, and teeming with shrubs and bloom. Everywhere the rock stones of the Islands are introduced with exquisite effect; and ferns of every conceivable variety seem to flourish amongst them to perfection. Then there is a fresh-water lake, stocked with feathered occupants of all kinds; and ostriches and emus, turkeys and peacocks, in the adjoining meadows in abundance. The House is built of granite, and is most substantial and pretty, but irregularly designed, and has evidently been added to, bit by bit.

Having thoroughly enjoyed more than an hour there, under the guidance of my chief boatman, we started back, and, with a strong wind in our favour, we spanked across under sail in next to no time. The sun shone brightly all the afternoon, and both at Tresco, and afloat, the varying lights and shades on the rocky islands, and on the green and brown verdure in some of them, were lovely; and I almost fancied myself once more in tropical regions. I got back in time for Evening Service, which was as nicely celebrated, and more fully attended than the morning one; and having taken a stroll on the Fort by moonlight afterwards, and written some letters, I once more resorted to the piano, to assuage my solitude till bed-time; for the Gentleman was still sick, and his wife, as in duty bound, attending him.

Monday, 15th October, 1866. – I was up at 6 o'clock, and made an excursion, past the Fort, to the western extremity of St Mary's, whence a very pretty view of St Agnes and the Bishop's Lighthouses is obtained; and the air was so clear and the soft feeling of the still downy coat of the sloping ground – verdant with moss, and heather, and furze, and ferns, in all varieties – so summer-like, that I lingered on it till the last moment; and when I returned to the Inn to breakfast before starting, I had only time to glance through the Visitors' Book, and select the following concluding stanza of some verses in praise of the Islands, as expressive of my impressions on leaving them –

> "Perchance my lot may bring me back
> Perhaps not, – I cannot say;
> I hope it may; – so here I check,
> My silly, Scilly, say."

It behoves me, therefore, simply to record, without further commentary remarks (except upon the breakfast, which consisting of very strong ducks' eggs, and awfully salt broiled ham steaks, which I did not much relish, in spite of the appetite my early walk had given me), that we started punctually at 8.30 (Scilly time, which is nearly thirty minutes west of, and therefore later than, Greenwich) with some twenty passengers, among them the invalid Gentleman, carefully tended by his wife, but looking as if he had won sixpence and lost eighteenpence; and several of the nautical persons who had spent the Sunday at our inn. The invalid seemed inclined to take refuge in the cabin, but I advised him to remain on deck, and though evidently out of sorts, he certainly brightened up soon after we got clear of the Islands, which gave us one of Nature's most lovely parting smiles, and we were rolling deliciously, on the broad Atlantic, on our way back to Penzance.

It was most pleasant to find that Mrs Gentleman was as indifferent to the fishes' importunities as myself, and quite as inclined as I to enjoy the brilliant morning afloat, and its bracing effect on our mental and bodily spirits. It is true we were both occasionally disconcerted at the Captain's reckless and very easy way of steering, sitting all the while, chatting with some of his yesterday's companions, and every now and then making an extremely close shave of vessels crossing our course. However, and notwithstanding wind and tide against us, we safely reached Penzance Pier in five hours, namely (allowing for the difference of time), at 2 p.m. I hastened off along the Esplanade, whence the view was exceedingly pretty in the full sunlight, to the Hotel to have some dinner (for I was quite ready for a meal after my voyage), but when I arrived there, I found all the servants of the Hotel assembled round the letter-box, with a smith, whether by profession black or white, I cannot say; but he seemed timid of doing his duty, which was to force the box somehow or other. At last he succeeded, but I had to content myself with a bason of soup, and then jump into the omnibus to save the train for Exeter, whithere I was bound, passing on my way the lodgings of my friends, who were sitting at the window, and nodded adieu. We started at 2.40, and, as far as Liskeard, I got a good view of Cornwall, passing through Redruth, Truro, St Austell, and Lostwithiel – all good-sized towns; and the country was very variegated and pretty, the first part being rather wild looking, and spotted with Mine shafts, and the latter more like Devonshire, with splendid apple orchards, the fruit still on the trees, well cultivated fields, and abundance of foliage, here and there, of the lovely autumn tints ...

MRS FLORENCE GLYNN
of
THE ISLE OF WIGHT, 1884

Tregothnan, *c.*1880

Isle of Wight Record Office, OG/CC/1361A–82A

Florence Glynn, known to her friends as Flo and to her husband as his 'dear little Pussie', and born Florence Boscawen and married John O. H. Glynn of the Isle of Wight. The following eighteen letters were written to her husband who had wished her well on her Cornish trip: 'I hope you have a nice cheery welcome tonight and will enjoy yourself ever so much in the home where your Cornish "forbears" lived so long. I hope they always behaved themselves "politely" and look nice and prim in their pictures and that the counterfeit presentments of past maiden aunts all look straight before their noses with no suspicion of tipping you sly winks.' Mrs Glynn visited Tregothnan, the 'Romantic Tudor' home of the Boscawen family and her relations (Viscounts Falmouth), Prideaux Place, the Elizabeth home, with eighteenth-century Gothic improvements, of the Prideaux-Brune family, and finally Antony, the early eighteenth-century home of the Carew-Pole family. Her travels began on 9 February and she left Cornwall three weeks later.

Tregothnan, Probus   Saturday [9 February]
My darling,

   I am beginning a letter to you tonight, while Marie is unpacking, in case I find tomorrow that the post goes out early. I hope you got my telegram. I sent it from Truro Station. My journey was very prosperous. Mrs Pole Carew was very pleasant (also Sir J. Duckworth, tho' I don't know if he knew who I was from Adam!) She & I reconnoitred at Swindon & Exeter etc. The Aclands [of Holnicote near Exmoor and Killerton near Exeter] got out at Taunton. I should have liked them if they had not been Radicals. After Plymouth I was alone, but before that I had begun to get very tired. However my journey was as good as could be [expected] only I missed you so. I was so glad to see you again at Paddington. I hope you will soon get more news. I keep thinking of them so. There was a very good fly to meet me at Truro & such a moonlight drive. I am longing to see it by daylight. It must be so pretty. I was received by enormous men & taken to a library (I think), where there was a little table ready for my dinner & in an instant Edith (not Mary who is upstairs with a cold) came to me & took me up to my room & then I came down again & she sat with me while I had my dinner. I did feel so small with those huge creatures & soon after I had begun Aunt Mary came in & greeted me most kindly & said they were very sorry not to see you (and so did Uncle Evelyn) & sat with me till I had had my dinner & then took me into the drawing room, where were Syd & Aunt Annie & various others. Soon after Rudy & Sydney & John & Sir F. Stapleton & some other men had come in. I have come up to bed. My room is very cosy, but of course I don't know which way it looks. I have sent

Maria to bed for she is very seedy, but will be allright tomorrow & so I am having a talk with my darling. Mrs Pole Carew said they were in rather an unsettled state, but would I write & let her know whether I could come to Anthony & she would say if it would fit. What shall I do? I don't feel much like going there. It is a pouring wet night now & blowing big guns. I do so hope dearest that you are warm & comfy tonight. Your loving, sleepy little wife, Florence Glynn

After breakfast, Sunday morning
... I slept well & came leisurely down to breakfast. Everybody is very pleasant & cheery. There have been heavy hail storms & bright gleams in between all the morning. I have not had time to look at the pictures. I am longing to, but I must soon go & get ready for church. I am so glad you had a pleasant afternoon with the "Old Man" & I daresay Edith's throwing you over made you more free. Now, darling, I must get ready to go to the church of my "forbears". Your loving wife, Florence Glynn
I am afraid the only reason Mr Acland changed his *Daily News* was because his father, Sir Thomas, had one!

Monday morning after breakfast
My own darling husband,
I was obliged to finish my letter directly after breakfast this morning & did not say half I wanted to say. The letters were put in two or three places this morning & mine was put at the foot of the wrong staircase & I thought when I went in to breakfast that there was none & a little lump [came] in my throat & then afterwards Margaret R. brought it to me, & I was oh so glad. Shall I tell you who is here? Aunt Annie & the girls (both pretty & bright, especially Evelyn), Sir F. & Lady Stapleton, Sydney & Syd, [Hon. Arthur Sydney Annesley & his wife Helen Sydney], Major & Mrs Dugdale (Miss Whatman) & Mr Glanville. Oh Jack, it is a pretty place. I don't mean the house, but the grounds & the river. My room looks on the bends of the river. Such a pretty view. Tomorrow there is rather a pleasant plan, & I should long for you to go, to go by water to Porthgwiddon & some go up to luncheon & others lunch in the boat & then on to Falmouth, but I think it will be wet. This morning we went to church & after the service Aunt M. came to me to show me the monuments which as you know interested me & E. showed me some. After luncheon Syd & Edith & I agreed to have a walk, the weather having improved & we had a lovely one down to the river thro' the woods home. Aunty Mary Towny joined us. Then we changed boots which were very dirty

& went out to a sort of summer house, which they call Appollo's Temple – a lot of us – & made a fire & sat for a time talking & laughing & then came in to tea & now I am resting in my room, before dressing for dinner for I am rather tired as can fancy. Tonight's sleep will quite wear off the journey. This morning at breakfast I suddenly found Sydney's head between mine & my neighbour's "You've been cutting your hair". He afterwards informed me that it suited me, the contour of my visage etc. I don't much care for Lady Stapleton – he is quite lame. Uncle Evelyn is much aged I think, but perhaps it is because I have not seen him for some time. I rather want you to come, darling, either this week or next. I will sound about that if I can. I don't know if you would be bored but I should rather like you to come, do you think there is a chance of it – don't forget about a coat. I am writing in a vague way, darling, but I am writing after breakfast on a Monday morning with everybody talking round me. Tell me when you write the origin of the word "Minster". What constitutes a minster, what a cathedral, i.e. York Minster, Canterbury Cathedral? Then there is another thing. Aunt Mary wants to get a connection with a colliery in the Forest of Deane, so as to have coals straight here by water (she does not like her present coals they come by water). I thought you might know something about it. The post goes here at 2.30 & I am told if I want to go on the water, I must be ready quick & may not be back in time to write more. I am putting all I have.

Monday afternoon [11 February]　　　　　　　　　　　Tregothnan
My own darling husband,

　　I seem to write to you at all sorts of odd moments but you see I do miss you <u>very</u> <u>very</u> much & as I cannot talk, I must write. I had to finish in a great hurry this morning & shut up my letter to you while I was dressing to go out, but it was the tide, not me! You would have enjoyed this morning's sail. John has got a little yacht, rather over 4 tons, & has lent it to E. for a day or two while he is away & often does – so Edith & Sydney & I started with lots of wraps & I in the new coat which is, I must say, very useful & we had a capital sail nearly down to Porthgwidden (the luncheon party having given up going because of the weather). We then demurred as to whether we should go up there & ask for luncheon or go on to Falmouth or go home. After a few minutes we settled to come home. I enjoyed it very much only I did so wish for you. It seemed to leave an empty space all the time. I do not think you would be bored here, if you had a sail, would you? I do not want to press you to come if you had rather not, but I should

like it. Do which you like doing & don't settle anything yet. I wonder
if you have any news yet again from Painswick. I know you will let me
know when you do. I must soon go down to tea, but am having a rest
& think people are hardly come in yet from their different occupations. Lady Stapleton is drawing from the tower – has been there
all day! I hear Mrs Dugdale drew well. They went today which I was
sorry for. He is a very nice man.

After dinner, Bed time. I went down to tea & sat & talked & worked
in the library, & sauntered about watching Sydney & Edith playing
Billiards, neither very well. I think I am a little disappointed in the
house, but not at all out of doors. The camelias are a mass of buds &
ought, they say, to be out now. I have one on my table – the coloured
primroses are out. Some of the girls gathered some today, but said it
was wet work. Rather a pleasant evening last night. I wore the new
white frock. I do think it is rather pretty. We had a discussion on fans
tonight. I wish I had ours here. I sang tonight, my voice rather
unsteady. Half the big room talks while music is going on, the rest
gathered round the pianoforte. I don't know what we are going to do
tomorrow. Some are going on the boat to Porthgwidden if it is fine,
but as I was out in her today, I ought perhaps not to go. You are, I
fancy, now just coming back from the Hornby's. I hope, my darling,
it is all bright & cheerful for you at home & that the maids take care
of you. I am afraid I write very stupid letters to you, dearie. I have
just been writing to Edith. I look so to the letter tomorrow morning.
You can't think how down cast I was when I went into breakfast on
Sunday morning, because I thought there was none. I shall think of
you tomorrow night dining with the "Old Man". I wonder what you
will have. Shall you feel like a bachelor again.

Tuesday. Your 2 dear letters greeted me when I came down this
morning, so instead of going straight into breakfast, I stayed in the
ante-room & read them greedily. Aunt Mary soon came in from
breakfast & began to read the papers & read me a bit of a letter from
Evie from the Horse-guards, bewailing the mess we are in & that tho'
Baker is not supposed to be sent by us yet he is recalled "to let one of
our men in". Aunt M. was much amused at your suggestion of the
G.O.M.'s going with £8,000 & an umbrella, said "Tell him thems my
sentiments'. Then I went into breakfast among the latecomers. Your
news about Lord Garmoyle caused great excitement & Sydney greeted
every fresh person with "Bradlaugh has been kicked out of the House
& Lord Garmoyle is going to marry Violet Cameron". I was so
interested in all you have been doing, my own darling. I hope you

are not very uncomfortable in the drawing room. I think it is rather hard on you. Perhaps it is wise to paper the whole dining room. I quite agree the room seems larger without the tapestry, but I think that beauty bit would not look so well anywhere else, do you? Isn't Mrs Alexander nice? I do like her so much, but you did not tell me what she had settled about the cook? (How do I leave out words). I am so glad of Nellie's card, so very, very glad. Do you know dear, it has occurred to me she will not have got my letter, if Mr Hightt's letters are unopened, as I enclosed it to him. I suppose I had better just wait & see what Mrs Brune says. It is probable that my time may not suit Mrs Pole-Carew. A nice young clergyman['s] son dined & slept here last night. – a perfect image of his sister Julia. I never saw anything so absurd. It is blowing a big gale. No one has gone sailing. Even Edith has stayed on dry land. You must not think because I ask you to come that I am not enjoying myself, darling. Do just as you think best. Sydney chaffs me in a good natured way as to what you are doing & says "of course you think you know, where he is dining tonight". He is just good natured tho' about my missing you. There is no news yet of Mabel tho' her nurse has been there a week or more. Look in Monday's *Morning Post* sporting Intellegence, & you see an account of a splendid great salver which Mark Dawson & Archer have sent Uncle E. Sydney is very anxious to send Uncle Evelyn (and so is Edith) some vulgar valentines. He wants you to send him three – about 1d. ones, direct them to Uncle Evelyn – all of course in different handwritings (write one address with your left hand). If you can get one of a young woman dancing, send it & write inside "from a Penny Gaff", & in another "from Ratcliff Highway". I wonder if you could write some verses or parody some. The other night at dinner Uncle Evelyn suddenly complained he had made seven jokes & none of us (the group near him) had seen them. He was quite plaintive about it. If you could write something, it would be great fun. Is there anything in Princess Ida? Do write something or if no Valentine would suit it – carricature something. Thursday is the 14th you know. Carrie Lloyd writes that her father is to stand for South Warwickshire. Her brothers are hopeful & say it would be a pleasant seat for him. I am writing [last page missing]

Tuesday afternoon   Tregothnan
My own darling,
    Just come in from a walk. The wind has not gone down a bit & pouring rain came on soon after we went out. I do wish it would blow & rain itself out & have done with it. It was too rough to sail with any

comfort, so various walking parties set out. Lady Stapleton & Edith & Syd & I setting off together, Syd & I walking together, but we only took a short walk & have come in much blown about. Will you tell me the name of the rather fast woman whom Leila met at the Thorpes. I want to know both her married & unmarried names (not that she is here!) I do not see much of May, which I am glad of. I fancy she goes away one day this week. I stopped writing just now, to go down to tea in the library, which by the way is a most dangerous room, for you can't see a bit who is at the other end. Sir Francis [Acland] generally ensconces himself in a large arm chair at the furthest end & one quite forgets the little thing is there. He is such a little creature. Now, I am glad to say, he has only taken me into dinner once. Mr Glanville took me in tonight & was very pleasant. He asked me various questions about Glynn & your old great uncle & seemed to admire the place so much & to regret that it had gone out of the right hands. I am thinking about you just about going home, you & the Old Man. We hear tonight thro' Mr Glanville the rumour of the fall of Sinkat! I am writing a stupid sleepy letter, so I had better get into bed. Goodnight my old darling.

Wednesday morning. Your packet of letters just come, darling or rather I came down to breakfast & found them there & read them before I went in to the same. I have had a kind note from Mrs Brune this morning asking me to come there on Friday week, if I do not mind them quite alone (of course I don't). I have just written to say I should like to come very much, asking to leave the day uncertain for a day or two because of you. I wonder if you will come down. Here I was interrupted by Sydney who wanted me to draw a Valentine for Uncle E. for some verses that I had written, so he & Syd carried me off to her room & I have just done. I did not please myself with the drawing, but they are very pleased, so that is all right. It is a sketch of Lady Stapleton who does make such eyes at him, especially at dinner. I hope she will never see it, but she is good natured & would not mind! I cannot say I like any of the photographs (and so they sent you the wrong woman!) But I like the profile best, the one with the least back. Anyhow it ought to be vignetted because of the folds in the gown, but will you not tell him to send you more positions to see before deciding. I was done so many more times than that. You poor darling, what a scramble you must have had yesterday & all the opinions about the Paper must have been hard work for you. I am sure I shall like whatever you do. I am rather excited about Edith Finch Hatton's letter as, if Mr Finch Hatton gets in, I shall have her in London. Another pouring wet morning, but we have hopes of its clearing eno' to let one get a little walk at least, but it is disappointing to have so much rain. Tonight I shall think of you dining at the Atherleys. Shall I write (if I go to Prideaux Place on the 22nd, to Mrs Pole Carew & propose Wednesday & Thursday following?) It seems a great deal to settle all by myself! I wrote such a lot yesterday that nothing seems left to say today except my own darling what you know, that I am always the same loving little wife. I hope that nose has been all right.

Goodbye now darling, your ever wife, Florence Glynn

Wednesday night, 11.30 p.m.   Tregothnan
My own darling husband,

We have had a pouring wet day without a break, so few went out. We spent the afternoon working (me?) & reading & chattering in the library. Aunty Mary provided me with Madame d'Abrantes in French (20 vols) & I must say it is a most terribly course. I never read anything like it. The afternoon passed quickly & this evening has been rather absurd. Aunty Mary & Mr Glanville who dined here again & Sir F. & May played whist, while Uncle Evelyn & Sydney & I sang Glees! They were most remarkable. Uncle Evelyn frequently stopping us with "stop a bit I haven't started. You two can't sing a bit". Sydney insisted that it was all Uncle Evelyn's fault, but amid much laughter from our audience we did accomplish three & now we have just come up to bed rather late, so I will not write much more. I mean to go over to Trelissick to see Mrs Brune on Tuesday, if I can.

Just out of bed & I cannot help writing to tell you what a lovely day it is, sunny & perfectly still & oh! the view from my window. The river perfectly still with reflections. Now I must stop, only it is difficult to leave the window.

After Breakfast. Rather in a hurry. I do not know what to say about your coming here & that is the fact. It is not because I am lonely, but I should rather like you to come, but then there is the expense of the journey. I quite see – the fly – 2 horses cost 15/6. I suppose you could have one horse. It is very tiresome you could not come tomorrow. Do just what you think best & feel inclined to do. If you telegraph, telegraph to me. If you come by the day train, I think I should be asked to be taken straight up to my room & dress quickly then they would give you your dinner. This I tell you in case you come. Do just as you like. I am writing with people talking & discussing all round me. I think I could stay here next week quite well, but then you see,

Mrs Brune asks me for the 22nd. She might, I daresay, put it off. I will write to Mrs Melville, if I can before post time. I am so sorry you are feeling the dinner parties. Jack, darling, how sad about Mrs Moss. (There was so much talking I have gone on with a pencil). I asked Sydney about the vet & he said at once Mavor, address, he thinks, South Audley Street. I am sorry about Jupiter. We are just off to luncheon at Porthgwiddon by water.

Your own loving wife, Florence Glynn

I am afraid you are very much driven. It was very good of you to do what I asked you.

Friday   Tregothnan
My own darling,

I am beginning a letter to you at once, as I do not like to wait for the clearance of a telegram, for fear of missing a post & I did not begin a letter to you yesterday evening as usual, because I was very tired with our day out. We started soon after 11 o'clock some driving, the rest in the little sailing boat, the *Cormerant* – the boating party consisted of Aunt Mary, Edith, the two Randolphs, Sydney & Syd & me. We have to run down through gardens & woods to a little quay where little boats wait & we are conveyed to the big one. Yesterday it was really perfectly lovely & I never enjoyed anything more except for one great exception that my darling was not there. I kept thinking that all day. We cut along at a capital pace & as we arrived off Porthgwidden too early we had a further sail in the Harbour – all of us very jolly (except Edith, who did not like being made to go up to the house for luncheon). Canon & Mrs Phillpotts were most cordial in their reception of me. After luncheon we had gone a party of 9, the Canon took some of us round his garden, which certainly is charming. We boaters had to leave rather early, so we had not much time. The sail back was equally delightful, sometimes we heeled over tremendously, so much as to frighten Syd, but Peter, our first mate is too good a sailor to put on too much sail. You would be amused to see how Sydney pulls away at the ropes. We got home at 5.40, very tired, but it was a most delightful day. Tea followed & then a little "reposez vous". I wish you had seen Dr Philpott for I do not like you not feeling well & I fancy it might have done you good to come here. I was so hurried yesterday morning that I got muddled.

Tuesday Night   Tregothnan
My own darling,

I have been thinking of you all day travelling, travelling, travelling.

I miss you terribly, but I know you were right to go. It was very bad having to say goodbye like that, wasn't it. I longed for a big hug & then the next minute you were besieged by Aunty Mary Townie! The field came very punctually & are all started off down the drive. However, Mary, Mrs Fletcher & I soon turned back & went down to the Lime Quay, where we took boat & were rowed to King Harry. It was rather rough part of the way & we had an amusing landing. We walked up to Trelissick & found Mrs Gilbert, but alas! no Brunes. They had put off coming till today, because of the rain. Wasn't it a pity. She made us stay to luncheon. I liked her very much. She is a dear old lady. She begged me to be most kindly remembered to you . We got home about 3 o'clock, I, very tired, & I can't tell why. Gradually the hunters began to come in. They had only found after 3 hours & a half, but seem to have had a good time. About 6 o'clock I started to come up to my room & on my way went to Sydney's dressing room to return the novel according to arrangement with him, & Syd called me to her room & I sat & talked to her till 7 o'clock. We have had rather a messy evening. I like Mrs Fletcher & was so glad she came with us today. I daresay you are snug in bed now & I must get in too, but there is nobody to wait for tonight. Goodnight, my own own darling.

Wednesday Morning. My darling, your letter has delighted me. It was so dear of you to write so much. I have devoured it first. It was really very trying for you being called at by somebody you did not know like that! Somebody has been whistling in the hall a little bit like you & quite made my heart jump. I suppose unless I can see my way to the "Bus" I had better drive the whole way. I am sorry it costs so much, dear, & also the tips. I will do what I can about that. I hope I shall do all right about them. Everyone is good natured & kind. Mr Wilkins took me into dinner last night & I sat between him & Sydney. I am so glad you like him. I told Brooks just now that you did not like your Fly & that he charged more which made him very indignant. John is very keen on my having a post boy, so between them all, I shall do, I suppose. There is a tremendous wind today & it has been raining a great deal, but only showers, I believe. Edith & the Randolphs & Miss M. are going in the *Cormorant* this morning. I have a horrid pain in my shoulder & feel chilly, so I have said I wont go & Syd advises now not to (she had promised me some stuff for my shoulder tonight). If you were here, perhaps I should go, but I suppose it is wise not to. I shall try & do all you say about my ticket. My boots have come this morning, greatly to my satisfaction. I must write now to Leila & to Edith Finch Hatton. Mind you choose a paper, for I am sure I shall like what you do.

Your own loving wife, Florence Glynn

I don't think anybody will sail! I have never got anything for E's birthday today!

Wednesday midnight, very sleepy   Tregothnan
My own darling husband,

Here I am, up in my room again, writing to my darling. We have had an uneventful but pleasant day. The sailing party was not a success as the Randolph girls were very frightened (it was a big gale) so they all came back. In the afternoon, Syd & Edith & I went for a walk tho' some woods, joined near home by Sydney. It did not rain the afternoon. After tea John & young Williams requested I would add five dogs to the picture, so it was fetched & we had great fun over it & finally it was finished to their satisfaction. I had to be particular, even as to the exact number of buttons on their gaiters. This evening Mrs Fletcher sang again so well & then Uncle Evelyn told me to sing again which I did, & he said he like it & my way of singing, when I said goodnight to him. Syd has given me some stuff for my neuralgia, which I am just going to put on & Edith has been in with some more stuff in case the other don't do! Between them all I ought to be cured. I think it is the constant damp & today the wind added. My darling I hope you still feel better. I shall be dreadfully disappointed, if I find you looking like you did, when you came down. Don't forget to take some quinine if you feel <u>low</u>. I must go to bed, my darling, good night.

Thursday. I am so glad to get your letter this morning & to hear that you were not so tired going back. I do think the change of air must have done you good & if so I am sure it was worth the expense. Indeed I did enjoy that sail & it just made the difference having you here. It was a different thing altogether. I will try & find out what the *Cormorant* cost to build, but it appears to be rather difficult to tell! I will also ask those questions about Peter <u>Ferris</u>. What fun it would be to do that ourselves. I am hoping to get a sail today, but the weather is, as usual, bad. Such a storm last night between 10.o'clock & 11.30, & it dropped quite suddenly. This morning brook half sunshine half rain & it was proposed that some should drive to the meet, 6 having ridden, but just as we were starting, a violent storm of rain came on, so I & Mrs Fletcher did not go, for tho' my pain is much better this morning, it was wiser not to go, & now I am glad for a note has just been brought to me from Mrs Brune to ask me to put off going there till Saturday (which Aunt Mary is most kind about my doing) & that they will take me in their own carriage meeting me at the lodge here – isn't that nice. I am so glad, darling, for now there will not be the expense of the Fly – of course I have said yes – It is very kind of them – Marie is to go by a certain van, which goes on Saturdays past this lodge to Padstow. Doesn't it all fit nicely. This has all stopped me in my letter to you. The at home party this morning were Edith, Mrs Fletcher & Aunt Annie. The weather improved gradually. I am so glad you have chosen the paper. I am sure I shall like it. Yes please, leave cards on Mrs Cubitt. Dear Carrie! tell her to write to me again & give her the address. Have you thanked Beatrice for her letter to you? I have had a letter from Glynn [Price] in re. coal which seems to contain some useful information. That is very kind of Lady Oglander. I am very glad you are to have Frank [Price]. It will give the boy some pleasure & I am sure you like to see him. I have had so many interruptions in writing my letter that I hardly know what I have written. I shall try & send Edith more primroses. Did Mrs Lloyd get what I sent? I am sorry Bassebe could not put your eyes right, but it is a nice picture & like my darling. I must not mind. Mrs Fletcher has taken refuge in the anti-room to read Altiora Peto, because Aunt Annie will talk in the drawing room, & now Aunt Annie has come in here! Jack, darling, Mrs Fletcher had the same sad experience as ours, with this difference that her Father's death killed her child at once & now they have two more, so there is hope for us. The sun is dazzling me, so I must stop writing. I am afraid another shower is coming. I shall think of you & Frank tonight.

Goodbye, my own darling, your loving wife, Florence Glynn

I have said to Mrs Pole Carew the 27 or 28th, forgetting till this moment that the 29th is the last day of the month. If I want to stay to the 1st shall I write to the Station Master at Exeter?

Thursday night   Tregothnan
My own darling,
Rather sleepy after her sail this afternoon. It was such a good one with only one draw back – that you were not there. I did so long for you. Our party at luncheon was very small, as none of the hunting party had returned & at 3, Edith & I started for the quay, where we found "Johnny" & the boat & he rowed us bravely out to the *Cormorant*. We expected after last nights storm to find a great deal of wind & there was a good bit, but not so much as we thought. We went right

out beyond the ships (beyond where they are thickest) but not right out to sea & were much interested in a ship which was wrecked off the point last night, having dragged its anchor. We pitched about a good deal & I am rather proud of feeling quite happy, but I am [an] uncertain creature. I am getting on, tho' I think. It was very cold & we were glad of the walk up to the house, which we reached about 7 o'clock. We had one violent shower, & took refuge in the cabin. We discussed [with] Peter as to whether there were yachts of the kind you said, to be hired in Falmouth. He seemed doubtful, but said there <u>might</u> be. I have not talked to John about it yet as I have only seen him at dinner, but I will not forget. I was near Uncle Evelyn at dinner & asked him what the *Cormorant* cost him. John said the cost [was] £160, but I fancy it is difficult to say, as the wood came from the place, though of course it is charged. I wish I could find some of those old sham bank notes people used to have & send him £150. Uncle Evelyn was so laughed at for not taking my handsome offer that at last he said he did not believe I had it! I wonder what you have been doing today. I hope somebody has taken care of you. I am glad you are to dine with the Burtons & sometimes I suppose you will dine at your Club. The Fletchers go tomorrow which I think everyone regrets. He says he should like to give you some trout fishing in North Wales. They are both very pleasant. Good night, my own darling.

Friday Morning. I am sure you will have said "My darling <u>was</u> sleepy when the part of her letter was written!" You will see by my letter this morning that the rheumatism was better & today it is quite right. I am <u>sure</u> it was not the sail on Monday that brought it on. I was so well wrapped up & it was not so cold as it was yesterday. I am very glad you got places at Drury Lane for last night. I am sure the boy will enjoy it. I have had a dear letter from Carrie this morning. She says she misses me very much & that Walter hopes I will return before he "slopes". You tantalize us with your account of the fine weather in London. Sydney says you have been dissipated & mistook the gas light for the sun! (Very impertinent of Sydney). However, this morning does realy seem inclined to be fine, if it will only last. I am glad you have heard from Leila. I suppose she has not got my letter. The exact plan of campaign tomorrow is this. Marie is to be ready with all the luggage about 9 o'clock & is conveyed to the Lodge where the carrier passes & will then be put into his vehicle. I am to be at the Lodge at 12 o'clock & shall then be picked up by the Brunes in their carriage. I shall send everything with Marie, – so as not to fill the

Brunes' carriage. It is so sweet of you to tell me not to mind about the money. Your tip to Brookes is very useful to me for he was very civil about <u>un</u>ordering my carriage, after he had taken trouble about it, & I shall get him to see that whoever takes Marie to the Lodge knows what to do with her. I went upstairs & found the writing tables occupied, so, like you, I shall finish in pencil. I am going for a little walk this morning & then afterwards for a sail. Think of me on the drive tomorrow. I am afraid I shall not be able to write on the drive tomorrow, darling, but I would, if I could.

Friday evening   Tregothnan
My darling husband,
    There seems very little fresh to tell you this evening & I am afraid there will not be much time tomorrow morning for writing, for I suppose I shall go off pretty early. This morning about 11.30 the Fletchers left & all were sorry, I think. I asked her to come & see us in London. I hope that was right. After they left I went out with Syd for a little turn before luncheon. The grounds here certainly are charming & everything seems to be growing so well, almost like things do in Italy. I came up to my room before luncheon & explained to Marie in what manner she is to travel tomorrow & tried to find the word for a carrier's van, finally told her it was what the French call a *Diligence* (knowing that Syd's maid speaks French). After a few moments she said "did Madam say I was going in a telephone". I tried to be grave but did you ever hear anything so comical. Directly after luncheon, Edith & I & some girls started off to the quay to go out in the *Cormorant*, but when we got to her, it was dead calm, so we had to come ignominiously back again. After dawdling I got a book & had a cosy read in the Library till tea-time, when tea & chatter & chaff with Sydney, & now I am come up to dress for dinner. I suppose you are just tying your tie to dine with the Burtons.

Saturday Morning. I am writing in the early morning for I was obliged to get up to give Marie my things. I got the house-maid to bring me my letters & have just got your dear one & a very cordial one from Mrs Pole Carew to say she will be very glad to see me any day next week, if I do not mind finding them alone, also saying she regrets not seeing you with me. So I suppose I had better go on Wednesday or Thursday – which? I am so interested in hearing all about Frank. I don't wonder you were distressed at having reduced him to tears, but I am sure you were quite right to speak to him as you did & you do not know what foolish things Laurie may not have said to him.

Certainly it is very good of him not to have spent all those tips. I remember Lady Oglander giving him that £1 quite well. I hope & trust the boy will do well & be steady. I like to hear of the boy being excited & anxious over seeing what he could of London. I am so glad you took him to Cinderella & enjoyed it yourself. Indeed, my darling, do not think I want a lot of amusement. You know I am happy – my own darling. My luggage & Marie just off on their way to the Lodge to join the "telephone". All kindly say they are sorry I am going. John (I sat between him & Sydney) suddenly realized the fact at dinner "Oh, I say, you're never going tomorrow – by Jove! I'm sorry." After dinner Sydney (old humbug, as I told him) put both hands on the arm of my chair & looked sadly in my face; "Dear Pussie, it's <u>very</u> sad that you are going tomorrow". He is very kind tho' & I am very glad of some talk I have had with him. You were quite like the Arabian Nights – leaving off just at the exciting moment about Cinderella! I am glad you & the "Old Man" are to dine with the Fitzgeralds. I hope it was pleasant last night. I was talking to Aunt Mary yesterday about a nursing Institution, which she helps to manage at Truro. They are in some difficulties about a superintendant, who is to be changed in two or three months. She has £50 per annum & her keep & looks after the nurses, but she ought to have seen work in a hospital to know what is right & what is wrong. Do you think Rose would care for this. I hardly think so & yet I fancy she might. Of course, a Paris Hospital would be as well as another to go thro'. It is not quite certain whether the Institution is to stay at Truro, but it would be somewhere on the G.W.R. Let me know by return what you think of this. They seem to be quarrelling rather, so perhaps it would be as well not to tell her of it. I must go down to breakfast now.

My darling goodbye, your loving little wife, Florence Glynn

I don't remember if there is a post from Prideaux Place on Sunday, but I shall write, if there is.

23 February, Saturday night   Prideaux Place, Padstow
My darling husband,

This letter will, I have just remembered, reach you at the same time as the one I wrote this morning, so this must be No. 2! Here I am, you see, quite safe after the long drive. Aunty Mary & the white pony & the out-rider conducted me to the Lodge this morning & very soon the Brunes appeared. Mrs Brune & Nellie & Mary. I thought we might get tired of one another on the long drive, but we didn't a bit! Mrs Brune was so pleasant & the girls most absurd, Mary was too killing & insisted upon eating apples nearly the whole time. We stayed some time at St Columb & went to look at the fine old church which has some very quaint old carved bench ends (rather like Fyne Court Church) & some very early brasses of the Arundels. We got here soon after 4 o'clock, when the other girls speedily rushed in to greet us, most cheery & noisy. I did not see Mr Brune till dinner time & he greeted me very cordially. He says he went to see you on Sunday & found the house very safely barred up. The girls were so merry at dinner. It seems so funny to be among them, just "en famille" after that big mixed party – I like it. They are very anxious about Mrs Charlie – poor little thing. She is in the family way, but all is not going well & she has been in bed since Christmas. I will explain it all to you when I come home. It is very sad for both the young ones as well as for the parents. There is a hope that he has got an adjutancy, but they do not like to say so yet. Anyhow if he does not get it, he will leave the Army. These girls are certainly very fond of each other. I like to see them together. We had a good deal of music tonight, but Nelly & I were glad to come early to bed. I have the same room we had before & it seems as if you must be coming up to the dressing room in a few minutes!

Sunday. Your letter came just before church & now there is not much time to write before luncheon. You poor darling! How <u>dreadful</u> for you to be shut out like that. Poor you. I can't help laughing a little bit, but it must have been miserable & such a bore to have to sleep somewhere else. Those maids sleep tight. I wonder if we should have heard. Thank you for sending me Leila's letter. I am afraid she is rather low altogether, don't you? Please return me Miss Fife's letter. I will settle tomorrow whether I leave here on Wednesday or Thursday & will tell you directly. I should think you would indeed be glad to get back to your own things, poor dear. It is showery here today, but I suppose it is doing its best! I am glad you sat next [to] Carrie Dickson. Why are they not going to Rome? I shall like to see her again very much. Did you have the hooks of the earrings kept? Tell me if the setting of the little tops shows very much. Marie arrived here quite safe & Mrs B's maid was in the same vehicle. Luncheon, so goodbye darling. Your loving little wife, Florence Glynn

Don't get locked out again. Sydney would have said it was sunshiny indeed!

24 February, Sunday night   Prideaux Place
My own dear husband,
    I daresay I shall have more time here for writing, yet I have got

into a way of sitting down every night to have a talk with you & I cannot do without it. I have to tell you what I fear, darling, you will be disappointed to hear. You can guess what it is. It came on Thursday night (3 weeks). I am taking great care, but I am sorry to come here, such a poor creature. I got through the drive pretty well, but was very tired today. I went to church this morning & for a little turn this afternoon in the gardens with Mr & Mrs Brune & laid down all the time they were at church tonight. I did not tell you today because – well tomorrow is Monday. I hope, darling, you do not mind <u>very</u> much. I want you send me a book by post to show Mrs Brune – that book you got for me last year – Bull (Isn't that the name?) It is in my bookcase, with a paper cover over the binding. Mrs B. is very uncomfortable about her daughter in law & I thought I might find something in that to allay her anxiety & she has not got the book. Lady Brabourne has not behaved at all well to Mrs Brune. We have had a merry evening, ending in music. I sang a little & I think they liked it. They have all been school-teaching today at intervals. It is very good of them. I must not sit up any more. Goodnight, darling.

Monday morning. A sunny morning with light clouds rather shimmery looking flying about. I feel stronger this morning darling (thought you would like to know) I think the delay may have been from what I told you, for I did feel so weak & ill, when Clere was with us the second time, but I suppose it is no use trying to find reasons. I made them all laugh very much by telling them at luncheon yesterday about your being locked out. It tickled them all immensely, tho' they were very sorry for you. Mr Brune has a very bad headache today, poor man. This afternoon I am to drive with Mrs Brune & go & see the Molesworths, I believe. I should think that would be rather amusing. These girls are certainly very good fun. They are irrepressably merry & impudent. Mary was so absurd driving. She & Nellie walked on a little to St Columb & just as we reached them were caught by a big shower. "My dear Mother, we are drenched to the <u>skin</u>!" "Get in, my dears, do get in." "Yes, but Mother, we're drenched to the <u>skin</u>", till poor Mrs Brune believed it. I think I will keep to Wednesday & will write to Mrs Pole Carew to that effect. She says she will send to meet me, if she can & if not she will see that a fly is there for me at Devonport Station. Marie's journey cost 4/6d. She is in the next room to mine, which I am glad of. The Brunes come soon to London & are beginning to think of packing. Gertrude has come in with two rampageous puppies to show me. The address at Anthony (note) is Anthony, Torpoint, Devonport. I am afraid Sandro's bus will not go the right time. I am so sorry.

Please send the book. I think you had better divide your letter tomorrow! They will not let me go till Thursday.

Monday night   Prideaux Place
My dearest husband,
I had to finish off in a great hurry this morning, as it was only just before Post-time, that they made a fuss & said I must not go on Wednesday. As there was no positive necessity, I said I would stay till Thursday. Nellie & Gertrude would not hear of my going so I shall go to Antony that day & to Eggesford on Saturday – do you approve, darling? I drove this afternoon with Nellie & Mary, first to call on Lady Molesworth, who was out & then we drove down to the sea & had a blow. Hamlin Bay – I think. The tide was high so we could not walk much, but the sea breeze was very refreshing. Then we came home & attended to the chickens. They made no company of me which is very nice. This evening we had a great deal of music beginning with two toy symphonies & I performed on the triangle! It has actually not rained today. It is colder, but it is such a comfort to have a fine day. I wonder what you have been doing today. Did you miss your little wife on Monday? It will not be very long before I am home again. What a deal we shall have to talk about. I have indeed a jaunt & my poor darling has stayed at home. Goodnight my own.

Tuesday Morning. Such a dear, dear letter this morning. My darling, you shall not miss me much longer (I think if I could not write to you, I should cry for you all day). It is very sweet to know that you do miss me so, but I do not like you to do it. What two cheery letters from Lady Oglander & Rose – the latter seems in good spirits. It is difficult to know what to say to Lady Oglander, because if you leave it till later you may not like to ask for it. How would it be to ask to have it to put in a Savings Bank for him [Frank Price], ready to buy the cart & horses or something of that sort, when he leaves the big farm. That seems the only way to me. I send you little Rosamunds letter of this morning. It is a very kind one & the brightest I have had from her yet. Another wet morning & not much prospect of clearing. I will certainly give Mr Brune your message. He has gone off early to *St Colomb*. I do see Gerty a great deal too, & I am getting to like her very much. She was the first to say I must not go tomorrow. There is something very honest about her. I will make them all squeak about that advertisement. How killing it is! I should like to know the date of the paper. Cinderella must be very good. No, the Charlie Brunes are not here. They are at Folkestone. The adjutancy he hopes for is to the "Inns of Court". They have asked him to some function on March 5th. (he was with Mr Brune when he came to call on you) so he hopes it is all right, but they do not like to be sure yet, or say so. If he gets it, they want a furnished house in our neighbourhood for a year. They are all unhappy about her, poor little thing. Mr Brune would, I am sure, be pleased to have another little Brune. I did not know Carrie was going away again. What shall we do with your holiday? It ought to be something you like very much. Paris would be much too 'spensive, so we must not think of it! (I can hear you saying "You naughty little thing, why did you put it into my head!") I am very sorry you could not go to tea with Mr Lloyd. I hope I shall not miss Miss Forster; if so & you see her do tell her how very sorry I am. I am sure I shall like the papers. The other poor rejected one must have been squeezed quite flat, if you & Edith both "sat" on it. No wonder it looked poor! No darling, I did not want the hooks sent to me. It is very sweet of you to have got the pins for your "putty". I do think Mrs Cockey is a nice woman & it makes one regret the paint the more. I think my rheumatics (you were quite right in saying that to Lady Molesworth) are really behaving fairly well in all this damp. Do you think I must go to any Baths this summer – if I had Mrs D. & the Baths at home every now & then? Of course, if cold winds come in March, I must expect to have some pain. Think about this, darling. Now I must stop writing, so goodbye. My own darling, your loving little wife, Florence Glynn

Kind as everyone is, I do so long to be with you again.

Tuesday Evening   Prideaux Place
My own dear heart,

I hope you have not missed your "Putty" quite so much today. It has been wet a great part of the day here, so we could not do much. This morning – after writing to my darling & to Mrs Pole Carew (whom I did not write to yesterday) I helped Gertie & Nellie to finish a screen they are making. In the afternoon, after we had read & talked a little, I sallied forth – as it had cleared a little, with Gerty for a walk & finally we joined the others to see after the chickens. They are much excited because their eggs have been stolen two or three times from the place far from the house – the kennels I think they call it, several which Beatrice left there in the morning were gone today. They are most amusing in their various plans to watch for the thief. Mr Brune has decided to send for the Police Sergeant. He (Mr B.) is much better & quite himself again. Lord & Lady Molesworth came to tea. What an oddity he is! She seems to be very kind to his children, spending her money on them & they are very fond of her. Tonight we had a great deal of music. I have sung a great deal. My darling, I want to learn the Violin. Are you quite horrified.

Wednesday morning. Your letter just come, darling & it seems to me rather a sad one. I am afraid my own you are very disappointed about your little wife, but I know you are right in saying it will come in his good time & we must not watch for it. Some day I feel the blessing will come. It isn't wrong to feel that, is it? We will do as you say, if we possibly can. It is very interesting to hear about the progress of the dining room! I am longing to see it & shall be very glad when you are comfortable in your own den again. Poor Louisa, it is dreadful when she breaks anything, but I am very sorry it is that dear little table. It is creepy & chilly here this morning. Perhaps one will be better for going out before luncheon. You did not send the Book – at least it has not come by this post. It may still come by the evening post. If you have not sent it will you send it to me at Antony. I daresay we might ask Mr Bentick to dinner. We will see when I come back. I wrote to the G.W.R. Superintendent at Plymouth about breaking the journey at Devonport & have had a most civil answer giving full permission, so that is all right. I have had another letter from Glynn [Price] this morning & must forward a copy of it to Aunt Mary Falmouth, so I had better write to her now, my own darling. Goodbye, I am coming home soon. Think about what I said about [my] not going to Baths this summer, & having Mrs D. at intervals instead.

Ever your loving little wife, Florence Glynn

Wednesday night   Prideaux Place
My own dear husband,

I have just finished packing my own little "Duds" & shall have a wee talk to you before getting into bed. We have had another rainy day! This morning, after my letters were done, I sang with Beatrice & in the afternoon, Mr & Mrs Brune & Gertrude & I (the others having gone other ways) settled forth in waterproofs & went down to the gardens & into the green houses. How nice they are, the things look so well. Then Gertrude & I came back together & walked about near the house & then came in to Tea. After tea I had a very nice little talk with Mrs Brune – the girls having left the room about 6 o'clock. In the evening I intended to go to church, but it poured so that I gave it up & stayed at home & dined with Mr & Mrs Brune & Gerty, a cosy little party. After the others came in, we had a great deal of music, beginning with the Toy Symphonies, in which we all took part & ending with my singing & Beatrice also. They are such a happy merry party. I shall miss them very much. If it is fine tomorrow they kindly propose to drive me & Marie (on the box) to Wadebridge & them I am to go into a little Fly & go on to Bodmin Road. My luggage is to go on early by the bus. Of course if it is wet this cannot be carried out. Do you like the plan, darling? It is getting late & I have to get up early for the luggage to go – so goodnight, my own darling.

Thursday. This morning looked so wet & cold that Mrs Brune & I had a conference in our dressing gowns & settled not to send the luggage & I am to go on the Paddington Fly. Your letter just come. I am so glad you opened poor Nelly [Hightt's] letter – poor, poor Nelly. I am so surprised tho' at the great progress Mr Hightt has made. Surely it is very sudden, but I am so thankful to hear it. First I forgot if I gave you the address at Eggesford – it would perhaps be better to put Lord Portsmouth's name, Eggesford House, North Devon. You tell me many bits of news. I am very sorry for poor Sukey. You do not say if you mean to sleep there. Perhaps you think that would fuss her. Tell me whether I am to write there. How very amusing about the Leap Year dance. I wonder how it will go off. We are much shocked about your proposal about after supper! I must go down to the Drawing room for the last half hour, before I start. Goodbye, my darling. I shall try & pass the long drive with reading Madam d'Abrantes.

Your loving little wife, Florence Glynn

Your party at the FitzGeralds must have been very pleasant. I fear dear Walter will have "sloped" before I come.

Thursday night   Antony, Torpoint
My own dear heart,

Here is your little wife, all alone in a big new place. Oh, it does seem so strange to be doing all this without you. It seems as if it cannot be me! I had a most cordial greeting from Mr & Mrs Pole Carew. I left Prideaux Place about 12.20 & had a very, very long drive to Bodmin Road. It seemed as if we were never coming to the "Church Town". It was so raw & cold, but the horses came a good steady pace & the man was very civil. When the train came, who should look out but the Randolphs on their way from Tregothnan to Pentillie, so I got into their carriage & so had company to Saltash. At Devonport the Pole Carews' carriage was waiting, which took me & Marie & luggage. We picked up Julia Pole Carew in the town & then came across the Ferry. We got here about 5.30 – or rather later perhaps – & found them all at tea. Two sailors were calling, one a Mr Smith Dorien. I wondered if he was the one we met on board the *Invinsible*. He went away very quickly or I would have asked him. This seems a charming place, such a nice great pannelled hall in which we sat most of the evening. I thought there were some nice pictures. I noticed one especially by Romney of an Honble. York, wife of a Pole Carew – a beautiful picture – the gown the same grey that he is so fond of. I never realized before how very pretty Julia P.C. is. She is most fascinating. She sung a good deal tonight & the youngest (whom we met at Prideaux Place) sung too & then they made me sing. I thought it foolish to refuse as there were only a man & his sister dining & not lots of people. I sung by heart & I think they liked it. We came off to bed as soon as the two people left. Mr Pole Carew is very tottly on his pins, but his memory & hearing perfectly good. I do so hope it will be fine tomorrow, but I have almost given up hoping for that. I wonder what you are doing tonight, my own darling, & what you did today. I hope you have not been driven. Goodnight, my own. I wish I could expect to hear your footstep in the dressing room next to my quaint old pannelled room, my own darling.

Friday morning. For a wonder, it is a beautiful sunny morning. It is so delightful to see the sun at last. This place is so pretty – glimpses of the water between the trees & in the openings. There are some very fine ilex & cedars. I have not been out yet, but I am to be ready at 11 to drive with Mrs Pole Carew to Mount Edgecumbe. I am so glad she is going to take me there. I am much interested to hear that you & Edith had that talk, so <u>thankful</u> she is in that mind about it. You must tell me about it when I come. I do feel as if I had got a bit nearer home here. They asked me to stay over Sunday, but I have refused. My darling, you do not send me the book I asked you for. Can't you find it? Mrs Brune had a better account of Mrs Charles yesterday, but she said she would still like to see the book as Lady Brabourne, tho' she says it is all Mrs Brune's fault (!) will not let her see a London doctor. Please let me have the book at Eggesford. It is in my book case with a paper cover over the binding. It is rather dreadful about E's cat, but I suppose it is right. It seems very cruel. I am glad you are to have the dining room & your own den again tomorrow. Pah! Those hangings must have been dirty. I hope the dirt did not get into your lungs, my darling. I am coming home soon, my own darling. Goodbye my own, your loving wife

(Was she <u>very</u> naughty when she was a little trot?) I hope you had a pleasant evening with my old cockle top.

Friday Night   Antony
My own dear husband,
  I have been trying to discover if there is a post from here, by which you can have this tomorrow night, but I am afraid there is not, so if there is a post from Eggesford on Sunday you will get two letters from me. I cannot describe to you the beauty of our drive this morning. It was quite lovely. I did so long for you, but I believe you have seen Mount Edgecumbe, haven't you? Mrs Pole Carew drove me in a pony carriage with such a charming pair of ponies. We went such a pace up & down such hills. Every now & then close to the sea, bits more like the Gulf of Genoa than anything English – at last we came to the lodge & then we went over the grass & drove to the edge of the Mount. Such a view, my darling, it was lovely. Trees of every description at our feet & then the great open sea & on our left Plymouth – the Dockyards – Stone-House – the great ships, all the creeks etc. Then we drove to the house by a long lonely road still at the edge through trees (quantities of stone pines & cork trees & great ilex, shimmering like olives) hanging over the sea. It was so beautiful. It was very unenglish! I did long for you. We found Lord Mount Edgecombe & one of his daughters at home & went in for a little while & then had a shorter but lovely drive home. It was beautifully sunny, but whenever we met the wind it was bitterly cold. It is such a comfort though not to have rain. In the afternoon I went out for a walk thro' the woods & by the water with Mrs Pole-Carew & Julia. Mr Pole Carew coming with us in a pony chair. This is a most charming place & so pretty. I do wish you could have come. I am so sleepy. It is past 12. Goodnight my own.

Saturday. I wish, darling, you could get this tomorrow. I do not at all like your not having a letter for a whole day. I believe there is a second post at Eggesford, which brings letters posted late at night in London. I did not think of telling you this before. I shall be in a state of "suffocation" about politics, so p<u>lease</u> send me a newspaper every day. I should like the *Morning Post* best. I mean, if I possibly can, to come home on Friday & would come before, if I could. I must see what poor little Rosamond says. I hope you found & read what you wanted about the cattle, & made a good speech for Mr Lloyd. I quite agree with you about the "working man". These explosions are most dreadful – please sit tight & don't be blown up – but seriously it is very terrible. I was to have gone with Mrs Pole-Carew, but it has begun to rain, so I suppose we shall not go. I was so sleepy when I wrote the first part of this letter, I hope I wrote 'scuse. Some young men [called Gresling, Hall & Bessell] came to dine & sleep last night from Plymouth, (to amuse me they said – by way of chaff.) The idea! One, a Mr Gresling, a nice little man about 38 said he was with Captain Fitzroy in Egypt last year & confirmed he was a very good & popular officer now; he seemed to think he was in London now – will not you call on him at his club? I quite know what you mean about the Old Admiral & his "Dotie". It is a great pity he does it. It is trying to clear, so I must see if Mrs Pole Carew wants to go. Let me have the paper & the book & letters to tell me all you are doing. I do so look for your letters & I am afraid I shall not get one on Monday. It seems to make the day begin a sort of dead dumb way with nothing from my darling, but I am coming home now.

My own darling goodbye, your loving little wife, Florence Glynn

I am glad I refused to stay here over Sunday, for that would have lengthened the time next week.

EVELYN BURNABY
of
SOUTHAMPTON, 1892

Liskeard, *c*.1855

Evelyn Burnaby, *A Ride from Land's End to John O'Groats*
(1893), 21–42.

Evelyn Henry Villebois Burnaby rode with a companion from
Southampton. Their horses were named Bonchurch and
Punch. He wrote that the tour was inspired by the ride to
the central Asian city of Khiva of his brother Frederick, a
well-known travel writer who died in the attempt to relieve
Khartoum in 1885. Burnaby also wrote that he hoped it
would be interesting to read and that it may 'help to fill up

a few leisure moments for those who have visited the many lovely spots in which our island abounds'. He added that he wanted to gauge public opinion for the upcoming General Election and that bicycles made such tours 'a matter of everyday occurrence'. Burnaby also wrote *Memories of Famous Trials* (1907).

We only spent one night at Plymouth, and rode on next day, crossing the Tamar by the ferry, to Liskeard. Here we had a novel experience of a Temperance house. No liquor was to be obtained on the premises, but the food was excellent and the beds clean.

From Liskeard to Bodmin, which also appeared to be in the very throes of election excitement, was our next stage, and thence we made tracks for St Austell, the neighbourhood of which seems to be given over to tin and copper mines. Talking of mines, I am reminded of an old friend at Ventnor, who formerly had been a large speculator on the Stock Exchange. His attention had always been directed to the Mining Market, and as the ruling passion haunts a man even unto death, my friend, after he left "the House," was ready to do a little outside business if the opportunity offered. Now there was a maiden lady residing in the Undercliffe, possessed of a considerable fortune and with a desire to increase her income. She consulted my friend as to a change in her investments. An appointment was made, and they met at an early hour in the morning. I was unfortunate enough to disturb the *tête-a-tête*, and I could not help overhearing the gentle insinuation, "Now what do say to a little mine." The unprotected female looked aghast, but firmly and calmly she expressed her intention of keeping her money in consols. My friend never forgave me for the interruption, and he always believed I had stopped his commission, and to this day he is known to his many friends as "the little mine."

From St Austell's, a ride of fourteen miles brought us to the cathedral city of Truro, where the memory of Bishop Wilkinson is as much revered as it is in his old parish of St Peter's, Eaton Square. "Clyma's Hotel," where we stayed, cannot be beaten. From Truro we continued our ride through Chacewater to Redruth, climbing the Granite Hill to Carn Brea, supposed to have been a Druidical resort in ancient days. The view from the summit was splendid, and to the north and south we could trace the coast-line of the Bristol and

English Channels. From Redruth to Penzance the country is barren and wild, relieved only by the coast scenery around St Ives; and almost as soon as we came in sight of St Michael's Mount, with its quaint little fortress home belonging to Lord St Leven, a straight road of a couple of miles brought us to Penzance.

It was a still, hazy kind of day, with the Scilly Islands indistinct but just visible through the curtain of mist which overhung the Atlantic when we reached Land's End, the goal for the moment, and the real starting-point of our tour on horseback. An hour was required to bait the nags, and we had time to look around before mounting for out expedition to the northward. The "Longships" alone broke the view, as, standing on the extreme ledge of English soil, we looked out to sea. I could not help recalling Thomas Carlyle's graphic description of the North Cape – its weird scenery with rugged headland and granite cliffs, the seagull pirouetting on the water's surface near the coast. There was "The slow heaving ocean, and the sun overhead, hanging low and hazy, as if he, too, were slumbering." There was no sound in this desolate and remote spot; nor any sign of habitation beyond the miniature Inn which faces the broad expanse of sea, and yonder the sequestered village of Sennen, protected from the wild north winds by the abrupt ridge of Cape Cornwall point, which is continued in long stretches of rock, wrought into very fantastic and grotesque shape, far away along the indented line of coast.

We had accomplished 270 miles since we started from the Dolphin at Southampton, and yet, despite vicissitudes and visits to various blacksmiths' forges, "Bonchurch" and "Punch" were as fresh as when they left their home circle in the Isle of Wight. When their heads were turned in the opposite direction which they had been accustomed for the last fortnight, they seemed to understand that there was to be a change in the order of events. I imagine they concluded it would be one for the better, judging by the style in which "Punch" negotiated a pretty stiff stone wall; but, then, my friend only rides 11st., and weight must tell after all. "Bonchurch" showed no desire to follow the acrobatic performances of his stable companion, and in that respect he did not resemble the camel "Romeo," which once carried my late brother, Fred, in the East, and which completely convulsed his rider's liver in his frantic attempts to keep pace with "Juliet", one of the same fraternity, with a more active gait. I verily believe horses have a kind of intuitive sense, and are more intelligent than many of the human race are apt to believe.

Few men had greater knowledge of a horse than the late Mr Baron

Martin, who was in the habit of riding the circuit, and always made a point, when the service at the cathedral was over on Commission Day, to canter over to any training stables which might be in the neighbourhood of the assize town. On one occasion the learned Baron, I believe, when at York was trying a case of breach of warranty, the animal in question being supposed to be suffering from an occult navicular disease. An old horse coper had been sworn, and was in the box. "Now," said the examining counsel, "tell my Lord, and the gentlemen of the jury, what is the disease from which they say this horse is suffering." With a knowing wink of the eye, and jerk of the thumb in the direction of the Bench, the witness replied, "Just you ask t'old 'un up there, and he will tell you." On another occasion Baron Martin's love of horse-flesh was singularly illustrated. He had ridden over from Monmouth, through the Forest of Dean, to the boundaries of the City of Gloucester, in company with his friend and marshal, the late Mr John Canning-Doherty. The Sheriff's carriage, with a splendid team of blacks, coachman and footmen, wigged and powdered, with their owner, had been waiting for some time when the learned judge appeared on the scene. The High Sheriff showed visible signs of annoyance, and his conduct to the representative of the law was not quite as courteous as it might have been. For this an apology was demanded, but when he remarked to Mr Baron Martin that he had been subjected to the jeering remarks of little urchins during the time he was awaiting his lordship's arrival, and that he had been at great expense in securing four match horses to do honour to the judge, the slight friction was healed in a moment, "Never saw a better team in my life," ejaculated the Baron. "I am not surprised, Mr High Sheriff, you resented the delay of our arrival."

From Land's End a short ride brought us to the "Logan Rock," part of the "Treen Castle" range, supposed formerly to have been a well fortified Druid Castle. An impulsive lieutenant in the navy, it is said, once had the temerity to move this huge boulder, which seems to swing on a pivot, and he slightly dislocated it from its normal position. As is well known, the Cornish are a most superstitious race, and owing to the outcry which this act of indiscretion caused among the population of the district, the culprit was called upon to have the "Logan" replaced on its original site. At Sennen the inhabitants are most primitive, and there are those amongst them who believe in witchcraft, sorcery, snake-charming and other fables of bygone generations; but, like the Norwegians, they are frank, hospitable, and yet as firmly attached to their traditional rights as when centuries ago they took up the sword in opposition to the conquest of Athelstane.

I heard a story of a miner who was employed on his work by night and took his rest by day, which proves that superstition is still rife amongst some of the Cornish people. Whilst he was sleeping he heard, or he fancied he heard, three distinct taps at his door. He immediately summoned the whole family to his bedside, and announced to them that the taps were a supernatural omen – that as far as this world was concerned they would have to pack up their goods and chattels and quit. At Helston on the 8th of May every year an annual floral festival takes place to commemorate the idea of a fiery dragon, which in remote history was supposed to have passed over the town.

We dismounted by the wall of Saint Buryan's Churchyard. Here Mr J. Richards, of Church Town Farm, proved a most excellent cicerone, and was well versed in the pariochial history. The church has been most beautifully restored, chiefly through the bounty of the Prince of Wales. It dates from the tenth century, when it was built by King Athelstane, who granted to it the privilege of sanctuary. The rood screen, which is decorated with quaint emblems, was a part of the old church. There are some curious crosses and inscriptions in the churchyard, and at the gate there is a flight of stone steps used by farmers in the ancient days for mounting and dismounting when accompanying their wives, who rode pillion with them, to Divine service. The same custom still prevails in Norway, in the Hardanger district of Vossevangen, and I remember assisting once at a wedding, when all the party rode to church, the bride and bridegroom's horses being joined together by coupling chains. There is a quaint epitaph within St Buryan's Church, on the tomb of Arthur Levelis, the squire of a family well known in Cornwall during the Middle Ages, and who died the 2nd of May, 1671:–

> "This worthy family hath flourished here,
> Since William's Conquest, full six hundred year,
> And longer much it might, but that the Blest,
> Must spend their *seavenths* in a blessed rest.
> This worthy gentleman, last of his name,
> Hath by his *vertues*, eternized the same;
> Much more than children could for books, for Love
> *Recordes* it here, in *Heartes* in Life above."

On a tombstone in the churchyard there appear the somewhat practical reflections – "To the Memory of Captain Nathaniel Doble":

> "Our life is but a winter's day,
> Some only breakfast and away,
> Others to dinner stay, and are full fed,

The oldest only sups, and goes to bed.
Large is his life who lingers out the day,
Who goes the soonest has the least to pay."

From Saint Buryan's through Penzance, our route was continued to St Ives. A very lofty erection was prominent on the wooded hill above the little fishing town. It turned out to be erected to the memory of a gentleman named Knill, who bequeathed a considerable sum of money to secure, after death, prayers for his soul. The terms of the will are rigidly carried out, and though the testator, I believe, is buried miles away from the spot, on a fixed day in every fourth year, the Mayor and other officials of the Corporation of St Ives attend at the monument in the wood, whilst twelve damsels in white dance around it and offer up prayers for the soul of their benefactor. From St Ives we rode on through the tin country; but all the inhabitants seemed to think more of politics than of their mines, and Mr Conybeare's chances of success in comparison with those of Mr Strauss for the Camborne Division, together with the grand victory of Mr Williams at Truro, seemed to be the staple theme of conversation. We passed one or two bacon-curing establishments, a novel venture in this locality, and a very lofty shaft was pointed out to as the site of an arsenic refining factory. I at once bethought myself of the "Maybrick Mystery" (at least so some people term it). No judge worked more patiently to unravel it than did Sir Fitzjames Stephen, and the exact number of dictionaries which he called into use, to enlighten the Liverpool jury as to the meaning of the technical medical term "Petechiæ," which, I understand, signifies a rash, will never be ascertained. During the eventful trial at St George's Hall I met the late Dr Tidy and Dr Stephenson on several occasions. The fact that "doctors differ" was, I should say, never more plainly established. Dr Tidy was so far carried away by his emotions, that he was about to state when under examination not only that he had made a post-mortem, but also created the subject thereof. An expression of bewilderment, however, from the learned judge enabled him to make the necessary amendment in his statement.

The north coast of Cornwall abounds in seal, and the chough is occasionally seen in the district, with his characteristic red bill to distinguish him from his partner in the famous song which will recall to many minds faded recollections of old "Evans," of hot potatoes at midnight, of learned Serjeant Ballantine pouring forth his fund of anecdotes to an attentive audience at a corner table, and last, but not least, of Paddy Green, with snow-white hair, silk pocket handkerchief, and the immortal snuff-box, chatting with group after group during the convivial evenings ere the "Falstaff" and the New Club had sprung up, flourished, and dwindled into decay.

At one of the hotels we come across a curious couple. They had evidently travelled far and wide on the Continent under the auspices of enterprising tour promoters. The ice was soon broken, and we entered into conversation. The gentleman seemed half inclined to apologize for spending his holiday on English soil. "You see," he exclaimed, "we have nearly done it all, though as for Niagara, we are going to do him last." He seemed to have a very vague idea of what he had seen, or where he had been, and his better half was not able to give him much assistance. His notions as to the locality of Genoa were very mixed. He was very proud of having made an ascent to the Pyramids, and descended in safety. "What," I asked him, "during your travels made the most impression on your mind?" "Now there," he said, "you have put me up a tree. But I take it that a storm on the Lake of Ouchy" – with a broad English expression of that lovely spot – "will take the cake." He was evidently not impressed by Cornish manners and customs.

We rode on through Redruth and Truro, over several miles of moorland, past the little "Victoria" roadside inn, and completed a long stage of forty-eight miles within the hospitable portals of "The Royal" at Bodmin. The capital town of the Principality, with its one long street and beacon, was more or less excited over the recent election. It had stuck to its colours, and sent back Mr Courtney to Parliament in preference to a comparative stranger. The Cornishman cares very little for Home Rule; he is wrapped up in tin and slate, though he is very clannish, and likes to support those who are of his own kith and kin. The advent of Her Majesty's Judge of Oyer and Terminer, and general gaol delivery, in the person of Sir Arthur Charles, formerly leader of the Western circuit, had caused a little life in the old town. We understood there were only seven prisoners to be tried, for the Cornish are as a rule a law-abiding and peaceable race. From Bodmin to Tintagel was our next move. The country here was wild and barren, and few habitations were visible. Here and there a church tower appeared as a solitary landmark, and "Brown Willy," a Cornish tor, at an altitude of about 1360 ft., kept reappearing at different stages on our route. It only required to be covered with snow to recall to one's mind the jagged appearance of the "Dent du Midi," as seen from Lake Leman, between Vevey and Clarens. The "Wharncliffe Arms" at Tintagel was our next resting-place. The remains of the old castle with which the rough seas of this coast have made havoc are associated with all kinds of romantic legends, and in the language of Lord Campbell in reference to the family of "Mar," its origin is lost in antiquity. It may have been the castellated fortress of some of the Cornish Princes, wherein they withstood foreign invasions; or perhaps it was the abode of the marauding tribes which infested the coast in the pre-Norman era. The path which winds up to the ruins is rather precipitous, with a yawning cavern beneath in some parts, and, like the Gemmi pass, it requires a steady head to face it.

These Cornish retreats, far from the madding crowd, are the resorts of painters, artists, and heterogeneous authors, who evidently derive inspiration from the wild scenery. I have a recollection of an eminent Canon of Westminster firing away with his ready pencil for hours at a stretch as he surveyed the Atlantic under a flag-staff on the heights above Bude. Though he gazed on northern seas, he was able to give to the world a vivid account of a shipwreck on the Mediterranean coast off Baiæ, whereby an Empress Queen fell a victim to no stress of weather, but to a foul conspiracy hatched by the fertile brain of the Nero whom she had caressed. Much of the Canon's choice oratory is associated with Monte Rosa, and scenes on the High Alps, though he often draws from the wild and picturesque spots in which this little scrap of Empire abounds.

From Tintagel to Bude was a stage of twenty miles. On the road we came across Mr Anderson, well known at Oxford to the frequenters of "Vincent's," and to the boating world as "Joe," now a fully-fledged parson. We stopped to bait at "Wainhouse Corner," an excellent hostelry by the roadside, kept by Mrs Cory, where I had stayed years ago; and with the towers of Marham Church and Week St Mary to mark the locality, we completed our three hundred and eightieth mile on dismounting at the "Falcon" at Bude.

Had Mr Pickwick and his companions selected the far West as the scene of their coaching expedition, they would not have made much progress. The various cairns, mounds, and crosses which abound in Cornwall would have demanded special entries in the notebook; whilst the quaint dialect and pointed expressions of the yokels would have excited the wonder of Nathaniel Winkle and Tracy Tupman. There are various kinds of tourists nowadays. There is the American, who likes to rush through the country. He is to be found one day listening to the organ at Lucerne, and long before you are up in the morning he is guessing and calculating outside your bedroom door as to whether he will reach Italian soil in time to visit some famous museum which has been sketched out as part of the day's programme. Whether or no he derives real pleasure from this hurry-scurry whirl of travel may be a subject of doubt. Then there is the *blasé* youth of the period, fresh from the stalls of the Gaiety with high collar and elaborate waistcoat, who the moment when he is landed at his hotel inquires as to whether there is a good music hall or concert room, and completely horrifies a pair of unprotected females armed with their "Murray" or "Bädeker," who are *en route* to some picture gallery or icy cold church.

However, to each man his own taste. There is certainly much to be learnt from the manners, customs, and conversation of the primitive Cornish folk. "What kind of day will it be to-morrow?" I inquired of a veteran labourer, who was putting the last bit of thatch on a hayrick. "There's n'ought telling," he replied; "de zun (the sun) he be going down red, but likely enough it will be a foxey morning." Sure and enough the diagnosis was correct, and it was a "wily" and windy day as we rode away from the "Falcon" at Bude. Solitude is the prevailing characteristic of the wild rocky scenery on our Cornish shores of the Atlantic, with nothing but the sea to separate you from the Western world, the bracing air being wafted direct and across from the Canadian coast. The absence, too, of railroad speculators has contributed to preserve the seclusion of the primitive little towns, nestling here and there in sandy coves between the Land's End and Hartland Point, each with its own natural fortress of huge rock and boulder, which rear up their heads like so many Centaurs along the shore. Mr Brendon, who reigns at the "Falcon," is purveyor for the various teams which are run to and fro in this remote district. Somehow or other on the various features of the travellers perched on the top of tourist coaches to me there always seemed a devil-may-care look, a kind of "I cannot-help-it," or "still-I-am-not-happy" expression. *The* vagaries of our English climate may account for it, but certainly in the Lake district and even in the sunny Isle of Wight, I have seen load after load blown in by the horn, looking as if they regretted they had ever left their hotel. It is in the Champs Elysees or the Bois that you see outward and visible signs of real enjoyment.

It was the good wife of our host at the "Falcon" who ministered to the Rev. John Russell, better known as "Parson Jack," after a long life run over the open, when the finish was at hand. Few men had such a host of friends, amongst all sorts and conditions of people. From Royalty and the Episcopal overseer of the diocese, in the person of the late "Harry of Exeter," down to the most humble follower of the Devon and Somerset staghounds on his shaggy Exmoor pony, he commanded respect. He could preach as well as he could ride to hounds, and he did not forget to obey the Royal command, and put a sermon in his pocket on his last visit to Sandringham. When the final illness came, and the end was near, his medical man inquired if he could relieve his suffering. "It is no good, Doctor," rejoined "Parson Jack;" "the machine is rusty and worn out; it's no use oiling it any more." He shared with Whyte-Melville a love for Nature and for sport. The rooms of his parsonage were decorated with trophies of the chase, and his chairs, supported by the antlers of warrantable stags, were mementoes of long runs, past Dunkerry Beacon, until the quarry went to sea at Porlock Weir, or, taking to the moorland, was brought to bay in the Doone Valley at Badgeworthy Water. Like the author of Katerfelto, "Parson Jack" has left behind a name which in North Devon will not soon be forgotten. As an old and valued friend of my late uncle, Mr Harry Villebois, "the Squire," he belonged to a bygone generation, of such men as Osbaldeston and Sir Henry Peyton, sportsmen who would more than hold their own with the representatives of our luxurious age. It is recorded that on one occasion when Jack Russell required the services of a curate, and an unfledged parson presented himself for inspection, he was interviewed by his master's old stud groom. "Can ye ride, zur (sir), to 'ounds," inquired the old stableman of the æsthetic divine; "because, if ye can't, Parson Jack will have nought to do with ye?"

Through Stratton and Kilkhampton our route lay upon leaving Bude. There was little to attract one's attention, except the announcement on various noticeboards that the Very Rev. the Dean of Rochester would preach in the neighbourhood on the following Sunday. He, too, though riding nearly 17st., used to be well up when hounds were running, and his graphic description of the pink coats glistening amid the oaks of Thoresby will be remembered by those who have read the author's "Nice and Her Neighbours," ere the "Rose King" of the Midlands had exchanged his home in the Rufford country to preside over the clergy in the cathedral church of Dickens's old city. Dean Hole possesses a keen sense of humour, and his reminiscences of *table-d'hôte* acquaintances are very amusing. The old boys who dye themselves black, and the old girls who dye themselves yellow and thrust their extremities into patent leather shoes fully two sizes too small, did not escape the notice of his observant eye.

What curious specimens of the human race I have encountered at various hotels on the Continent, and in one's own country, too! It is a study worth cultivating to watch the faces of a family of four – father, mother, and two grown-up daughters – when the *fricassée* of *poulet* is being handed down the line by the waiter. The glances askance at the wings, which are gradually disappearing, whilst the legs alone remain to testify to the dismemberment of the once crowing poultry-yard bird are very significant, and the look of disgust of the portly head of the family when the drumstick fell to his lot will never be effaced from my memory. Then there is the gentleman somewhat advanced in life, with a stiff leg and an eyeglass, who is on the look out for a second partner to share his joys and his sorrows. Again, I met a lady, a widow indeed, who ere the ice had hardly been broken confided to my ear the nature of her various investments. She was decidedly of a speculative turn of mind, dearly loved miscellaneous flutters, was a firm believer in "Bryant and May," and looked upon the Automatic Sweetmeat Company, whose wares are to be met with at every railway station, as simply a treasure amongst financial quotations. And "you know," she added, "my daughter will only have what I like to leave her, and my poor Henry had such implicit confidence in me that he left all his money to me absolutely." I could not help thinking that in her husband's lifetime the securities had been of the usual preference and guarantee stocks, and that he never had the rashness to dabble in chocolate cream or barley sugar. I also met a kind venerable old gentleman who told me he had had four wives, and each had died from natural causes. No, he was not a bigamist. Talking of that offence, I am reminded of the finest expression of satire which was ever uttered, and which, I believe, may be attributed to the late Mr Justice Maule. A wretched culprit, who could neither read nor write, was convicted on his own confession of intermarriage ere the seven years' limit had been passed, and whilst his first wife was still alive. There was no doubt that he had been driven to extremities by circumstances over which he had no control, and that his former partner, like Mrs Weller, had predilections for a member of the Stiggins's persuasion. When the culprit was called up for judgment Mr Justice Maule addressed him in scathing terms: "Prisoner at the bar, you stand convicted on your own confession of this terrible and heinous crime. You say that your first wife treated you badly, and I dare say she did; but then you had the noble profession of the law at your command, and you should not have taken matters into your own hands. You ought to have consulted one of those gentlemen down there," pointing to the well of the court, which was occupied by a long row of solicitors, "and he would have charged you several sums of six-and-eightpence, but would have done you little good. He would have passed you on to one of those gentlemen in wig and gown over there, and after you had spent about twenty pounds, your case would have been heard in open court. I don't disguise from you the fact that I know you would have lost it, but then you would have been advised to carry it a step further to the Court of Appeal, and finally to the House of Lords, when in all probability, after years of waiting, you would have been allowed to marry the lady. But, prisoner, you have not done all this; you have not taken advantage of the law, but have acted contrary thereto. You are liable to transportation beyond the seas for a long term of years, but I sentence you to a nominal day's imprisonment; you can go." Those who have had experience of offices in Lincoln's Inn Fields, of interviews with Dodson and Fogg, and of Counsel's chambers, will appreciate the force of this masterpiece of satirical utterance. Perhaps in the dim and distant future, a fusion of the two branches of the legal profession under the auspices of Sir Edward Clarke may tend to render the machinery of the law more speedy, and less cumbersome and expensive to worn-out suitors ...

ETHEL
1902

'A Cornish Fish-Wife'

Postcard, *c*.1902, private collection

To: Miss Mathews, 9 Ashchurch Park Villas, Shepherds Bush, London

Glandower 13/7/02

Glad you arrived up safely. Lovely here today. I got a very nice pair of white gloves as the light ones were not [a] pretty shade. John just off to Land's End. Ethel

AUNT LILY
1903

'Fore Street, Redruth'

Postcard, *c*.1903, private collection

To: Ernest Punchard, Chord House, Deans Court, London

Dear Ernest, I do hope you will like this view, it is the principal street in Redruth. There is very little to choose from, by the way, of cards here but will send you the best I can find. This is a most lovely spot to spend a holiday in, there being such pretty country around & sea within a few miles. Aunt Lily

M.B.D.
1903

'Penzance from Newlyn'

Postcard, *c.*1903, private collection

To: Thomas P. Wren Esquire, Church Road, Lelant

Awfully sorry we could not come today, it was really too wet, was it not. If tomorrow turns out fine you can expect us, wire if it is not convenient. M.B.D.

ANNIE STOOK
1907

'Mary Kelynack of Newlyn, at 80 years of age, walked to
London to see the Queen'

Postcard, *c*.1907, private collection

To: Miss Alys MacDonald, 3 Hope Terrace, Chard, Somerset

8 South Terrace, Penzance

A Happy New Year to you & may you see as many as the original of
the portrait on the back, yours etc., Annie Stook

BILL
1912

Two views of Mount Edgcumbe

Postcard, *c*.1912, private collection

12/12/12

Dear Mabel, Just a line to say I have to make a start after dinner, a few of us is starting today & some Monday morning but not all who were standing off. With love, I know what you mean, from Bill xxxxx

J. O.
1921

'Land's End Hotel'

Postcard, *c*.1921, private collection

To: John Stockton, 109 Nooley Moor Road, Rochdale

Penlee Villa, Penlee View Terrace, Penzance March 20 1921

Sir, I received the papers this morning and for which I thank you, we leave here in the morning for London, then home on Wednesday. Will come and see you on Thursday. Alls well, hoping you are all the same & home. Yours very sincerely, J.O.

CYRIL
1928

'St Michael's Mount, Penzance'

Postcard, *c*.1928, private collection

To: Mrs H. Robbins, 11 Hayford Avenue, Vauxhall, London

18/7/28

Have sent you on rail this day 1 tin cream. Love from all, having fun,

Cyril

GLADYS
1928

'Lizard'

Postcard, *c*.1928, private collection

To: Miss M. K. Waller, 66 Abbots Park Road, Leyton, London

2/8/28 Channel Views, Lizard, Cornwall

Dear Kath,

Thanks for your card. We had quite a budget awaiting us yesterday on our return from Land's End. This is one of the many coves round here. Perhaps you prefer the human variety. We are not returning till Monday, so shall not see you over the weekend. With love, Gladys

MAY
1929

'St Michael's Mount, from the air'

Postcard, *c*.1929, private collection

To: Miss Ivy Dawson, 463 Manchester Road, Crossfoot, Sheffield, Yorkshire

Penzance

My dear Ivy, Thanks, your letter received this a.m. I am glad you enjoyed the cream. We are having a nice time, the country is so beautiful. We had a Cornish pasty last Thursday for dinner. I should think it was about a foot long. How I got through it I don't know but I did. I felt like bursting. Love, May

WINNIE
1931

'Perranporth, Cliffs'

Postcard, *c*.1931, private collection

To: Miss Raitt, 5 Moseley Road, Fallowfield, Manchester

Perranporth

Dear Aunt,

How would you like scrambling over these rocks. All the coast is like this. It is very pretty but so quiet. Not so much life as at home. I hope you are keeping well & taking care of yourself. Jack is looking like a lobster, we are having glorious weather. With much love, Winnie

MR HUNT
1933

'Porthscatho'

Postcard, *c*.1933, private collection

To: Master M. P. Hunt, Carman, 10 Burdon Road, Chean, Surrey

Thursday

Dear Michael,
    Just received Mary's card, am very pleased to hear you are such a good boy. We can see this place from our window when we are having dinner. It is very good for sailing & fishing. The river is fine & a lot of large boats in it. There are plenty of creeks which you can row up in a boat. Don't forget to water my beans round by the garage.
Love, Dad

ALICE
1933

'Lostwithiel Street, Fowey'

Postcard, *c*.1933, private collection

To: Mrs Lee, 71 Woodlands Gardens, Isleworth, Middlesex

Pentewan, 12/7/33

Not charmed with Cornwall so far but perhaps I'm not in the mood for it. It seems very colourless. The weather was very bad until today, now the sun is shining but the wind is high. Have been soaked through twice already. Our hotel is extremely comfortable & the food good & perfectly cooked. Thank you for your comforting letter dear. I think you are right. It seems such an unreasonable attitude to adopt. I don't think it can last. Will send again shortly, heaps of love, ever yours, Alice

MURIEL
1935

'Padstow, the quay'

Postcard, *c.*1935, private collection

To: Miss Helen Butcher, Broadfields, Farnborough, Kent

Wednesday

Dear Helen,
   How would you like to play with these little children and their boats! Tell your mother I wish she were here with me – the days are delightful for walking and I shall be out all day on Friday walking to Bedruthan & back. I'll write again soon, much love, from Muriel

MRS MARGARET HALSEY
of
YONKERS, NEW YORK, C.1937

Cornish fishermen, 1934

Margaret Halsey, *With Malice Towards Some* (New York, 1938), 161–6.

Mrs Halsey, originally from Yonkers in New York, was the wife of an American academic who was working at the University College of the South West, subsequently the University of Exeter, during the winter of 1937–8. Her account is disarmingly perceptive while at the same time it was obviously intended to amuse the reader. But the frankness with which she wrote of Exeter, and particularly of the college, must have scandalized the city when it was

printed, particularly given it was printed by a leading New
York publisher. Mrs Halsey was in her late twenties when
she visited Cornwall. Purford could have been Kingsand.
Mrs Halsey died in 1997 at the age of 87. Her other publications include *Color Blind: a white woman looks at the Negro*
(1946) and *The folks at home* (1952).

September 14th
We left Plymouth as soon as possible, having a grudge against it, and
crossed the Sound to Cornwall. The original plan was for us to spend
the rest of the time before October first, when we move into Mrs
Turney's house, proceeding at leisure down the coast of Cornwall.
But Mr Primrose's car, which had all it could do to drag the pageant
of its bleeding heart across the hills of Devon, lost conciousness
completely when confronted with the hills of Cornwall. We had to
lift it to the sofa and unfasten its stays. When this debacle occurred,
we were in a little village called Purford [sic], just across the Sound
from Plymouth, and Purford being decidedly appetising of aspect,
we decided to stay here for a while.

September 15th
Purford has less patience and sweetness about it and more severity
and guts than English villages seem customarily to have. It stands on
a hilly little peninsula which, having Plymouth Sound on one side
and the Atlantic Ocean on the other two, is instinct with horizons.
Purford itself has been boldly tacked to the side of a steep descent
which plungest suicidally into Plymouth Sound. The streets of this
village are virtually perpendicular, and are rendered still more
improbable by being in addition so narrow that a four-year-old child
with a pail in its hand constitutes a traffic jam. Sprinkled in among
the white cottages are others which have been plastered in burnt
orange or salmon pink or tan, departures from the norm which give
the village a remarkable air of independence. Along some of the
streets, a sea wall with purple-flowering vines growing over it inter-
poses benevolently to keep you from falling over on to the dark,
malign coastal rocks below.

Though a shelter of woods flanks Purford on either side, tall, green
hills rise baldly up at the back of it. These, combined with the
stretched-out pieces of water, make the houses, which in other English

villages seem to be rubbing up against each other like puppies in a basket, seem in Purford to be huddling together for the definite purpose of protection. This blue-browed and rock-ribbed Cornish austerity makes a pleasant change after the lushness of Devon. I think we will stay here until the long-awaited first of October.

September 17th

The English hotels we have stayed in so far always seemed to me expressly planned to discourage people from remaining away from home overnight. The red plush. The black walnut. The framed engravings of lovers' quarrels. The Pampas grass. The fireplace blocked up with nastly little brutes of gas heaters. Whenever we checked out of a hotel this summer, it was with the moral certainty that the manager immediately retired to his office for a few minutes of private rejoicing. 'There,' he would say, looking out of the window after us, 'that'll teach 'em to go gadding about!'

But the hotel we are staying at in Purford has wide, light staircases with brown oak chests on the landings. Set on the hill above the village, it is a big, rambling stone house, formerly a private residence. We have been given a large room with a southern exposure and tall casement windows. There is a white mantel over a bona fide fireplace, a four-poster bed with a faded canopy, and a cushioned window seat where you can sit and look out over the roofs of the village to the liners standing sedately in the Sound and being milked by tenders.

September 19th

The owner of the hotel, a retired naval officer, has just been up to the room and built us a handsome fire. He is a strong-and-silenter. He builds fires and worms dogs and whittles out boats and evens off tennis courts, performing these and similar offices with an air of manifest enjoyment, and he never wastes a word – largely, I suppose, because he does not have to. His shrewd, weather-beaten face is a conversation in itself. Two of his sons are in the navy, and two more are still at the stage of leaving spare mizzenmasts and strings of dead fish on the drawing-room chairs, a habit which adds perceptibly to the informality of the atmosphere. The two sons appear briefly, dry, in the morning and reappear briefly, dripping sea water, at six in the evening. They have beautiful manners, which maintain a sort of warring equilibrium with a strong conviction that people who cannot sail boats ought not to be allowed to waste the time of people who can.

September 21ˢᵗ
Mr Primrose's car is able to get about a little again, and yesterday we ventured to drive down the coast as far as a little place called Mevagissey. It was a beautiful drive, all cliffs and clouds and rainbows and dark rocks and wide blue stretches of sea, though, as Henry pointed out, when you try to put it in words you only sound as if you were describing a black eye. I had though Purford precipitate, but we saw other villages which were considerably more so. It feels as if one were either reading or dreaming, to look at those rugged and colourful Cornish villages, stepping down brusque hillsides into their Morte d'Arthur coves. But the inhabitants, Henry's colleagues in Exeter say, are so inbred that in some places fifty per cent of the schoolchildren are either morons or nearly so. Handsome is that handsome does.

September 22ⁿᵈ
I went into one of the crowded, stuffy little shops of Purford today – it was not much larger than a good-sized dog kennel – to get some oranges with which to outflank the hotel carbohydrates. By borrowing from the neighbours, the shop managed to get together a dozen oranges, but they were hardly bigger than walnuts, and when cut into, proved to be filled with a vegetable equivalent of absorbent cotton. However, we are having a full moon, and this landscape by moonlight is so beautiful that Henry and I, going for our nightly walk, almost have to bring each other home in pails.

One of the pleasanter things about coming to England is the number of hitherto skipped-over little phrases which suddenly takes on meaning. 'Draw the curtains', for instance. The English, instead of window shades like ours, have heavy curtains at the windows which are pushed aside during the daytime and drawn together at night. In this hotel, though, there are no curtains at all, and we go to sleep at night in a beatific combination of moonlight and firelight. I go to sleep, that is. Henry explains sombrely that it keeps him awake. Of all Henry's beliefs, perhaps his favourite one is that he cannot fall asleep if there is so much as a pinprick of light or a hair-scrape of noise in the room. Actually, he drowses in bolier factories and nods off under klieg lights, but he gets so much simple pleasure out of being resigned to an insomnia he does not have, that I have abandoned the heartless statistics of the situation and given the legend its innocent head.

September 25th
Henry has gone up to Exeter for the opening of the college, but I am staying on in Purford until the first of the month.

September 29th
Tomorrow we move into Yeobridge [sic], and from now on there will be a whole house to spread out in and I shall wear ironed underwear again. Whee! …

Index of Personal
and Place Names

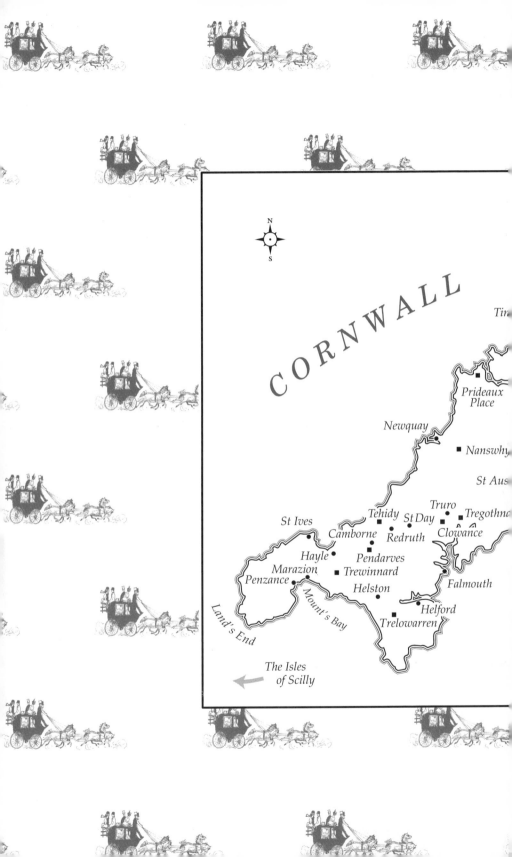